Mubarak Al-Sabah

Mubarak Al-Sabah

The Foundation of Kuwait

By Souad M. Al-Sabah

Translated by Laila Asser

Edited by John King

I.B. TAURIS
LONDON · NEW YORK

Published in 2014 by I.B.Tauris & Co. Ltd
6 Salem Road, London W2 4BU
175 Fifth Avenue, New York NY 10010
www.ibtauris.com

Distributed in the United States and Canada
Exclusively by Palgrave Macmillan
175 Fifth Avenue, New York NY 10010

ISBN: 978 1 78076 454 2

A full CIP record for this book is available from the British Library
A full CIP record is available from the Library of Congress

Library of Congress Catalog Card Number: available

Typeset by Data Standards Ltd, Frome, Somerset
Printed and bound by CPI Group (UK) Ltd, Croydon, CR0 4YY

MIX
Paper from
responsible sources
FSC
www.fsc.org   FSC® C013604

To my immediate family; to the spirit of my husband Sheikh Abdullah Bin Mubarak; to my children Mohammed, Mubarak, Omniya and Shayma; to my grandchildren and to my larger family, the people of Kuwait – I dedicate these pages devoted to the history of our founder and the rise of a nation.

Table of Contents

List of Plates

———◆◆◆———

1   Sheikh Mubarak in 1901.
2   Sheikh Mubarak with officers of the Russian naval ship *Varyag*, 1901.
3   Sheikh Mubarak, mounted, receiving Lord Curzon, 1903.
4   Sheikh Mubarak and his friend Sheikh Khaz'al of Muhammurah, 1907.
5   Sheikh Mubarak standing on a bridge that connected the old and new sections of Al-Seif Palace.
6   The Summer Palace, 1907.
7   Sheikh Mubarak in his outdoor council.
8   Sheikh Mubarak with Emir 'Abd al-'Aziz Al-S'aud on his right hand, among a group of the two families, 1910.
9   Sheikh Mubarak, 1912.
10   Sheikh Mubarak in his last years. Standing at the back to his left is his son, Sheikh Jaber.
11   Sheikh Mubarak with the commander of Basra forces, most likely before the battle of Basra, 1914.
12   Mubarak's seal and signature, in the archives of the Kuwaiti Research and Studies Center, 1908.
13   A certificate issued by the Sheikh attesting to the identity of Kuwaiti merchants and a certificate issued by Sheikh Mubarak for Kuwaiti ships, 1908.
14   A document prepared by the Sheikh to prevent the dealing of arms in Kuwait, 1900.
15   A document showing the Sheikh's approval for British and Iranian ships to be inspected and searched for smuggled weapons, 1900.

16 A certificate issued by Sheikh Mubarak authorizing weapons for self-defence onboard ships.

17 The Sheikh pledges to oppose the arms trade, 1900.

Preface

This book seeks to throw new light on the life of Sheikh Mubarak Al-Sabah and his reign, which ran from 1896 to 1915. While most works on this period concentrate on mere chronology without giving due credit to the significance of certain events, I have sought to provide a different perspective on the internal social and political situation in Kuwait during Sheikh Mubarak's reign. With unprecedented access to primary sources, this publication seeks to shed new light on the life and character of the Sheikh. It offers an analysis of the history of the period, and explores social and economic developments as well as the military campaigns and developments in foreign relations that punctuate Kuwait's history. The book's central theme is that of the construction of the state. This is inevitably linked to the demarcation of its political boundaries and international relations. Sheikh Mubarak insisted that Kuwait should have autonomous control over its internal affairs, and he also strove to enhance the country's influence in the Gulf and the Arabian Peninsula.

The book not only deals with political and military matters, but also closely examines the factors constraining social and economic development. It covers the beginnings of Kuwait's opening to aspects of modern life in various social spheres, such as education, the introduction of postal and telegraphic services, the development of healthcare, the organization of customs services and taxation and the facilitation of economic and trade activities. It also seeks to place political and social development in Kuwait in the context of regional and international changes taking place contemporaneously in the Gulf, examining the increasing strategic significance of Kuwait at the close of the nineteenth century and the international rivalries in which it played a part.

The text draws upon a wide variety of primary sources, as well as published books and studies hitherto little used. I am aware that the history of the Gulf in this period makes extensive use of the diplomatic correspondence of the great powers. When the subject of study is the international struggles in which Kuwait was concerned this is, of course, a valid approach. This book, however, places emphasis on Kuwait itself and developments within the state to give a new perspective of the nation, drawn from Kuwaiti sources. The issues at stake relate to Sheikh Mubarak's internal, regional and international policies, and how he strove to achieve independence for Kuwait.

In my portrayal of Sheikh Mubarak, I have attempted to give a picture of a man who was obliged to work under difficult and complicated circumstances, but who contrived, nevertheless, to preserve the independence of his country (whose economic and strategic importance was increasing) amidst conflict and competition between the European powers who sought to impose their influence in the Gulf region. Sheikh Mubarak's compass was always directed towards the independence of Kuwait, to the enhancement of its wealth and trade and to the introduction of modern life into the country. He skilfully made use of the rivalry between European countries to achieve these aims.

In writing this book, my aim has been to offer the new generation in Kuwait a picture of the events that took place a century ago but whose importance remains undiminished for understanding the nature of Kuwait today and its position in the world.

Souad Al-Sabah

March 2014

Introduction

The Role of Sheikh Mubarak in Founding the Modern State of Kuwait

In their contemplation of nations, historians have focused on certain moments because they are turning points between one period and another. One of these turning points in the Gulf and perhaps the whole Middle East took place on 17 May 1896, when Sheikh Mubarak became the ruler of Kuwait, which he led from that day until 28 November 1915. He was the seventh sheikh of Kuwait to belong to the Al-Sabah family. During his reign and thanks to his efforts the foundations of the state were laid and he attracted the sobriquet 'Mubarak the Great' and has been credited as the founder of modern Kuwait.

Mubarak laid down the principles of sovereignty in the country. He established Kuwait's independence in its internal affairs and boosted its role in the area to a degree that led some to believe he sought to make himself the emir of the whole of Arabia. When Sheikh Mubarak became the ruler of Kuwait, a new period in the history of the region began. This was a time marked by fierce international rivalry and continuous interference on the part of the Ottoman Empire, together with local struggles and wars. The Sheikh was to steer his ship skilfully to guarantee Kuwait's independence.

Sheikh Mubarak, like all founder-leaders of states, has generated his share of glorification. One Kuwaiti historian has written: 'Mubarak is all of Kuwait. He is the one who raised it above its peers and made its reputation in various countries. Mubarak is the one who let his name be known in the capitals and cities of the world and made it prominent in forums and conferences. It is through his efforts that Kuwait achieved fame and prosperity. His reign was one of security and safety, a time of power and respect. Upon his death, Kuwait lost a courageous man, who did not fear death. Without him, Kuwait would have remained obscure. [...] Without him, its reputation would not have travelled throughout the desert.[1]

Sheikh Makki bin Azzouz described Kuwait during Mubarak's reign thus: 'In those days, Kuwait was as famous as Basra. Anyone who was involved in politics knew about its emir, Mubarak Al-Sabah. They knew his country, Kuwait, because Kuwait became known through him.' Stanley Mylrea, who worked in Kuwait for several years, described him as follows: 'Sheikh Mubarak was a man who was ahead of his time by a generation. He was very interested in the art of war and his skill in using maps astonished me.' In April 1914, Omar Fawzi, the Ottoman minister of war, called him 'the sheikh of politics'. The British Political Agent in Kuwait from 1929 to 1936, Harold Dickson, described him as a first-class ruler, military leader and diplomat.

Mubarak combined fighting skill with political acumen. He was bold, adventurous and brave. At other times, he was patient, stoical and a brilliant negotiator. Between war and politics, fighting and diplomacy, he became one of the founders of the state. William Shakespear, British Political Agent in Kuwait from 1909 to 1915, remarked in 1911 that as Kuwait was still under Sheikh Mubarak's strong fist, it was the most secure and best ruled in the Gulf.

Mubarak's task was to lay the foundations for his country's independence within the framework of the complex international relations prevalent in the last decade of the nineteenth century. This period witnessed a surge in European colonialism, in the context of which rivalry to divide up the legacy of the Ottoman Empire took several forms. This international contention was most evident in the Gulf in general and in Kuwait in particular; so much so that the historian Briton Busch dedicated part of his book *Britain and the Persian Gulf, 1894–1914* specifically to the issue of Kuwait.

While Mubarak steered Kuwait's ship through the shoals of this international conflict, he also sought, with deliberate patience, to build Kuwait's prosperity and further its trade. Although the landmarks of Mubarak's life appear as a series of military battles and raids, his overriding objective remained the achievement of the necessary security and stability for trade to flourish. Trade was the backbone of Kuwait's society. Kuwait had the best harbour on the Arabian side of the Gulf, which served as the entry into the heart of Najd and the Arabian Peninsula. He was conscious that trade would prosper only through security and stability. For this reason, he prioritized strong rule and furnished himself with the necessary military means to deter those who coveted Kuwait.

With security in place, the merchant fleet of Kuwait developed and Kuwait's trade with India and eastern Asia expanded. Mubarak made an agreement with the British-India Steam Navigation Company to send a ship once a week to transport passengers and goods. Sometimes he even financed these ships himself in order to encourage trade between Kuwait and other countries.

In this and other ways, Sheikh Mubarak actively intervened to support Kuwait's merchants and provided them with a propitious environment for the growth of their business. He respected their needs and looked after their interests because he realized that the growth of their trade served to augment the fortunes of Kuwait as a whole. They were making a key contribution to the country's economy, and so he never hesitated in supporting the merchants financially. His objective was for their trade to grow and their wealth to multiply, and when they needed funds he opened his treasuries to them and gave them ample time to repay their loans. If a merchant fell on bad times so that bankruptcy loomed, or lost fortune to a merchant abroad, Mubarak would intervene to protect Kuwaiti interests.

Mubarak was aware that the growth of trade would not merely bring profits for the merchants but would also afford job opportunities for the people of the country. In May 1899, to ensure that the state would benefit from the enhancement of prosperity he sought to promote, he set up a customs system through which the Government levied a duty of 5 per cent of the price of imported goods, including those from Ottoman ports. This later increased to 10 per cent on certain items.

In the context of its atmosphere of security and stability, Kuwait began its journey towards modernization. In 1911 the first hospital was opened as part of the American Mission. The first doctor to work there was Dr Arthur Bennett and the first female doctor was Dr Eleanor Calverley, who was known in Kuwait as Khatun Halima. After this, the Al-Mubarakiyya School was established. Ustadh Omar Assem Al-Izmiri became its headmaster, and among its first teachers were Sheikh Abdul Aziz Al-Rashid and Sheikh Yussouf Al-Qinai. In 1913 the Charitable Society was established, with the objective of sending students to study abroad. This is now regarded as Kuwait's first benevolent organization. In addition, a public library was opened, money was distributed among the poor and the people were provided with free health services.

All these achievements demonstrate Mubarak's success in setting Kuwait on an independent footing, free of Ottoman rule, despite the Ottoman Empire's continuing determination to exercise its power throughout the Arab lands with the appointment of governors to administer provinces on behalf of the Sultan. What enabled Mubarak to achieve this was his relationship with Britain, which allowed him to prevent the Ottoman Empire from exercising any real power in Kuwait, despite its continued theoretical sovereignty.

Despite the autonomous course he steered, however, the Ottomans treated Sheikh Mubarak with respect. In 1911, the empire awarded him the Majidi Order, First Class. Two years later, the Sultan awarded him the Ottoman Order, First Class, one of the highest decorations awarded by the Ottoman authorities to persons of distinction. He was also the recipient of other honours from Britain. In 1903 King George V appointed him as a Knight Commander of the Order of the Indian Empire, and in 1912 Lord Curzon, the Viceroy of India, awarded Sheikh Mubarak the rank of Knight Commander of the Star of India.

With the outbreak of World War I in 1914, Kuwait's status underwent a momentous change when Britain recognized Kuwait as an independent emirate under British protection. In that year, when Mubarak visited his friend Sheikh Khaz'al on board his private yacht, the *Mishrif*, he ordered a red flag to be flown with the word 'Kuwait' written on it in white. This was adopted as the official flag of the emirate.

Old age was beginning to tell on Mubarak by this time, and signs of physical weakness were becoming evident. At the beginning of 1915, his health began to fail in earnest. At around 8.15 pm on the evening of Monday 28 November 1915, Sheikh Mubarak died at the age of 71. His rule had lasted for 19 years. The whole of Kuwait came out to walk behind his coffin, and he was buried next to his brothers Muhammad and Jarrah in the emirate's new cemetery. He had seven sons: Jaber, Salem, Subah, Fahd, Nasser, Hamad and Abdullah. The Kuwaiti poet Hamad bin Abdul Latif Al-Maghlouth took part in the funeral, which he commemorated in a poem in which he movingly described the Sheikh's life and his role in the rise of Kuwait.

With the death of Sheikh Mubarak, Kuwait suffered a huge loss. However, though the man passed away, as a symbol, model and example he has remained. To this day, Kuwait follows in the footsteps of its founder in much of its internal and foreign policies.

~1~

Making a State

He was the maker of modern Kuwait, a man of long vision
and great ability [whose] influence extended far out into the
desert.[1]

From the memoirs of Dr Stanley Mylrea, who came to
Kuwait in 1911

There are two kinds of leader: one makes history, while the
other is overwhelmed by it. A ruler of the first kind views the
environment in which he finds himself as a challenge and seeks to
mould it to suit his dreams and ambitions. For the second kind of
leader, his circumstances constitute an unavoidable fate from which
he cannot escape. He therefore surrenders to it and accepts things
as they are, to his inevitable detriment. There is no doubt that
Sheikh Mubarak, who reigned in Kuwait from 1896 to 1915, was
a ruler of the first kind. He was obliged to cope with a situation of
great complexity, where Kuwait's internal situation interacted with
the regional circumstances of the Gulf and with the policies and
long-term plans of the major European powers. Internally, as will
become clear in this chapter, Sheikh Yusuf Al-Ibrahim, an
implacable enemy of Sheikh Mubarak who was related by marriage
to Mubarak's predecessor, Sheikh Muhammad, sought for as long

as he was able to dislodge Mubarak from power. In this, he attempted to enlist the support of regional parties such as the Al-Rashid in Arabia, the ruler of Qatar and certain Ottoman officials. The region was, at the time, the scene of a struggle between the Al-Saud and the Al-Rashid for power in Najd, and control over the remainder of Arabia. At the same time it also witnessed repeated attempts by the Ottoman Empire to re-establish its authority and reaffirm its influence over the Arab sheikhdoms of the Gulf.

At the close of the nineteenth century, this Ottoman ambition found itself in opposition to the increasing power of Britain in the Gulf, in both political and military terms. The confrontation culminated with the installation by Britain of a number of protectorate agreements with the sheikhs of the Arab Emirates. While the Anglo-Ottoman conflict was the primary axis of political interaction in the Gulf during this period, the struggle was also influenced by the rivalry among other European powers in the region, with Germany, Russia and France each growing more adventurous. The number of different parties involved, together with the diversity of their interests, led to a complex series of conflicts and rivalries on the one hand, and to a variety of alliances and friendships on the other. The parameters of these conflicts fluctuated, with roles and positions evolving according to the varying interests of the parties over time.

Sheikh Mubarak was obliged to steer Kuwait through troubled waters, as the situation constantly evolved. He had to calibrate carefully his relationship with all parties so as to serve the interests of his country. First, there was the primary issue of his relationship with the Ottoman Empire. He opted to maintain his formal link with the Empire, in part at least because it was identified with the Islamic caliphate. He utilized this relationship astutely to safeguard Kuwaiti interests, including the protection of the property of the Al-Sabah family in the Faw area, and the security of Kuwaiti merchant shipping in those Gulf ports that were still controlled by the Ottoman authorities. He was ready to allow this connection to persist for as long as Istanbul refrained from interference in

Kuwait's internal politics and affairs. However, he consistently refused to receive any official Ottoman representative in Kuwait. Second, his relationship with Britain was increasingly important and he entered into a close relationship with the British Government, which was the strongest and most influential power in the Gulf. His objective here was to protect his country from being sucked into the quicksand of potential Ottoman interference in its internal affairs. Third, however, he developed an awareness of other European powers that potentially represented a danger to Kuwait but might also have benefits to bring. He received representatives of the major European powers and listened to what they had to offer. At the same time, he was always careful to let the British authorities know about such contacts. In part this was a way of signalling to the British that he was not a prisoner of British diplomacy, and that he had alternatives to which he could turn when necessary. Briton Cooper Busch, a historian of the Gulf, pays tribute to the Sheikh's mastery of diplomacy.[2]

Sheikh Mubarak's early years

Sheikh Mubarak was born in 1844. He was a son of Sheikh Al-Sabah and succeeded his elder brother Sheikh Muhammad to the throne in unclear circumstances. At the age of five, his grandfather, Sheikh Jaber, took charge of his education. Sheikh Jaber appointed a religious scholar to teach the young Mubarak the principles of the Qur'an and religious sciences. At the age of 12, he began his education in shooting and riding. Within two years he had completed his training in horsemanship and had surpassed his peers and friends. As an adult, he became one of Kuwait's most accomplished horsemen, and as a marksman he rarely missed his target. He also began at an early age to attend government meetings. In his younger days, before he took power, he spent much of his time participating in military expeditions in the desert and became an expert in military arts and strategy. In 1871, for example, when he was still only 27, his eldest brother, Sheikh

Abdullah Al-Sabah, who had succeeded as Sheikh of Kuwait in 1866, appointed him to lead the Kuwaiti contingent that assisted the Ottoman forces in the Al-Hasa campaign led by Nafidh Pasha. Sheikh Abdullah himself headed the naval campaign, designating Mubarak to lead the land forces. In 1871, he met the Ottoman Governor of Baghdad, Midhat Pasha. It was at this time, in appreciation of Kuwait's role in the Al-Hasa campaign, that Midhat Pasha granted the ruler of Kuwait ownership of an area of palm groves in the Shatt Al-Arab region, with perpetual tax exemption.

In 1892, Sheikh Muhammad Al-Sabah, another of Mubarak's older brothers, succeeded to the leadership of Kuwait, after which he sent Sheikh Mubarak to head a number of desert campaigns. Sheikh Mubarak's first task was to lead a punitive campaign against Majid Al-Duwaysh, one of the leaders of the Mutayr tribe, who had been attempting to seize the property of tribes who were favourable to Kuwait. Later the same year, he led a force sent by Sheikh Muhammad to support Ibn Suwayt, the head of the Al-Dhufayr tribe, against a rebel leader from the same tribe. In 1893, he led a Kuwaiti detachment sent to support Ottoman troops in Qatar. He also led campaigns ordered by Sheikh Muhammad against the Al-Sa'id, who had attacked various tribes attached to Kuwait. Mubarak pursued the Al-Sa'id and confronted them in the Al-Khanqa area, where he defeated them and recovered property they had stolen. In 1894, Sheikh Mubarak led the force sent by the Sheikh of Kuwait against the Bani Hajar tribe, who had raided Kuwaiti boats in the Gulf and stolen their cargo. He confronted the Bani Hajar at a location between Al-Qatif and Al-Hasa, where he overcame them and retrieved the booty they had stolen. In most of these battles, the standard-bearer was Abdullah bin Muhammad Al-Mizyan. His son, Ibrahim, shared this duty with him and continued after his father's death.[3] Mubarak derived great benefit from the part he played in these battles. He learned the art of desert warfare, forged close relationships with the heads of the Bedouin tribes and enhanced his personal standing through his leadership of the Kuwaiti forces.

Contemporaries describe Mubarak as tall and tanned, with dark eyes, commenting that he was a sure-footed man with a firm stride, who was strong but slender. As to his abilities, Hafez Wahbah describes him as having 'a long memory and a strong will'.[4] Hussein Khalaf Al-Sheikh Khaz'al remarks that he had a scar on his forehead from a sword, which made him appear even more fearsome, adding that,

> he was intelligent and sensitive and was highly energetic. He thought deeply but spoke little. He had a long memory and never forgot a face, no matter how much time had passed.[5]

Abd Al-Massih Antaki, the owner of the Egyptian magazine *Al-Imran*, who met Sheikh Mubarak in 1907, described him as,

> tall, slender, with muscular arms, dark hair and attractive black eyes, which radiated intelligence and resourcefulness. His beard was short and sparse. He has a good memory, remembering all the events he has experienced or heard of. If anyone mentions an event in front of him, he immediately corrects any error and will then recount the story in minute detail.[6]

Mubarak's grounding in the traditions of the desert tribes had inculcated in him a love for the land and a strong will. Each time Sheikh Muhammad sent him to the desert, his task was to impose order among tribesmen who were accustomed to freedom from constraint and rejected the interference of any outside authority. Mubarak carried out his orders, though the necessary financial support was often only grudgingly provided. This commission was both a testing and a useful experience for Mubarak, during which he cultivated strong relationships with certain tribes, including the Ajman and Al-Rashaydeh. This led to lasting attachments of loyalty between him and the tribes. When he came to power, he was proud to describe himself as the sheikh of Kuwait's tribes, and he was able to take advantage of his strong links with the tribesmen to establish a military force capable of defending Kuwait, deterring its enemies and supporting its friends.

In power, Mubarak's guiding principle was in the first place to consolidate his authority, although he was beset by a morass of conflicts and conspiracies. He took pains to construct a formidable military force for Kuwait, taking advantage of the international rivalry between the major powers and the Ottomans to protect the independence of his country. He was the first to define Kuwait as a nation, raising the first national flag carrying the name of 'Kuwait' and demarcating the geographical borders of the emirate.

Consolidating the state

Mubarak came to power in difficult circumstances, amidst a series of testing political and military events that culminated in the deaths in obscure circumstances of his brothers, Muhammad and Jarrah. In this context, the early years of his reign were marked by a sequence of political disturbances and military clashes, including attempts from Kuwait to drive him from power.

The internal conflict in Kuwait was influenced by regional and international considerations. On the international front, there were constant attempts by the Ottomans to intervene in the affairs of the nation in order to counter the growing influence of Europe. Meanwhile, European activities reflected the rivalry between Britain, France, Russia and Germany. A further factor was the regional struggle in Arabia, and in particular that between the Al-Saud and the Al-Rashid for control of Najd and Al-Hasa. Amidst all these external pressures, Mubarak strove to bring into play all the diplomatic and military resources he could muster to strengthen the basis of his authority in Kuwait.

At the heart of his troubles was his quarrel with his brothers Muhammad and Jarrah. The conflict continued even after their deaths, as Mubarak's implacable adversary Yusuf Al-Ibrahim gave sanctuary to their sons. Yusuf Al-Ibrahim, also known as the

Sheikh of Dora, was one of the wealthiest pearl merchants in Kuwait; he was related to the Al-Sabah by marriage and had enjoyed great influence during the reign of Sheikh Muhammad. His constant goal was to undermine Mubarak's rule. He allied himself with certain Ottoman officials as well as with the Al-Rashid. Yusuf Al-Ibrahim's antagonism was a major factor in Kuwaiti–Ottoman relations during the first years of Mubarak's reign, and it came to an end only with his death, on 25 January 1906.

Yusuf Al-Ibrahim attempted to recruit the support of Hamdi Pasha, the Governor of Basra, for his campaign against Sheikh Mubarak, bringing to bear all the diplomatic wiles he had at his disposal. In his relations with the Ottomans he took care to convey the impression that Mubarak was a supporter of the British while claiming that he himself, once in power, would restore Ottoman control over Kuwait. At the same time, in a letter he sent to the British Consul in Basra and to the British Resident in Bushire, he promised the British that he would request British protection over Kuwait if London were to intervene to end Mubarak's rule. He made full use of his wealth in his bid to achieve his aims. In addition to his political connections and financial resources, Yusuf Al-Ibrahim also resorted to force on a number of occasions, mounting several military expeditions against Kuwait.

The Ottomans welcomed Yusuf Al-Ibrahim's efforts. Sheikh Mubarak's refusal to accept an Ottoman military garrison or political agent, and his insistence on the internal independence of Kuwait, meant that the nation was an obstacle to the geographical continuity of the Ottoman Sultan's control over the Gulf coast. Kuwait lay between the two provinces of Al-Hasa and Basra, both of which belonged to the Ottoman Empire, so its position presented a physical blockage that disrupted Ottoman control.[7] An instance of Sheikh Mubarak's resistance to an Ottoman military garrison in Kuwait took place in September 1899, when an Ottoman admiral arrived in Kuwait with a retinue of five military personnel, whom Sheikh Mubarak received as guests in his residence. The admiral's reply when asked the purpose of his mission in Kuwait was that Hamdi Pasha, the Ottoman Governor of Basra, had assigned him to be Kuwait's naval commander. The Sheikh's reply was swift and decisive. 'Kuwait', he declared, 'had no need of a naval commander, and he should therefore return whence he had come, none of his cargo should be unloaded, and he should take his leave that very night.'[8]

For his part, Mubarak did not remain inactive. He observed Yusuf Al-Ibrahim's machinations and took steps to counteract his schemes, using similar methods and stratagems. He reassured the Ottoman authorities of his loyalty and reiterated his desire to maintain relations with them. He spared nothing in his gifts to Ottoman officials, warning them that the British had designs on his emirate. He raised the Ottoman flag over his palace. He asked Rajab Pasha, the Governor of Baghdad, to persuade the Sublime Porte to regard any internal disturbance within Kuwait solely as a feature of its internal affairs, which should not be allowed to affect relations between Kuwait and Istanbul. Mubarak's aim was to consolidate his position inside Kuwait and keep the Ottomans out, discouraging them from backing his rivals. A further aim was to safeguard his possessions in Basra.[9] However, he was ready for the possibility of an invasion and had made the necessary preparations. At the same time, in anticipation of any unexpected development, Sheikh Mubarak maintained his discreet lines of communication with the British so as to be in a position to confront anticipated pressure from the Ottomans.

The year after he took power, 1897, was eventful, with frequent confrontations with Yusuf Al-Ibrahim, who, as we have seen, was encouraged by Ottomans keen to reassert their influence in Kuwait. In February 1897, the Governor of Basra appointed an Ottoman official to run a quarantine centre in Kuwait. This purportedly innocuous move in fact represented an attempt to change the emirate's status, which Mubarak was not prepared to accept. Henceforth, Mubarak also began actively to seek outside support, particularly in the light of threats made by Ibn Al-Rashid and Yusuf Al-Ibrahim, who still aspired to become Kuwait's ruler. Indeed, that very month, Sheikh Mubarak met a representative of the British Political Resident in the Gulf, to whom he conveyed his wish to place Kuwait under British protection in order to preserve it from Ottoman control. Britain, however, did not make an immediate response to his proposal, since, in order to conclude an agreement with the ruler of Kuwait, Britain would need to recognize his status as independent of the Ottoman Empire, and this in turn would imply that Britain was stepping back from the recognition it had given in 1878 to Ottoman sovereignty over the Arab Emirates on the northern coast of the Gulf.[10]

Despite Britain's caution, Yusuf Al-Ibrahim believed that the Sheikh was seeking a way to thwart his ambitions. This led him to resort to military action. In June 1897, he prepared a naval flotilla to invade Kuwait, made up of 14 ships, with some 1,500–1,800 men on board. Mubarak, however, received intelligence of the plot and was able to confront Yusuf Al-Ibrahim's ships at sea, where he overpowered the would-be invasion force. Mubarak demanded that the Governor of Basra arrest those who had planned the invasion, but the Ottoman authorities refused to take the matter seriously. The Governor of Basra also refused Mubarak's request that his naval forces be allowed impunity to pursue Yusuf Al-Ibrahim in both Ottoman and Persian waters.

An account of how Mubarak discovered this plot is provided by Sheikh Abdullah Al-Nuri, who records that as a merchant named Ali Sulayman Abu Kahil was returning by ship to Kuwait his vessel was ambushed and captured on the high seas by Yusuf Al-Ibrahim's men. He was brought before Yusuf Al-Ibrahim, who questioned him about the situation in Kuwait and pressed him to provide information about Sheikh Mubarak. Abu Kahil was later released, and when he eventually arrived in Kuwait he hastened to tell Sheikh Mubarak that a naval expedition was in preparation. When the ships arrived, therefore, Kuwait's own vessels were deployed in force ready to meet them. Afterwards, Mubarak asked Abu Kahil to say what he wanted as a reward, and though Abu

Kahil asked for nothing, Mubarak gave him a ship called *Al-Maymun* as a reward for his good deed.[11]

Despite this setback, however, Yusuf Al-Ibrahim did not abandon his plans, mounting a further attack, supported on this occasion by Sheikh Jassem bin Muhammad Al-Thani, the ruler of Qatar. An attack by both land and sea was set to take place in November 1897, but Sheikh Jassem thought better of it and the plan was not put into action. Afterwards, Yusuf Al-Ibrahim turned for support to Abdul Aziz bin Mut'ab Al-Rashid, the Emir of Ha'il and Najd, who was known as the 'Emir of the Mountain'. Ibn Al-Rashid had his own reasons for seeking to undermine Kuwait because, from 1892, Kuwait had given sanctuary to the Emir Abdul Rahman Al-Faisal Al-Saud, bitter enemy of the Al-Rashid. Isolated incidents had already led to armed clashes between the two sides. However, the British were monitoring events and warned Sheikh Mubarak against the consequences of attacking the Al-Rashid. The British administration in India contacted Mubarak's agent in Bombay warning him of the consequences of such an attack, but the Sheikh refused to accept this advice.[12]

Eventually, it appeared that the Ottoman authorities came to see that Sheikh Mubarak had a firm grip on power in Kuwait and that any attempts against him by Yusuf Al-Ibrahim would continue to be fruitless. In December 1897, the Sultan issued an edict appointing Sheikh Mubarak as *qaimaqam* over Kuwait, with an annual salary of 150 *kara* of dates,[13] which was commuted to an annual salary of 300 pounds sterling.[14] Sheikh Mubarak by no means always maintained the upper hand in his intermittent confrontations with his enemies, however, and armed clashes between Mubarak and Ibn Al-Rashid continued. The most serious setback for the Sheikh came with the battle of Al-Sarif in March 1901, when Mubarak's forces were defeated. This will be discussed in detail below. The defeat was a resounding one, and the door seemed once more to be open for the Ottomans to attempt the reimposition of their direct authority over Kuwait. The following year, Qasim Pasha, the Sultan's son-in-law and commander-in-chief of Ottoman forces in Iraq, marched to Basra at the head of a military force. The plan was that this force would then move on to Kuwait to depose Sheikh Mubarak.

London objected to this move on the part of the Ottomans, which opened the possibility of a confrontation between Britain and the Ottoman Empire. Muhsin Pasha, the Governor of Basra, however, took a diplomatic initiative that was crucial in halting the escalation, no doubt at the behest of Istanbul. On 18 May 1901, Muhsin Pasha paid a friendly visit to Kuwait, accompanied by Qasim Pasha, certain notables from Basra and a small force of 150 soldiers. He declared that the objective of this visit was to ameliorate the state of relations between Mubarak and Ibn Al-Rashid. However, when Muhsin met Sheikh Mubarak, he also tried to persuade him to offer his submission to the Ottoman Sultan's orders, on the grounds that the emirate was a *sanjak* of the Ottoman Empire.[15] Muhsin also made another attempt to persuade Mubarak to agree to have an Ottoman garrison in Kuwait, but the Sheikh maintained his refusal.[16]

Despatches from the Russian embassy in Istanbul record that the visit lasted for four days, and that the Sheikh received Muhsin Pasha with true Arab warmth; however, it was reported that from the moment he arrived, he was given clearly to understand by Mubarak that he was receiving him not as the Governor of Basra or an envoy of the Sultan, but simply as an old friend who had offered him much help during hard times. A later report by Alexander Adamov, the Russian Consul in Basra, stated that on this occasion Mubarak told Muhsin Pasha explicitly that, because of the threat he was facing from the Ottomans, he had agreed to place himself under the protection of a foreign power.[17]

However, Mubarak was still careful not to sever his ties with the Ottoman authorities completely. In response to the Governor's request that he travel to Basra to declare his allegiance to the Sultan, Mubarak agreed to go to Faw but not as far as Basra, and only on condition that he did so on board his own private yacht.

On 23 May 1901, the Sheikh's yacht set sail, accompanied by one other ship carrying companions and guards. Meanwhile, the Sheikh had taken care to contact the British Political Resident in the Gulf to inform him about his intention to travel to Faw, asking the British official to monitor developments. Once in Faw, he sent a telegram to Istanbul renewing his loyalty and allegiance to the Ottoman Sultan.[18]

The Ottoman archive in Istanbul includes a number of documents that demonstrate the vacillation of the Ottoman leaders in the years 1899–1901 between a diplomatic approach to Kuwait on the one hand, and the use of force on the other, in order to obtain the allegiance of Sheikh Mubarak. One of these documents, dating from 1899, records the decision of the Ottoman cabinet to,

> dispatch the Naqib Al-Ashraf[19] of Basra to Kuwait at the order of the Sublime Porte to counsel Mubarak Al-Sabah to be obedient and subjugate himself to the higher authorities, to warn him of the foreign ambitions in Kuwait and its surrounding area, and to indicate what great harm the fulfilment of these ambitions would bring to the Empire and to Islam.[20]

There is also a memorandum by the Head of Scribes in the Imperial Divan, written in the same year. This comments that,

> Mubarak Al-Sabah must be made to understand, wisely and through correct and efficacious words, that if the British are successful in fulfilling their ambitions to expand into Kuwait, this will bring great harm to the Empire and to Islam ... Owing to his connection to the Imperial State and his mission to preserve the rights of Muslims, he must take the necessary measures to prevent these foreign ambitions from being achieved.

The document adds that if Mubarak were to do so, and also send a written undertaking to remain faithful to his promise and to his relationship with the Imperial State, he would be accorded high ranks, honours and privileges.[21]

After the Ottoman had fulfilled his duty, the Governor of Basra sent a memorandum to the interior ministry on 31 January 1900 in which he noted that the Naqib had returned the previous day from Kuwait to Basra carrying a letter and a pledge of allegiance from Mubarak Al-Sabah. The Governor of Basra asked that Mubarak should be honoured with the rank of 'mirmirat' and be granted a medal befitting this rank,[22] and that his annual grant from the Ottoman state, which had been withheld, should now be paid.[23] Subsequently, however, with no clear progress taking place in relations between Kuwait and Istanbul, the Special Council of Ministers under the Grand Vizier, Rifat Pasha, met to discuss sending the Naqib Al-Ashraf of Basra once more to communicate with the Sheikh.[24]

Following Mubarak's defeat at the battle of Al-Sarif, the Special Council of Ministers had once more discussed the matter of the official Ottoman presence in Kuwait. A special committee reported on the issue to the council, saying,

> Mubarak Pasha now leans towards the British after his defeat by Ibn Al-Rashid. There are two British navy ships in Kuwaiti waters and two naval agencies in Kuwait which display the British flag. This is because the Imperial State has so far neglected to establish official departments there such as customs offices and a port.

The report also remarked that the Ottoman interior minister had informed the Sultan that the governments of France and Germany were in agreement that the Ottomans should set up official departments in Kuwait, 'to confirm its legitimate authority over this part of its Empire'.[25]

At the same time, Muhsin Pasha wrote to Istanbul, commenting that the British had been waiting for several years for an opportunity to take the Sheikh of Kuwait under their wing. In his words:

As a result of the defeat suffered by Mubarak Pasha at the hands of Ibn Al-Rashid, the Marshal of the Sixth Imperial Army came to Basra to inform officials there of the formation of a military force to be sent to Kuwait under the leadership of Mirliva Muhammad Fadel Pasha.[26] He made statements which specified various threats that had been made to Mubarak Pasha.

The Governor of Basra added that there were rumours that Ibn Al-Rashid was preparing for an invasion of Kuwait, and that this situation could have the paradoxical result of leading to the rise of British influence in Kuwait. He explained that during his visit to Kuwait two months previously he had witnessed with his own eyes a British naval ship stationed in the waters of Kuwait, with other naval ships paying visits periodically. Although he had tried to persuade Mubarak to allow an Ottoman force to land in Kuwait and to allow the establishment of Ottoman offices there, he had been unsuccessful. He was also personally prepared to initiate military action to guarantee what he called 'the sacred rights of the Exalted Sultanate in Kuwait'.[27]

Muhsin Pasha continued to take a lively interest in developments regarding Kuwait. He sent a cable in cipher to Istanbul in which he reported that he had written to Mubarak Al-Sabah Pasha demanding to know why British merchant ships were coming to Kuwait in such great numbers, and why the British were building a lighthouse and harbour facilities. He reported that he had received a reply from Sheikh Mubarak in which the latter said:

> The purpose is to help with the importation of essential goods for the people of Kuwait, including rice and other commodities. These ships will not be allowed to come back to Kuwait after they have made one or two more trips. As regards the allegations that a work permit has been given to a British trading agency, that a lighthouse and a pontoon have been built and that the British flag has been flown, and that contact has been made with a ship afflicted with communicable

diseases, these are all lies and there is no truth in them. All Kuwait is decorated with Ottoman victory banners, and this can be verified by sending an envoy to Kuwait.

The Governor of Basra added that he would send the ship *Zahhaf* as soon as its renovation was completed to investigate the matter. The Governor repeated what he had declared previously in regard to 'his readiness to lead a military force with the aim of rectifying matters in Kuwait, either by persuading Mubarak to submit to the Imperial Sultan or through defeating him by military force'.[28]

The Ottoman Special Council of Ministers was convened under the leadership of the Grand Vizier, Rifat Pasha, to discuss this memorandum. It was agreed that 'Mubarak Al-Sabah Pasha would be invited to Basra and that his security would be guaranteed by suitable means. Discussions will be held with him to persuade him to allow an imperial military force to land in Kuwait and to set up port and customs authorities there. The Ministry of the Interior wil inform the governor of Basra of this decision after it is ratified by the Sultan.'[29]

On 26 August 1901, the Governor of Basra sent a cable in cipher to the Sublime Porte. It said that the commanding officer of the ship *Zahhaf*, which had arrived in Kuwait two days earlier,

> had been met by the commander of a British naval ship there who informed him that Kuwait was under British protection. The British officer threatened the Ottoman captain with military reprisals if he attempted to land troops or unload munitions.

The captain of the ship added that he had gone to meet Sheikh Mubarak, who denied the existence of British protection but added that he was prepared to accept it if compelled to do so.[30] Captain Pears, the commanding officer of the British ship, the *Perseus*, warned the captain of the *Zahhaf* against any attempt to land troops, adding that if he did so he would be fired on.

According to the British documentary record, the British captain's report says that the Ottoman officer informed him that there were no troops on board his ship and that he had simply come to negotiate with the Sheikh. The Turkish captain also pointed out that Kuwait was Ottoman territory, that the Sheikh was an Ottoman subject, and that foreign countries had no right to interfere in Kuwaiti affairs. The next day, the captain of the *Zahhaf* met Sheikh Mubarak and declared his intention to stay in Kuwait. Mubarak replied that he could do what he liked as long as he did not attempt to land any troops. The officer repeated the threat that he would inform the Ottoman authorities in Faw of what had happened and would return with more ships and troops. The Sheikh answered that he should do whatever he saw fit.

The Ottoman Special Council of Ministers met on 28 August to discuss the claim made by the captain of the British ship to the effect that Britain had declared its protection over Kuwait. It was agreed that instructions would be issued to the Ottoman embassy in London to contact the British Government, 'to urge it to stop officials from making such statements which are in contradiction to the good relations between the two countries'.[31] This was approved by the Sultan on 31 August.

On 4 September, as a result of the long absence of Lord Landsdowne, the British Foreign Secretary, because of illness that had caused him to remain in Ireland, the Ottoman ambassador met a Foreign Ministry spokesman to express his country's surprise at such behaviour by the British, which, he pointed out, was not in accordance with existing agreements. The British official replied that what had taken place was a misunderstanding between the captains of the two ships and that he would put the matter to the Foreign Secretary upon his return and would let the ambassador know his reply.[32] The Ottoman ambassador returned to the Foreign Ministry in London the very next day to insist on the necessity of 'preserving the legitimate rights of the Imperial State in Kuwait', pointing out that 'any agreement by the British government made separately with *qaimaqam* Mubarak Al-Sabah would be considered illegal. However, if it wishes to make a separate agreement to protect its merchant ships, then this must be made with the Sublime Porte.'[33]

Britain expressed its objections to the Naqib of Basra's mission to Kuwait. The British chargé d'affaires in Istanbul was received by the Ottoman Foreign Minister, whereupon he issued what amounted to a threat, namely that,

> unless orders are not sent immediately to the aforementioned Naqib to return to Basra immediately and never again to presume to undertake such an action, the British government will withdraw the safeguards it has given to preserve the status quo in Kuwait. The Sublime Porte will be responsible for the consequences.[34]

What increased the anxiety and irritation of the British diplomats was that a blanket of secrecy had surrounded the Naqib's mission. When they questioned Mubarak about the mission, he gave expedient answers, which he deemed necessary in order to maintain his relations with both the Ottomans as well as the British.[35]

The following day, on 6 September 1901, the Ottoman embassy in London forwarded to Istanbul a memorandum from the British Foreign Office that condemned the Naqib of Basra's trip to Kuwait and the threats he had issued to Mubarak Al-Sabah. The telegram included the report sent by the British naval captain in Kuwait, which said, as it was quoted by the Ottoman memorandum:

> If Ottoman officials continue to create difficulties, the British government may have to seek a different kind of arrangement which might be less in keeping with the interests of the Imperial State.

On the same day, the Ottoman Foreign Minister sent a telegram to his embassy in London regarding his meeting with the British ambassador in Istanbul. The ambassador had confirmed, that his government would not consider occupying Kuwait or imposing protection upon it if the Imperial State will refrain from the dispatch of any military force to the country and will guarantee the preservation of the status quo there.

The minister had reassured the British ambassador that the Ottoman Government was not planning to send a military force to Kuwait at that time and that it was committed to the status quo there, but that Britain must reciprocate by promising neither to occupy Kuwait nor to impose protection on it.[36]

On 13 September 1901, the Ottoman embassy in London responded with a despatch to Istanbul that included the response of the British Foreign Secretary given on 11 September 1901:

> The British government confirms the assurances given by the British ambassador in Istanbul to the Foreign Minister of the Imperial State that Britain will not occupy Kuwait or impose its protection on it on condition that the status quo is preserved and the Imperial State does not send a military force there.[37]

Owing to Ottoman fears that British influence in Kuwait was growing, the Sublime Porte issued an imperial edict whose provisions included the voluntary exile of Sheikh Mubarak from Kuwait. The Sheikh would be obliged to take up residence in Istanbul, where he would be appointed as a member of the state Shura council, or alternatively he could travel to any other Ottoman territory, where he would receive an annual pension. If he were to refuse to do this, he would be removed from Kuwait by force and would be, as the edict phrased it, 'treated harshly'. The Governor of Basra, Mustafa Nuri Pasha, then sent a copy of this edict to the Sheikh.

When Sheikh Mubarak received Nuri Pasha's letter, he dealt with it calmly and shrewdly, sending a response in which he detailed all the support the Al-Sabah had afforded to the Ottoman Empire and confirmed that his sentiments towards the Empire were unaltered. Mubarak was certainly aware that the Governor of

Basra had no power to implement the imperial order, but in any case, by sending a response, he sought to gain time through prevarication. He also wrote a letter to the British Political Resident informing him of what had transpired. The latter promised his assistance.

The *Zahhaf* reappeared off the coast of Kuwait on 1 December 1901, carrying Rajab Al-Naqib, the Naqib Al-Ashraf of Basra, along with Miralay Najib Bek,[38] the brother of Mustafa Nuri Pasha, the Governor of Basra. With them was an Ottoman military force sufficient to enable them to compel Sheikh Mubarak to carry out the imperial order of which he had been notified. He had been informed that if he did not implement it willingly, he would be removed from Kuwait by force.

The British response was swift and decisive. Orders were given to HMS *Pomone* to sail to the port of Kuwait, followed by HMS *Sphinx*. This was intended to demonstrate clearly the extent of British support for Mubarak against the Ottoman threats. Both captains told the Naqib the same thing, namely that they would bombard Kuwait City if Mubarak was obliged to succumb to the threat.[39] The Naqib had no choice but to retreat, sailing back to Basra on board the *Zahhaf*. The British Government lodged a protest with the Ottoman Government, as the British regarded the Ottoman actions as a flagrant violation of the Sultan's promise. The British declared that Her Majesty's Government was prepared to support the Sheikh, and that it would not permit an Ottoman attack on Kuwait.

The Ottoman Foreign Minister sent word to his embassy in London, explaining that the purpose of 'the Naqib of Basra's visit to Kuwait was not to put pressure on *qaimaqam* Mubarak in any form. He simply took the opportunity of *Zahhaf*'s presence to go on board the ship.' As for the British Government, he remarked that 'it would be a sorry state of affairs to consider the presence of high officials of the Imperial State in Basra in a city belonging to the Empire to be a violation of the status quo in Kuwait'. He continued: 'If the British government insists on regarding this as a violation then we are prepared to take it to arbitration to prove the justice of our case.' The minister asked that these clarifications be conveyed in person on the next occasion the ambassador had to meet Lord Landsdowne.[40]

The matter did not end there. On 15 December 1901, the Ottoman Foreign Minister asked his embassy in London to make enquiries about information received according to which the captain of HMS *Pomone* had hauled down the Ottoman flag, which had been flying in Kuwait for 300 years. Reportedly, the captain,

> threw it to the ground and raised instead the flag made specifically for Kuwait, which has black and white vertical stripes. He asked Ottoman officials in Kuwait to leave the country according to what he claimed was the agreement between the Imperial State and Britain over the independence of Kuwait.

The Ottoman Foreign Minister expressed his regret over this strange behaviour and said that his country was ready to take the matter to arbitration. He insisted that the Ottomans were determined to defend their political rights in Kuwait and once more asked his ambassador to make the Sublime Porte's position clear to the British Foreign Secretary.[41]

On 18 December 1901, the Ottoman embassy sent word to Istanbul of Lord Landsdowne's reaction to the information he had received. The Foreign Secretary reportedly said that the account of events given by the Ottoman Foreign Ministry was 'a fantasy that the mind could not grasp', adding that 'it was impossible that the captain of a British navy ship should behave in this way without him being reported'. He added that he would demand an explanation of this matter from the Admiralty and assured the Ottoman ambassador that the British Government seeks to 'preserve the status quo in the area'.[42]

On 30 December, the Governor of Basra, Nuri Pasha, sent an encoded cable to the Sublime Porte, marked 'very urgent'. This reported that he had forbidden the export of dates, rice and grain from Basra to Kuwait 'because Mubarak Al-Sabah had strayed beyond the circle of obedience and friendship'. He reported that he had sent the Naqib of Basra and the Miralay Najib Bek back to Kuwait on board the *Zahhaf* for a second time, 'to advise Mubarak Al-Sabah to return to the fold of obedience and submission to the Imperial State'.[43] However, Sheikh Mubarak had not agreed.

The next day the Grand Vizier, Sa'id Pasha, sent a memorandum to the Sultan concerning the British ambassador's request that the embargo on sending foodstuffs to Kuwait be lifted. This request was supported by the German ambassador, who pointed out that 'a prohibition on sending foodstuffs to Kuwait pushes it into the arms of foreign powers, which is undesirable'. The Grand Vizier added that the ban on exports to Kuwait had been ordered by the Governor of Basra, and that the Sublime Porte had not issued any instructions on the matter. The Grand Vizier asked for the Sultan's permission to lift the ban. On 3 January 1902, 'the Imperial Will agreed to do so'.[44]

Mubarak's defeat at the battle of Al-Sarif provided an opportunity for his old enemy Yusuf Al-Ibrahim to renew his efforts. He harried the Kuwaiti tribes who were loyal to Sheikh Mubarak, stealing their cattle and camels. In September 1902 he organized a naval campaign to invade Kuwait, which had the endorsement of the Governor of Basra. Despite Yusuf Al-Ibrahim having cloaked the preparations for this campaign in the utmost secrecy, it became known to Mubarak's son, Sheikh Jaber Al-Mubarak, who was in Faw at the time and gathered information about Yusuf Al-Ibrahim's movements. Jaber sent a messenger to his father warning him of the plans being made. He also sent a telegram conveying the same information to the British Political Resident in the Gulf.

The expedition, however, went ahead, and two large ships set sail transporting 150 men armed with guns. The intended disembarkation point for this force was at Ras Al-Ajuza, directly to the east of Kuwait City. However, the invaders were astonished to discover that the authorities in Kuwait knew all about the planned invasion. They also found themselves facing the British vessel HMS *Lapwing*, and its captain, Commander Armstrong, who was also apprised of Yusuf Al-Ibrahim's plans. This bid, like those Yusuf Al-Ibrahim had made previously, ended in failure. After armed exchanges, the two invading ships, together with all their supplies, weapons, ammunition and grappling ladders, were seized.[45]

Sir Nicholas O'Conor, the British ambassador in Istanbul, believed that this operation provided a clear demonstration of Britain's determination to defend Kuwait. The British Foreign Office protested about the incident to the Ottoman authorities, informing them that in future Britain would do whatever was necessary to guarantee its interests. Istanbul apologized and said that the events had taken place without their knowledge. However, the Ottoman Empire continued in other ways to put pressure on Sheikh Mubarak. In one instance, they encouraged the Sheikh of Al-Zubayr to seize livestock belonging to him.

The turbulent relationship between the Ottomans and Sheikh Mubarak never reached the point of complete rupture. Each side was careful to maintain its links with the other. Co-operation was intermingled with confrontation, and even conflict, paradoxically sometimes at the same time. For example, in early 1905, at a time of some improvement in the Sheikh's relations with Istanbul, the Ottoman authorities made a series of proposals that included the deployment of a military garrison, the opening of a post office and the establishment of a quarantine office in Kuwait. The Sheikh rejected all these initiatives. He did, however, agree that a telegraph line to be constructed from Basra to Al-Qatif could pass through Kuwait, which he perceived as a potential advantage. He also agreed that Ottoman mail from the Governor of Al-Hasa could be transported across Kuwait. In the same period, Sheikh Mubarak made sporadic contributions to the cost of building Turkish military installations in Basra. He also signed an agreement to return escaped criminals to the Ottoman authorities, were they to be apprehended in Kuwait. The Ottoman authorities responded to this by allowing Sheikh Mubarak to build a harbour in Faw, opposite the land owned by Kuwait. The only factor interrupting these exchanges was the intermittent disturbances created by Yusuf Al-Ibrahim. With Yusuf Al-Ibrahim's death on 25 January 1906, his attempts to interfere in Kuwait ended and Mubarak's rule was thereby strengthened.[46]

Those who were hostile to Mubarak among the Ottoman officials did not, however, give up the hope they retained of dislodging him in favour of a more amenable candidate. They encouraged an attack on Kuwait by the Sheikh of Al-Muntafiq, Sa'dun Mansur Pasha. He had been persecuted by the Ottoman authorities in 1903, and had sought refuge in Kuwait, living there for a period under Sheikh Mubarak's protection, so knew Kuwait well. On 10 June 1910, he was victorious over a Kuwaiti force led by Sheikh Jaber Al-Mubarak and Emir Abdul Aziz bin Saud at a pitched battle at Hadiyya. When the news reached Sheikh Mubarak, he commented that he would prepare an army twice the size of Sa'dun Mansur's forces and would take revenge on the Sheikh of Al-Muntafiq. This is precisely what took place five months later at the battle of Mazboura, where Kuwait and its sheikh were amply compensated for the defeat at Hadiyya, and the Sheikh of Al-Muntafiq was heavily defeated.[47]

These occasional vicissitudes in the relationship between Sheikh Mubarak and the Ottoman Empire resonated in the Arabic press at the time, where journalists backed either one side or the other. For example, Sheikh Rashid Rida wrote an article on the matter in *Al-Manar* magazine under the title, 'The Question of Sheikh Mubarak's Relationship with the Ottoman Authorities and the British'. He defended the Sheikh, affirming that he was 'an Ottoman who dearly loved the Commander of the Faithful and that the British interference in Kuwait was the result of bad administration by the Ottomans'. Rashid Rida quotes Sheikh Mubarak as saying, they proposed to me that I should choose a flag to fly over my country and declare my independence under their protection, but I refused. And every day you can see the Ottoman flag flying over my head.[48]

In the same vein, Abd Al-Massih Antaki, the owner of *Al-Imran* magazine in Cairo, wrote several adulatory articles about Sheikh Mubarak, drawing attention to his presumed loyalty to the Ottoman Empire. One of these was in the form of an open letter to Sultan Abdul Hamid, asking him not to neglect those who were loyal sons of the Ottoman nation such as Sheikh Mubarak. He said that, despite all that the Sheikh had done for the Imperial State, he had not been immune to the imputations of the malicious and the allegations of disloyalty, adding:

> This madness cannot be taken seriously by any rational person and only the ignorant would do so. It has been denied by all those who know Sheikh Mubarak or know anything about him, whether regarding his adherence to Islam or his dedication to the support of the Ottoman Caliphate.[49]

Antaki accompanied Sheikh Mubarak on his trip from Al-Muhammara to Kuwait in 1907. During the trip, Antaki sent 23 letters about his experience back to Cairo, which were published in *Al-Imran* magazine under the collective title, 'The Flowery Gardens between Kuwait and Al-Muhammara'. The following year, he published a book in which he affirmed yet again the loyalty of the Sheikh to the Ottoman Empire and his desire to revive the glory of Islam and the Muslims. He commented that the tense relations between the Sheikh and certain Ottoman officials were no more than the result of the miscalculations of the officials and their repeated misjudgements in their relationship with Arab leaders.[50]

Despite the strengthening relationship between Sheikh Mubarak and Britain that was developing at the same time, which Mubarak used as a balancing factor against Ottoman threats, British diplomats deduced from Sheikh Mubarak's care not to compromise his links with the Ottoman Empire that the Sheikh had his own plans and ambitions that did not always coincide with British interests. In a memorandum dated 21 March 1902, Lord Landsdowne expressed his anxiety over the Sheikh. In regard to Mubarak's activities, he noted: 'The situation in Kuwait has become more critical. It is time to confront him directly and frankly.' He also said that, while Britain had committed itself to Sheikh Mubarak, 'it is clear that he is not trustworthy. No one knows where his land begins and ends. Our obligations towards him are like the borders of his country, unspecified.'[51]

In October 1902, Mubarak asked the British Government in India to supply him with two artillery pieces, which he planned to deploy in the area of Al-Jahra in response to tribal attacks there. The request was forwarded to the Foreign Office in London, with a suggestion that it should be rejected on the basis that the British Government had promised to protect Kuwait and that Mubarak therefore had no need for such weapons. Lord Landsdowne agreed to the request, but made it a condition that the borders of Kuwait should at last be clearly delineated.

Meanwhile, on occasion, the Ottoman authorities were still taking steps to improve their relations with Sheikh Mubarak. On 11 October 1910, the Governor of Basra sent a letter to 'the revered noble sir, *qaimaqam* of Kuwait, his excellency the blessed Sheikh Mubarak Al-Sabah', informing him that there were annual allowances set aside for the *qaimaqam* of Kuwait and asking him how he would like to receive them, and whether he wished them to be allocated from the budget for the Faw area or the main treasury in Basra.

Sheikh Mubarak replied on the same day, signing his letter 'Ruler of Kuwait and the head of its tribes', the title Mubarak used in preference to the appellation '*qaimaqam* of Kuwait'. In his letter the Sheikh noted that he had not received the monetary allowances alluded to for many years past, but that this had not prevented him from loyal and faithful co-operation with the Ottoman authorities, adding that he saw no reason to burden the budget of the Ottoman state with such an expense.[52] Thus, Mubarak refused to receive the monthly allowances accorded to him by the Ottoman Empire. His motive was to retain his hard-won independence regarding the administration of Kuwait's internal affairs, and to lay stress on the principle that his relationship with the Ottoman state was solely a moral one and implied no financial obligation. However, Ottoman officials hostile to the Sheikh continued to try to embarrass him. On 11 May 1912, the newspaper *Al-Dustur* in Basra published a report claiming that a monthly salary of 20,000 piasters had been allocated to Sheikh Mubarak Al-Sabah. This was denied by the Governor of Basra in the same newspaper on 22 May.[53]

In the second decade of the twentieth century, however, the constant stream of attempts by the Ottoman authorities to extend their control over Kuwait continued. In 1911, the Governor of Basra informed the Sheikh that the Ottoman Government was prepared to issue a *firman* that would guarantee his position, adding that they would refrain from interfering in Kuwait's local affairs on condition that Sheikh Mubarak registered his people as Ottoman subjects. The Sheikh did not respond to this proposal, so the Ottomans reiterated it in 1913. The Governor of Basra proposed to Sheikh Mubarak that he would consult him in all matters to do with Basra and the Arabian Desert, and would help him control his own desert tribes. Sheikh Mubarak was not unaware that the aim of this proposal was simply to tie him more closely to the Ottoman state, and concluded that it would lead to problems with the tribes. He excused himself from entering into any obligation, citing his old age and his preoccupation with the affairs of his subjects and country.[54]

Exploiting international rivalries

Since the accession to power of Sheikh Sabah Al-Sabah, the first ruler of Kuwait from the Al-Sabah family, the rulers of Kuwait had followed a cautious policy aimed at preserving their country's independence: this included the exclusion of any official foreign presence. In the preceding period a number of external challenges had threatened Kuwait. The most important of these was the British East India Company's attempt to increase its role in Kuwait's affairs, with British support. The rise in the influence of the Wahhabi movement in Arabia was also a challenge, as its followers attempted to extend their influence into Kuwait and to disseminate their ideas there.

Faced with these challenges, the rulers of Kuwait used their links with the Ottoman Empire as a means of balancing power. However, Istanbul never appointed a local ruler in Kuwait, in contrast to its policy of imposing Ottoman governors in the Fertile Crescent and Egypt. Instead, the Ottomans had accorded recognition to the existing Sheikh of Kuwait and had granted him financial allowances. The authority of the Ottoman Sultan over Kuwait remained on a moral and nominal basis. Yet this did not prevent various Ottoman officials, particularly the Governor of Basra, from interfering from time to time in the affairs of the country, especially when they felt that the ruler of Kuwait was facing a crisis and needed Ottoman support.

At the beginning of Mubarak's period of rule, Hamdi Pasha, the Governor of Basra, as has been seen, inaugurated a new phase when he attempted to extend Ottoman influence over Kuwait, making a bid to change the relationship from merely nominal control into one of real power. This clashed with Sheikh Mubarak's ambition to preserve Kuwait's independence and his own autonomy. It also clashed with British interests, as the British desire to maintain the Gulf as an unhindered sea passage to India necessitated that they would attempt to prevent the intrusion of any other external influence into the region, whether Ottoman or European.

It was in the 1870s that Kuwait began to represent a major concern for British diplomacy and strategy. A report by a Colonel Bailey focused on the special maritime features of Kuwait harbour, pointing out its commercial and strategic importance for Britain. In

1871, a British parliamentary committee recommended that a railway be built linking Alexandretta (İskenderun) on the Mediterranean with Kuwait City. Later, on 16 September 1904, the correspondent for the Cairo *Al-Ahram* newspaper wrote about the increased strategic importance of Kuwait, and Britain's focus on it:

> Kuwait is crucially important because it is the gateway to the whole region. It is the only route into the heart of Arabia. From Kuwait, the road to Iraq and Mesopotamia begins. The road from Kuwait into Iraq avoids the obstacles present in Shatt Al-Arab and its channels.[55]

Furthermore, the changing international situation, and rising European rivalry over the Gulf, enhanced the strategic importance of Kuwait.

We shall examine in what follows how the interests of Sheikh Mubarak and Britain coincided, leading on 23 January 1899 to the signing of the protection agreement. From the outset, the Ottomans circulated rumours about Mubarak's relationship with the British. Some said his first contact with a British representative was made in Bombay, where he had lived for some time before assuming power. Istanbul accused the British Political Resident in Bushire of organizing the events that led to Mubarak taking power. For their part, the British dealt with Sheikh Mubarak as an independent ruler, responsible for the behaviour of his subjects. For instance, when some of the Sheikh's men were accused of piracy in the waters of the Shatt Al-Arab, the British Foreign Office placed responsibility on the Sheikh of Kuwait because 'he is an independent ruler who only nominally recognizes Ottoman authority'.[56]

With the spread of reports about Mubarak's ambiguity towards the Ottoman Empire, which at the time was seen as the symbol of Islam and the unity of Muslims, a controversy began over the Sheikh's attitude, with some regarding him as less than loyal to the

Islamic community. Some publications referred to the matter as the 'fitna of Kuwait'.[57]

In fact, it was in 1896 that Mubarak first reached out to the British when he asked them to protect the independence of Kuwait from Ottoman influence. At this time, he was under pressure from Yusuf Al-Ibrahim's incessant conspiracies and interference, which were not discouraged by the Ottoman authorities. However, Sheikh Mubarak was careful always to show overt loyalty to the Ottoman Empire. This was why, on 3 July 1896, he refused to board the British ship HMS *Sphinx* when it docked in Kuwait. The HMS *Sphinx* had been sent by the British Government in India to discover the truth about the events in Kuwait that had led to Sheikh Mubarak's rise to power.

In his report on the visit, the captain of the HMS *Sphinx*, Commander Baker, mentions that the ship's arrival in Kuwait had caused many problems. Mubarak had not wanted the visit to take place and had ostentatiously flown the Ottoman flag over his palace. When Baker questioned him on this, he was evasive to such an extent that the captain thought that Kuwait had fallen under Ottoman authority and that Ottoman influence must have increased after Sheikh Mubarak came to power. However, despite Mubarak's demonstrations of loyalty, the Ottomans themselves did not trust him, suspecting that he was attempting to break away from their sphere of control. In fact their level of mistrust seems to have prompted him to go further in seeking protection from the British than he might otherwise have done.[58]

According to British documents, the first actual contact was made by the Sheikh on 15 February 1897, through his friend Muhammad Rahim bin Abdul Nabi Safar, the British Political Agent in Bahrain. Safar conveyed to the British authorities Sheikh Mubarak's wish to meet one of the British officials in Bushire. Britain's policy at the time was not to make contact with local sheikhs in areas that Britain considered to be part of the Ottoman Empire, so Sheikh Mubarak received no response to his request.

At the end of March, Sheikh Mubarak sent word to his friend in Bahrain again, reminding him that he was still waiting for a reply.

After long discussions between British diplomats, in which the British Political Resident in Bushire, the British Government in India and the Foreign Office in London all participated, it was agreed that a channel of communications would be opened with Sheikh Mubarak. Muhammad Rahim Safar was instructed to arrange a meeting in Al-Muhammara between Mubarak and J. C. Gaskin, the Deputy Political Resident in Bushire. The meeting was set for 29 April, and although Gaskin arrived at the agreed time, Sheikh Mubarak did not. It is uncertain why Mubarak absented himself from the meeting he had long sought. Perhaps he had simply failed to receive the invitation. Alternatively, some political consideration, and in particular the ongoing attempts by Yusuf Al-Ibrahim to invade Kuwait and remove him from power, may have prevented him from attending. For his part, Mubarak wrote to the Political Resident explaining that he was unable to travel outside Kuwait and preferred not to send a delegation to meet Gaskin. He suggested that the Political Resident should send an envoy or a representative to Kuwait to discuss matters with him.

Some months elapsed, but in due course, on 5 September 1897, Gaskin travelled to Kuwait on board HMS *Lawrence*. He held two meetings with Sheikh Mubarak in the presence of the captain of the ship, Captain Hewitt, and wrote a detailed report to the Political Resident, Colonel Meade, who forwarded it to the British Government in India on 25 September 1897. The report said that the two meetings took place on shore because Sheikh Mubarak had been reluctant to board the ship, fearing that this would cause him difficulty with the Ottoman authorities at a time when London was still undecided about British protection over Kuwait.

According to the report, the purpose of the meeting was to warn the Sheikh against the repercussions of becoming involved in piracy and to point out to him that the British authorities would hold him responsible for any acts of piracy committed by his subjects against British-protected ships, such as the attack on the Indian vessel *Haripasa* in 1895 in the Shatt Al-Arab. The Sheikh of Kuwait denied that any of his subjects were involved in such acts and claimed that the source of the piracy was the other side of the Gulf. The Sheikh added that Kuwaiti boats had been raided and plundered more than once, and declared that he was prepared to co-operate in fighting piracy. The Sheikh then said that he and his people wished to place Kuwait under British protection, in the same way as Bahrain and the sheikhs on the Trucial Coast had done. He added that in order to achieve this he would be ready to co-operate with Britain in the maintenance of law and order in the areas under his control in the Gulf. He asserted his belief that the Ottomans wished to fully absorb Kuwait, and that he desired British protection in order to guard against this.[59]

However, having read the report of the meeting, Colonel Meade commented that he was suspicious of Sheikh Mubarak's intentions and his apparent desire to enjoy British support because of his continuing links with the Ottoman Empire and the financial contribution he continued to make to it. His conclusion was that the Sheikh's motive for wishing to develop a relationship with Britain was to exert pressure on the Ottoman authorities in order to prevent them from interfering in Kuwait's internal affairs. Nevertheless, the Government of India forwarded the Sheikh's request for British protection to the Foreign Office in London. The request was rejected, in accordance with the Foreign Office's policy not to interfere in Kuwait's affairs as long as the security of the region was not under threat or in danger.

As international rivalry grew, however, and after the Ottoman Empire granted a concession on 30 December 1898 to an influential Russian, Count Vladimir Kapnist, to build a railway from the Syrian city of Tripoli on the Mediterranean to Kuwait, British views changed, and the British Foreign Secretary, Lord Salisbury, prioritized the signature of an agreement between Kuwait and Britain. He asked Colonel Meade to go to Kuwait to sign the agreement. Meade arrived on 21 January 1899 on board

HMS *Lawrence*. At the time, the Ottoman vessel *Zahhaf* was in the port, but it left the following day.

Four considerations that led to this change of mind on the part of the British and the signature to an agreement with Kuwait can be identified. First, Britain had become aware that Ottoman forces were being mobilized in Basra in preparation for an invasion of Kuwait that was intended to remove Mubarak from power. Second, the Russian embassy in Istanbul was agitating against the British, and in the context of Russia's plan for the construction of a railway to Kuwait it had asked the Ottoman authorities to build a coaling station in Kuwait where trains could be refuelled. Third, Germany, which had already made economic and commercial inroads into the Ottoman Empire, was also seeking to construct a railway. This line would run between Berlin and Baghdad with a continuation to Kuwait. Finally, Britain's view had changed with the accession of Lord Curzon to the position of Viceroy of India in 1898. Curzon was one of a group of British diplomats who always stressed the importance of the Gulf to British interests, and he was anxious to impose British control over the region. Curzon went as far as to say that he regarded British control over the Gulf as crucial to the security of India. He therefore took the view that no other European power should be allowed to encroach on British influence in the area. For this reason, Curzon's policy towards the Gulf differed from that of his predecessors, and he took the decision that it was necessary to enter negotiations with Sheikh Mubarak in order to place Kuwait under British protection.[60]

On the other side, Sheikh Mubarak had his own reasons for continuing to want a treaty with Britain. These included the ongoing conflict of interest between Kuwait and the Ottoman Empire, and the unsettling role played by his old enemy Yusuf Al-Ibrahim, who had been working hard to arouse the hostility of Hamdi Pasha, the Governor of Basra, towards Mubarak. In the Arabian Peninsula, Ibn Al-Rashid, another Ottoman ally, also presented a threat to Kuwait. The alliance between Sheikh Jassem, the ruler of Qatar, Ibn Al-Rashid and Yusuf Al-Ibrahim was a further threat. In the face of all these dangers, Mubarak wanted a guarantee of Britain's military and political protection in order to safeguard the position of the Al-Sabah family in Kuwait. Mubarak may have believed that British protection would afford Kuwait sufficient security and stability to enable him to exercise an active and effective regional policy.

The agreement between Kuwait and Britain was signed on 23 January 1899 by Sheikh Mubarak, the ruler of Kuwait, and Colonel Meade, the British Political Resident in the Gulf. The witnesses were Muhammad Rahim bin Abdul Nabi Safar, the British Political Agent in Bahrain, and J. Calcott Gaskin, the assistant to the British Political Resident. Three copies were made. According to the agreement, the Sheikh of Kuwait undertook 'on behalf of himself, his heirs and successors not to accept any other country's or government's agent or *qaimaqam* in Kuwait or in any other area within its borders without the permission of the British Imperial State'. He also committed himself and his heirs and successors not to give up, sell, rent, pledge, mortgage or give away for the purposes of ownership, or for any other purpose, any part of his land to any other government or the subjects of any other country without the agreement of the British Government. When Colonel Meade asked Mubarak to sign this agreement, he refused to do so without further guarantees from Britain. He demanded that there should be a written statement specifying Britain's agreement to protect Sheikh Mubarak if Kuwait should be in danger.

Colonel Meade explained to the Sheikh that he could not include this condition in the clauses of the agreement because he was not authorized to do so, and also pointed out that such a text was not included in any other agreement that Britain had made with the sheikhs of the Gulf. But Mubarak insisted on this demand. The matter was eventually resolved by adding an appendix to the agreement that included a letter from Meade to Sheikh Mubarak confirming that Britain would offer its 'good offices' if any danger were to threaten Kuwait. A further clause was also added to the agreement, at Mubarak's request, which extended Britain's commitment to Kuwait to cover any other territories owned by the Sheikh, even if such territories were under the sovereignty of other states. The intention here was to indicate that Britain would regard itself as committed to guarantee that the date farms in Faw would remain the property of the Al-Sabah family. This appeared to answer the reservations of Sheikh Mubarak's brothers, who had refused to sign the agreement, apparently in order to put pressure on Britain to protect the property of the Al-Sabah family that lay in Ottoman territory. Finally, Meade insisted to the Sheikh that the agreement should not be made public, in order not to provoke other countries.

In June 1899, to ensure that the British Political Resident in Bushire would be in a position to continue monitoring the situation in Kuwait, as well as Sheikh Mubarak's activities, Ali Gholoum Rida was appointed as 'news' agent in Kuwait. It was part of Britain's diplomatic practice in the Gulf to appoint what were known as 'native' agents and informants to work for them in the Gulf sheikhdoms under the cover of being engaged in trade. One of Gholoum's earliest letters was sent on 4 September 1899, written in Persian. The last was sent on 10 May 1904. This was less than a month before the first British Political Agent was officially appointed in Kuwait.[61]

The agreement between Sheikh Mubarak and the British authorities could not be kept secret, however. Ali bin Gholoum's letter of 18 December 1899 says, 'The people of Kuwait are secretly discussing news of an agreement between Sheikh Mubarak and the Political Agent.'[62] The news had also reached the Ottomans. As a direct response, Anis Pasha, who had been an ineffectual governor in Basra, was replaced by Hamdi Pasha, who remained in the office until the beginning of 1897, finally leaving only because of Sheikh Mubarak's hostility towards him, which had been prompted in turn by the Governor's own antagonism. The Russian Consul in Baghdad commented on Anis Pasha's dismissal by saying, 'The Kuwait issue played the major role in

changing the governor of Basra.' This seemed to be confirmed
when the new governor began to make military preparations and to
prepare the ground politically for the subjugation of Kuwait. He
wrote to the Sublime Porte stressing the importance of increasing
the strength of the Ottoman navy in the Gulf.[63] Both the German
and Russian Empires regarded the accord between Britain and
Kuwait as a new episode in the extension of British control over
the Gulf, which called for political action on their part to reinforce
the influence of the Ottoman Empire in Kuwait. This may be why
the Germans pressed ahead to reach agreement with the Sublime
Porte on the licence granted to Germany to build the Baghdad
railway, which was concluded at the same time.

Nevertheless, the agreement was not officially made public until
1903, when Lord Landsdowne at last made a statement to
Parliament to the effect that the Sheikh of Kuwait had concluded
an agreement with Britain relating to British protection. This was
the first official announcement of the extension of British
protection over Kuwait. The agreement remained the basis of
Anglo-Kuwaiti relations until Kuwait gained its independence
in 1961.[64]

Despite the obligations placed on Sheikh Mubarak by the
protection agreement, and his belief in the importance of the
British role in protecting the independence of his country against
Ottoman interference, he still avoided a complete severance of his
links with the Ottoman Empire. Sheikh Mubarak was well aware
that Kuwait still had major interests that would be safeguarded by
the maintenance of relations with the Ottomans – for example, the
protection of the property of the Al-Sabah family, including the
date farms in Faw, and a guarantee of the safety of Kuwaiti
shipping in Gulf ports. In consequence, he did what he could to
maintain ties with Istanbul at the same time as developing a new
relationship with the British. He renovated and improved a
mosque in Kuwait and asked permission from the Sultan to
dedicate it in his name. A document in the Ottoman Archive in
Istanbul indicates that a memo was sent concerning this matter on

18 September 1900, and that an 'Exalted Will' was indeed issued agreeing to the appellation of the mosque.[65]

In 1904, when Mukhlis Pasha, the Governor of Basra, built a naval base on the Shatt Al-Arab, Sheikh Mubarak was swift to offer financial support from Kuwait's revenues. In the same year, he offered to give a subvention for the construction of a garrison at Al-Ishar, which prompted the official newspaper that was now being published in Basra to compliment him and bless his efforts. The newspaper referred to him as 'Sheikh Mubarak who upholds the Enlightened Hamidi throne', and continued, 'This generous gift and zeal is a clear indication and proof of his noble self with all its attributes of honesty and sincerity … to our Majesty Abdul Hamid Khan II.' In the same year, Mubarak donated 500 Ottoman lire as a contribution to the construction of the Hijaz railway. He donated a similar amount for the same purpose in August 1906.[66]

Sheikh Mubarak's various donations were an expression of his desire to maintain good relations with the Ottoman Empire and to display a symbolic loyalty towards it. In 1911, after the great fire that had destroyed much of the centre of Istanbul on 11 February, he gave 5,000 Ottoman lire for the restoration of the city. This contribution was made in response to an appeal organized by Hussein Jalal Bek, the Governor of Basra. The Sheikh transferred the money through Saud Al-Khaled Al-Khudayr. In the same year, he donated 3,000 Ottoman lire to assist the Ottoman war effort in Tripoli against Italy. He wrote to Hasan Rida Pasha, the Governor of Basra, expressing his desire to see an Ottoman victory over the Empire's enemies and adding that he was ready to send fighters to support them. The Governor of Basra replied in a letter thanking him for his offer and for his concern for the Empire. In 1912, he donated 1,000 Ottoman lire to the Hijaz railway. He also donated to support the Ottoman Empire in its struggle to maintain its hold over the Balkans. When war first broke out in the Balkans, committees were formed across the Empire to collect donations for the army. Al-Sayyed Taleb Al-Naqib became the head of such a committee in Basra and Sheikh Mubarak was quick to give 11,000 Ottoman lire towards this cause. He wrote to Al-Sayyed Taleb Al-Naqib expressing his expectation that the Ottoman Empire would show its appreciation of the service he was offering:

> We have done our duty towards the state we obey. We await your fairness in that which suits our honourable status because of the financial and physical services we have given. In any case, we hope that they will be appreciated.

The Ottoman controller of finances, Abdul Rahman Pasha, replied to Al-Naqib:

> It is our duty to express our highest appreciation. I convey our most faithful thanks to the Muslim people of Bahrain and to the honourable Mubarak Pasha Al-Sabah, who has, in his patriotism and enthusiasm, hastened to provide assistance, with that dutifulness which is natural for such a person.

As a reward for his services, the Sultan decreed the award to Sheikh Mubarak of the Majidi medal, first class. On 3 February 1912, the acting Governor of Basra, Ali Rida Pasha, informed Sheikh Mubarak of the award, and, knowing that the Sheikh was not in good health, he expressed his regret that he could not himself come to Kuwait to present it. Instead he sent the medal with a delegation headed by the Mufti of Basra, Sheikh Abdul Malik Efendi Al-Shawwaf.[67] The delegation also included Hajj Mahmoud Pasha, Naim Bek, head of the elementary court, and Hajj Taha Glaybi, a member of Basra's administration council. The Sheikh was invested with the medal in a solemn celebration held in front of Al-Seif Palace.[68]

The following year the Governor of Basra, Sulayman Shafiq Kamali, suggested to the Sultan that the Sheikh should also be awarded the First Ottoman Medal, in return for the constancy of his services to the state. The Sultan agreed and sent a delegation headed by Sami Bek, the Mutasarrif of Al-Hasa, with a number of high officials from Basra. He was awarded this medal in 1913.[69]

The Ottoman Archives include a number of documents that illustrate Sheikh Mubarak's desire to convey the impression to the Ottomans that he was a loyal and supportive subject. In a cable sent in 1913 in cipher by the acting Governor of Basra, Ali Rida, to the Ottoman interior ministry, Ali Rida notes that,

> Sheikh Mubarak, the *qaimaqam* of Kuwait, visited me today to confirm his friendship with the Imperial State and his preparedness to sacrifice money and soul in its service, standing alongside the Islamic Caliphate.[70]

Another cable sent in cipher from the Governor of Basra to the interior ministry in the same year, reports that Sheikh Mubarak visited Sheikh Khaz'al, the Emir of Al-Muhammara, at his place of residence. There he met with the British consul resident in Al-Muhammara and the British consul in Basra. The conversation concerned the outcome of the Balkan wars, in which the Empire had lost territory. The two consuls remarked that this was bad for the Sublime Porte and would certainly have an effect on 'the Arab element, and will inspire it to declare independence in Yemen, Najd and elsewhere, especially with the foreign support the Arabs are receiving'. Sheikh Mubarak replied, patriotically, that millions of Arabs, from the Syrian Desert and Aleppo, to the Sea of Oman and Persia, were waiting only for a small sign from the Caliph of the Muslims to rise as one man against foreign intrigue and attempts at secession, sacrificing their blood and all that they possess to defend the Imperial State.[71]

~2~

The Building of a Nation

The recruitment and arming of Kuwait's military forces

Sheikh Mubarak was acutely aware of the need for a strong military force to consolidate his control over the desert tribes, while also confronting the regional dangers and threats faced by Kuwait. To this end, he made use of his relationship with Britain to procure armaments. Despite having signed an agreement in 1900 with the British Government of India prohibiting the import and export of weapons and the transport of armaments through Kuwait, the British authorities were in practice lax about preventing weapons from reaching Kuwait.[1]

Lorimer maintains in his *Gazetteer of the Persian Gulf, Oman and Central Arabia* that in 1899, a large cache of weapons was imported openly into Kuwait from Muscat, on which customs duties were levied. In the early years of the twentieth century, Kuwait became in fact a centre of the arms trade. The Sheikh imposed a specific tax on rifles brought into Kuwait, which became an important source of income. This action was a demonstration that Mubarak was able to maintain some independence from the British, and that he would be able to play an important role in tribal conflicts in the neighbouring desert.[2]

A French merchant named Antonin Goguyer played a key part in this trade. Both a businessman and a political figure, with wide-ranging links and relationships with French officials, Goguyer was not just an arms trader but also worked for the interests of France.[3] In April 1904, he paid his first visit to Kuwait, where he arrived disguised as an Arab trader, calling himself Abdullah Al-Maghrebi. He was accompanied by another man, named Hajj Dhahaba. During this visit, Sheikh Mubarak accommodated Goguyer for three months in one of his palaces, until his departure for Muscat, and was attentive to Goguyer's views regarding the intentions of the great powers and their policies in the Gulf region. The Frenchman realized that he had gained the Sheikh's confidence. Apparently it was during this visit that Goguyer concluded his first arms deal with the Sheikh. At the end of April 1904, shipments totalling 2,000 rifles arrived in Kuwait on board several ships from Muscat. Thereafter Goguyer's shipments entered Kuwait regularly, without hindrance or obstacle. Hajj Dhahaba would receive them and distribute them.[4]

In the first week of August 1904, 12 crates of weapons arrived in the port of Kuwait. In the same month, a further shipment of 29 crates found its way into the Sheikh's storerooms. At the end of August, a further 800 rifles were imported, to be resold in Persia. By the beginning of 1905, the importation of weapons was taking place at an average of 1,000 rifles a month, most of which came in on Kuwaiti ships.[5] Due to the extent of this trade, Mubarak was able to strengthen his army, increasing its numbers and enhancing its capability, which raised its status in the region. Consequently, he was in general able to defeat his enemies in most of the military confrontations in which he found himself engaged.

Britain's lack of rigour in enforcing the prohibition on the sale of arms was consciously intended to enable Mubarak to furnish himself with the military capability needed to face the threat on his southern frontier from Ibn Al-Rashid, whom the British regarded as a tool in the hands of the Ottomans. It was also meant to assist Abdul Aziz Al-Saud, Mubarak's ally, to strengthen his position after his recapture of Riyadh in 1902. The wider goal was to weaken Ottoman control over the Gulf coast. Britain also wished to conciliate Mubarak. This deliberate negligence emerges clearly from a memorandum sent by the Government of India to the British Political Resident in the Gulf asking him not to interfere in the arms traffic to Kuwait for a certain period.[6]

This interpretation gains further credibility from an Ottoman report of a meeting between the British ambassador in Istanbul and the Foreign Minister, Tawfik Pasha, where the conversation focused on the current conflict between the Wahhabis and Ibn Al-Rashid, which, according to the Ottomans, was being exacerbated by the quantities of weapons and military equipment that were being imported by way of Kuwait. The Ottoman Foreign Minister said to the ambassador:

> The role being played by Kuwait in transporting weapons to the area is regrettable. Ibn Al-Rashid, who has been discouraged by the Sublime Porte from responding to Kuwaiti provocation, might consider this action to be directed against him. This may lead in turn to dire consequences for which the Sublime Porte will not accept any responsibility.[7]

On 16 September 1904, the Muscat correspondent of *Al-Ahram* reported that Sheikh Mubarak was supplying many of the lesser sheikhs who were in revolt against the Ottomans with whatever weapons and ammunition they needed. The report suggested that, without Mubarak's backing, none of the minor sheikhs would be able to continue their rebellions:

> Once a week, the British mail arrives in Kuwait from Muscat. With every delivery, Kuwaiti merchants consign hundreds of rifles and large amounts of ammunition to their agents in Kuwait. Their way of accomplishing this is notorious: they label the crates of rifles as boxes of sweets and the crates with ammunition as dried lemons. The British and French officers are aware of this and obstruct customs officials in all transit ports from inspecting these weapons or from preventing their onward passage to Kuwait.[8]

In September 1910, after the defeat of Mubarak's forces at their battle with the Sheikh of Al-Muntafiq at Hadiyya, the British allowed him to buy a further 1,500 rifles from Muscat. Mubarak, however, considered this amount to be insufficient to replace the weapons and munitions he had lost in the battle and claimed that he needed more.[9]

The archives of the British Agency in Kuwait reveal further communications between the Sheikh and the British on this issue, illustrating the Sheikh's insistence in demanding more weapons. For example, on 12 January 1911, the Political Resident in Bushire, Lieutenant Colonel Percy Cox (later Major General Sir Percy Cox), wrote to Sheikh Mubarak, relaying Britain's advice about the weapons he needed to buy from Muscat, indicating that he would be obliged to store them there and that an agent of his should make contact with the British Agent to arrange for consignments to be sent on to Kuwait from time to time according to the Sheikh's needs and in coordination with Britain.

The Political Agent in Muscat reported that, according to the instructions Mubarak sent to his agent Hajj Najaf, the quantity of weapons and ammunition he wanted to buy had increased. His requirements now included 500 five-shot rifles, with 400 rounds of ammunition for each, 2,000 Martini rifles, each with 200 rounds, in addition to a further 100,000 rounds for the five-shot rifles and 600,000 for the Martini rifles. The Political Agent added that he had given instructions to Hajj Najaf to go to Muscat to enter into negotiations for the purchase of these weapons. He further noted that Britain might find it difficult to understand the reason for these increased quantities, and advised the Sheikh that, in order to avoid any misunderstanding with the British Government, he should not insist on the additional arms. He said that he was confident that the Sheikh would recall the opinion he had expressed in a previous letter dated 8 November 1910, in which he stressed the importance of avoiding any unnecessary rumours that might arise from the Sheikh's insistence on buying these kinds of armaments in such exaggerated quantities.

On 14 February 1911, Sheikh Mubarak replied to Colonel Cox, clarifying once more the reasons for such a large quantity of weapons and ammunition. He pointed out that Kuwait was the sea outlet for Najd and that its commerce was based on exports from the land and imports by sea. While the sea route to Kuwait was safe thanks to the presence of the Royal Navy, the land route was not at all secure. The Bedouin were accustomed to attacking merchants and travellers, seizing their goods and plundering their property. Since Kuwait's commercial interests were largely dependent on the land route, the Sheikh had seen fit to station men to secure it. Despite this, attacks on land caravans bound for Kuwait had continued. This had necessitated an enhancement of the Sheikh's forces, which implied an enlargement of their requirements in terms of weapons and ammunition. He added that the importance of this issue was such that he had placed his son, Sheikh Jaber, at the head of 3,000 fighters, with a further thousand to be led by his other sons charged with conducting the necessary security operations. The Sheikh remarked that it was also necessary to arm the general populace of Kuwait so that they could defend themselves, if necessary.

The Sheikh offered a further justification for his need for the arms. He noted that the number of young men at school in Kuwait had increased to between 1,200 and 1,800, and that he was determined to arm them and force them to do military service. He also indicated that he had ordered his agents not to buy illegally smuggled weapons and had banned the illegal import of arms in accordance with the agreement he had signed with Britain. He concluded that if Britain was concerned with Kuwait's interests and determined to ensure its protection, as he believed, then his hope was that the British authorities would permit him to buy all the weapons he required. Finally, he noted that the weapons he had already received had been used to arm his tribes, but that he needed more.

As for the volume of ammunition required, the Sheikh explained that this was because the tribes were continuing to use their weapons to hunt animals, despite the fact that he had urged them to desist. He had sent an inspector to check on this, who had discovered the practice was continuing. He insisted that after he had distributed all the ammunition at his disposal to his troops and to the tribesmen, he had only six crates remaining, which contained 9,000 rounds. This, he explained, was why he was asking permission from the British Government to transport to Kuwait 150,000 bullets purchased by his former envoy to Muscat, Ismail bin Muhammad Rafih, as soon as possible. The Sheikh promised to distribute the ammunition to Kuwait's troops and to the tribes. He added that this quantity should be sufficient for a year.[10]

Mubarak made preparations to receive the additional supplies even before he received the Political Agent's agreement. On 10 May 1911, he wrote to Major S. G. Knox, the British Consul in Muscat, reminding him that he had already bought weapons from Muscat, with Britain's agreement, to arm his soldiers. He noted that some rifles had been bought without the correct ammunition, rendering them useless, and explained that he had sent a request to the Political Resident for approval to purchase this ammunition, adding that he had asked his agent, Mirza Hussein bin Abdul Baqi Najaf Asfahani, to ask Knox to inform him when the licence had been received. He suggested two ways to ship these rifles to Kuwait: they could either be brought by a ship specially chartered for the purpose, or sent with the regular mail steamers. Mubarak's preference was for the regular steamers, because the owners of chartered ships might seek to make use of the licence in order to ship other weapons on their own account.[11]

The Sheikh was nothing if not persistent in his efforts to obtain more weapons. On 29 September 1911, he wrote to William Shakespear, the Political Agent in Kuwait, explaining that the agreement reached with S. G. Knox in Muscat was that the Sheikh would be licensed to have 2,500 rifles, with 400 bullets for each, along with 200,000 bullets per annum as supplementary ammunition. He related once more how these weapons would be distributed, noting that some would be assigned to the young men who had completed their studies, since Islam instructs that they should be trained to carry weapons. These weapons would be distributed on condition that they were registered in their names and that they were used only to maintain security. A further quantity would be distributed among those who worked on the pearl-diving boats to protect themselves against pirate attacks, and the remainder to the Sheikh's personal forces.

Ostensibly, Mubarak was anxious to obtain British approval for the additional arms to protect the trade of the Kuwaiti tribes from raids by other armed tribes. The Sheikh attempted to reassure Shakespear, adding that he would keep him informed as to how the weapons had been distributed. He repeated that a large proportion of the weapons he had already received had gone to the sheikhs of the Kuwaiti tribes, whom the agent knew personally.[12]

On 4 October 1911, Mubarak reiterated his arguments in a further letter to the Political Agent, adding that the people of Kuwait and the tribesmen had been accustomed to buying weapons for themselves and that they had ceased to do so only to comply with the wishes of the British Government and in accordance with the Anglo-Kuwaiti Agreement. Their hope was that Britain would permit them to acquire the additional weapons they needed. In response to a request from Shakespear that the Sheikh should declare what weapons he already had, Mubarak sent a detailed list of the rifles and ammunition in the possession of the tribesmen under his control and that of his sons.[13]

Shakespear replied to Mubarak the same day, expressing his concerns over Sheikh Mubarak's requests, as specified in his letters dated 29 September and 4 October. His letter reflected the British Government's concerns over Sheikh Mubarak's reasons for obtaining these weapons. Shakespear said it would be necessary to know precisely how such weapons and ammunition would enter and exit Kuwait, noting that the demands expressed in writing and verbally by the Sheikh had been conveyed to the British Government. He maintained that the Sheikh's insistence on obtaining further weapons and ammunition may not be of benefit to him and could become a source of anxiety for the British authorities, but that he would in any case inform his government of all these matters.[14]

It seems that the British Government took its time to consider this issue and to reach a decision. On 15 October 1912, a year after the correspondence began, Percy Cox sent a letter to Sheikh Mubarak in his capacity as Political Resident in the Gulf, in which he expressed the British Government's appreciation of the Sheikh's respect for the special regulations imposed on arms trading. Cox made it clear, however, that in the short term the Sheikh would not be able to obtain any more consignments of weapons owing to the large size of the last consignment approved by the British Government. In his letter, Cox expressed his hope that the Sheikh had grasped what Shakespear had told him concerning buying arms from Muscat and pointed out the necessity of adhering to the rules pertaining to it, which dictated that each rifle purchased should have a serial number and that a note should be retained of the store where it was to be kept. He added that these rules applied to everyone without exception. He made it clear that no accusation was being levelled against anyone in particular. The British documents indicate that Cox sent copies of this letter to both Al-Muhammara and to Kuwait because he was not sure of the Sheikh's location.[15]

The correspondence over the purchase of the weapons did not end there, however. On 7 November 1912, Sheikh Mubarak replied to Colonel Cox reminding him that during his last visit to Kuwait, he had informed him that his practice was to stamp all rifles distributed among his people with his personal seal. They themselves would then apply their own seals in order to register the name of each gun's owner, to facilitate their distribution in case of an emergency in which weapons needed to be given out for a military campaign. As for the rifles distributed among the tribes, no other seals were put on them other than the Sheikh's personal seal. Sheikh Mubarak's following remark appeared to indicate the emergence of a new difficulty. The Sheikh informed the Political Resident in the Gulf that the people had refused to receive a consignment of weapons that carried the seal of the Muscat arsenal, and that when he tried to persuade them to accept these rifles they strongly refused to do so.[16] This was a new development.

On 15 November, Cox repeated his insistence that he could not comprehend why the Sheikh's subjects might object to the seal of the Muscat arsenal. Their refusal to receive the weapons gave the impression that the people of Kuwait had no real need of them for their personal use. The Resident reiterated that there could be no exception to the application of such a seal as an identifying mark on weapons exported from Muscat with the approval of the British Government. He said that if the Sheikh's subjects were unwilling to accept the seal then it would be better for them to remain without the weapons.[17]

On 12 December 1912, the Sheikh wrote to Cox renewing his requests and offering yet further justifications for the scale of his requirements. Kuwait's main source of revenue, in addition to pearl diving, was the seaborne trade with India, whence goods of all kinds were imported. This required vigilance, as many trade routes were insecure, and it was for this reason that the Sheikh was asking for additional weapons. The Sheikh requested that the 2,600 guns to be distributed to the tribes should have no markings and that the marked rifles already received would be distributed among the Sheikh's soldiers. Kuwait needed to buy an extra 600 rifles each year because of the increase in its population and the expansion of the pearl trade. The Sheikh added that if he was compelled to accept the seal of the Muscat arsenal on guns supplied to him from there, his alternative proposal would be that the guns be bought directly from London.[18]

On 31 December 1912, in a further letter to Sheikh Mubarak, Colonel Cox reiterated once more the British Government's position. He explained that it was impossible to make any exceptions or to be less rigorous with regard to the previously agreed condition and that the Sheikh's request for guns without seals was a matter that was beyond his responsibility and authority. Cox noted that the British Government was grateful for the Sheikh's co-operation in fighting illegal arms trading and that he would convey Sheikh Mubarak's request to the British Government. He added that they would find it difficult to respond favourably to this request, but that he would convey the Sheikh's suggestion that he should buy arms directly from London. The Political Resident once again expressed his inability to understand the objections of the Kuwaiti tribes to weapons carrying identification marks.[19]

With remarkable persistence, however, despite this discouragement, the Sheikh continued to make similar demands. On 22 January 1913, he wrote to the Political Resident in the same vein. Once again, he said that the rifles carrying the seal of the Muscat arsenal were still being held by customs authorities, because the people of Kuwait did not wish to use them. The Sheikh asked Cox to approve their return to Muscat for sale, or alternatively he suggested that they could be sold to Sheikh Khaz'al, the Emir of Al-Muhammara, who was also in need of weapons.[20] In two letters, dated 29 January and 2 February 1913, Colonel Cox again informed the Sheikh of the British Government's position, repeating that the agreement between the two sides to import 6,000 rifles from Muscat stipulated that the weapons should carry the seal of the Muscat arsenal. He said that the British Government had asked him to inform the Sheikh that it could not regard the reported objections of his subjects to the 'Muscat seal' as plausible and that the Sheikh should compel them to accept the weapons if they were in genuine need of them. The British authorities explained that the application of the seal to these weapons was not an act directed specifically against the Sheikh or his subjects but was a general rule applied by the Muscat arsenal, and that were the Sheikh's demand for exemption from this rule to be granted it would lead to similar requests from other importers.[21] Even after all these exchanges, Sheikh Mubarak tirelessly repeated his need for the weapons. On 18 May 1913, he wrote to Cox emphasizing the need of those who worked in the pearl-diving trade to have weapons to protect themselves. He wrote that they were poor and that diving was their only source of income but that they were exposed to piracy, putting their lives in danger, as they had insufficient weapons to defend themselves.[22]

The Sheikh was well aware that the British officials mistrusted his intentions and feared that if he got hold of the unmarked weapons he desired, they could be used to expand his sphere of influence and extend his territory. From time to time, the Sheikh attempted to allay the doubts of the British on this issue. For example, in 1910, he informed Shakespear that the ship *Fath Al-Khayr*, which flew the French flag, was smuggling weapons and ammunition from Muscat to Kuwait. Shakespear wrote to the Sheikh on 7 May 1910 expressing the thanks of the British Government for this information. He proposed that the Sheikh should take personal charge of these weapons for safekeeping. Mubarak replied the next day informing Shakespear that the ship had arrived in harbour and that the weapons had been forcibly unloaded and stored in the customs area, where they would be kept until a decision had been taken about how to dispose of them.[23]

For their part, the British certainly wanted the Sheikh's support in the fight against arms smuggling. For example, on 20 February 1912, Shakespear informed the Sheikh that he had received a letter from the Deputy Political Resident in Bushire, indicating that the illegal trade in weapons was on the increase in the northern part of the Persian Gulf, and that British ships would intensify their monitoring of traffic there. He called on Sheikh Mubarak to assist in the fight against illegal arms trading, asking him to urge his subjects to avoid this activity. The Sheikh replied the next day confirming that he was committed to all the promises he had made in this matter and that ships belonging to his subjects were never permitted to carry weapons without a licence. He said that he had asked his agent in Muscat, Yusuf Al-Zawawi, to make it clear to Kuwaiti captains that they should not transport unlicensed weapons 'either to ourselves or to anyone else', and that whomsoever disobeyed this order would be subjected to severe punishment.[24]

In this context, Sheikh Mubarak continued to do all he could to reinforce his army and provide further weapons and ammunition for the population and tribes of Kuwait. His primary consideration was to maintain his insistence that the British authorities agree to his demands on the matter of the quantity and supply of weapons and ammunition. He wrote tirelessly on this same issue, reiterating the same arguments over and over. Finally, he sought to do what he could to diminish the anxiety of British officials in relation to his intended use of the military power at his disposal, and their concern that it could lead to the expansion of his ambitions in Arabia.

Mubarak did not lose sight of the need to emphasize, on appropriate occasions, his commitment to the three separate agreements he had signed with the British on 23 January 1899, 24 May 1900 and 28 February 1904. He did not hesitate to point out the discrepancy between Kuwait's adherence to the ban on illegal arms trading and the practice elsewhere. An instance of this may be seen in his letter to Percy Cox on 16 May 1912, in which he wrote that while the people of Kuwait had adhered to the rules on arms trading, arms were being traded illegally in Qatar and Al-Bu'aynayn, and that anyone from Kuwait who wanted to buy weapons illegally could obtain them from Qatar. They only refrained from doing so, he said, because they respected the Sheikh's authority and were aware that it would distress him.[25]

A flag for Kuwait

The flag of any country is a symbol of loyalty and commitment around which its citizens unite. Countries are distinguished by their flags. Historically, armies had their own banners and flags. Later, with the advance of maritime trade, ships began to display the flags of the country to which the owner belonged. When Kuwait first built up its commercial fleet in the eighteenth century, Sheikh Abdullah I bin Sabah, the second ruler of Kuwait to come from the Al-Sabah family (1746–1813), flew the first specifically Kuwaiti flag on his ships. This was the red Sulaymi flag, the same flag flown on the ships of the followers of Utub Al-Khalifa in 1762, when they left Kuwait for Al-Zubara. Kuwaiti ships continued to fly this flag during the reign of Sheikh Jaber I bin Al-Sabah (1813–1859).

In 1871, Sheikh Abdullah II bin Sabah, the fifth ruler of Kuwait from the Al-Sabah family, raised the red Ottoman flag. This expression of Ottoman patriotism was prompted by the erstwhile harassment of Kuwaiti ships by the Ottoman authorities. He also aimed to enjoy the economic privileges associated with the expression of Ottoman allegiance, such as exemption from customs duties and the guarantee of the safety of Kuwaiti property in Ottoman territories. It was the first time an Ottoman flag had been flown by Kuwaiti ships. The practice continued throughout the reign of his brother and successor Sheikh Muhammad bin Sabah, into the first years of the reign of Sheikh Mubarak, who, as one Kuwaiti author has noted, 'erected a high flagpole near the coast and a smaller one over the house he lived in. On both, he raised the Ottoman flag.'[26]

The Kuwaiti flag went through more than one version during Sheikh Mubarak's reign. When Lord Curzon visited Kuwait in 1903, a red flag was raised, printed with the phrase 'In God we trust' ('tawakkalna ala Allah'). In 1905, the Political Agent suggested that Kuwait should fly a flag of its own on its ships. He proposed that the flag should be red, with the name 'Kuwait' written in the Latin alphabet as 'Koweit', and also in Arabic. Mubarak refused to have words written on the flag in anything but Arabic because he believed that this was contrary to Islamic tradition. The Agent also suggested that a special seal be designed for official papers and that a certificate of nationality be carried by Kuwaiti ships. The Sheikh accepted both these suggestions.[27] In

1914, Mubarak began to fly a flag of his own invention unique to Kuwait. This was a red flag with 'Kuwait' written in Arabic across it. It came in three forms: a triangular one for the emirate, a square for government departments and a rectangle for ships.

British documents reveal that the Sheikh and Colonel Cox repeatedly discussed the question of the flag. They considered the importance of Kuwait having its own national flag, and the British put across the view that it was no longer possible to fly the Ottoman flag unmodified.[28] The Sheikh's argument was that when he and the sheikhs of Kuwait who had preceded him flew the Ottoman flag it was not so much a sign of their subordination to the Ottoman Empire but rather that they considered the Ottoman flag to be a symbol of Islam. At the outset, therefore, the Sheikh's belief was that the Ottoman flag should continue to be used, in the same colour and with the crescent and star, but with the addition of the word 'Kuwait'. At this stage, however, in 1905, there was no agreement on a new form for the flag of Kuwait, and the Ottoman flag continued to be flown.

The British continued nevertheless to demand that Kuwait should in principle have its own flag, as an indication of its autonomy from the Ottoman Empire. The Sheikh stood against making a change, since he wished to continue to use the Ottoman flag to safeguard the interests of Kuwaiti shipping in other Gulf ports belonging to the Ottomans and was also anxious not to jeopardize the status of the Kuwaiti farms in Faw. He therefore continued to fly the Ottoman flag until the outbreak of World War I in 1914.

In the intervening period, however, there was at least one unfortunate incident when a Kuwaiti ship belonging to Hajj Hamad Al-Saqr was fired on and halted by a Royal Navy ship during a trip between Basra and Kuwait because it was flying the Ottoman flag. When it was made clear that the ship was owned by a subject of Sheikh Mubarak, the British allowed it to continue its journey, but only after its captain was asked to lower the Ottoman flag and warned not to fly it again on pain of having his ship destroyed and sunk.[29] This incident finally led the Sheikh to agree that the Kuwaiti flag had to be different from the Ottoman flag. In 1914, he visited Sheikh Khaz'al aboard his yacht, *Mishrif*. Mubarak ordered the Ottoman flag to be lowered and instead flew a red flag with the word 'Kuwait' written across it in Arabic script in white. This was the first national flag, and long remained the symbol of Kuwait.[30]

Kuwait's frontiers

Historians concur that the notion that countries must have defined frontiers is a modern idea linked to the rise of the national state in Europe, with all its associated concepts of nationality and the authority of the state over its subjects within its geographical boundaries.[31] In this context, the borders of the sheikhdoms of the Gulf were in general concerned with the geographical area inhabited by those tribes who had sworn allegiance to the local sheikhs and owed them loyalty. The consequence of this system was that in practice the borders of such sheikhdoms changed, from time to time, in accordance with the power of the ruler and his ability to enforce his authority over the areas inhabited by the various tribes.

The demarcation of the borders of Kuwait was not easily accomplished, nor was it achieved without challenge. Sheikh Mubarak was obliged to carry on a constant struggle with the Ottomans to protect the borders of his country, while the Ottoman authorities, who were concerned to restrict Kuwait's autonomy, sought to limit the area belonging to Kuwait. The Ottomans aimed to extend their influence, with the support they had newly gained from Germany, over the area that the Germans required for the completion of the Berlin–Baghdad Railway with its extension to Kuwait.

The border crisis between the Ottoman Empire and Kuwait began in 1902, when Ottoman forces occupied the island of Bubyan and the areas of Umm Qasr and Sifwan, in addition to other areas adjacent to Ras Khor Al-Sabiyya, close to the north-eastern corner of the port of Kuwait City, which constituted the safe outlets for Khor Abdullah. The occupation was a demonstration of the Ottoman claim to the area, but also had a practical purpose since this was land on which the Baghdad railway would be built. The Ottomans claimed that the areas concerned were outside the agreed borders of Kuwait. There was, however, an apparent contradiction inherent in the Ottoman position. On the one hand, they claimed that they had legal sovereignty over the whole of Kuwait's territory. On the other hand, having failed to impose this sovereignty in practice, they resorted to the punitive severance of Kuwait's peripheral areas. This could only have positive implications for Kuwait, as it implied recognition on the part of the Ottomans of the independence of Kuwait and its ruler.[32]

Sheikh Mubarak protested against the Ottoman occupation, insisting that all the areas occupied were within the boundaries of Kuwait. Britain gave him an assurance that the occupation of these areas would not bestow any legal rights over them to the Ottoman Empire. The British ambassador in Istanbul, Sir Nicholas O'Conor, protested to the Ottoman authorities that as part of its agreement with the Sheikh, Britain must support his stand and that the Ottomans had violated the status quo. In practice, however, Britain took no action beyond lodging a protest, and the Ottomans remained in effective control in the occupied areas.

A number of documents from the correspondence between Britain and the Ottomans over this issue are to be found in the Ottoman Archives. A memorandum by Tawfik Pasha, the Ottoman Foreign Minister, recording his meeting with Sir Nicholas O'Conor, notes that the British ambassador had informed him that Britain took the view that the deployment of Ottoman troops in Umm Qasr and Sifwan and the expulsion of Sheikh Mubarak's forces constituted a breach of the status quo agreement on Kuwait and represented a direct threat. The ambassador had asked the minister for a clarification of the

Ottoman position, to which the minister had replied that he was unfamiliar with the areas concerned and had no information about troops having landed there. Tawfik Pasha informed the British ambassador that he would need to seek clarification from Basra in order to speak definitively on the matter. He added that the Sublime Porte enjoyed absolute authority to land its troops anywhere within its territories if the need arose.[33]

In a further meeting with the Ottoman Foreign Minister, Sir Nicholas O'Conor raised the matter again, this time issuing a warning that there would be consequences if the situation were to continue. The minister replied once more that he had no information about the situation, but that he could say definitely that Umm Qasr and the island of Bubyan did not belong to Kuwait. The British ambassador pointed out that these places were adjacent to Kuwait and were considered part of it, and again said that sending Ottoman troops there would lead to grave consequences.[34] Four days later, the ambassador met the minister again and conveyed Britain's opposition to Ottoman troops being sent into regions appertaining to Kuwait,

> where this may lead to an armed confrontation between them and forces belonging to Sheikh Mubarak on the ground. If the status quo was to be altered, Britain would no longer be satisfied simply with the protection of Kuwait but would occupy it.[35]

British documents also reflect the development of the country's position on the issue of Kuwait's borders.[36] One document indicates that questions had begun to be raised in 1902 over the geographical limits of the Sheikh of Kuwait's authority. The delineation of the borders had not been discussed during negotiations over the status quo agreement between the Ottoman Empire and Britain in 1901, so their position remained uncertain. In February of the same year, Britain sought to verify its intelligence regarding the presence of Ottoman forces on territory belonging to the Sheikh of Kuwait, sending a warship to inspect the areas. The ship's captain reported back that there were Ottoman bases in Umm Qasr, which is situated on Khor Abdullah, and on Bubyan island, north of Kuwait. Britain regarded this as a violation of the status quo and subsequently filed a complaint with the Ottoman authorities.

In regard to the island of Bubyan, the British documents indicate that Sir Nicholas O'Conor urged Istanbul to withdraw the Ottoman garrison, threatening that if the Turks did not remove their installations, the British would build a base there on behalf of Sheikh Mubarak. This threat went no further, however, as the Foreign Secretary, Lord Landsdowne, opposed measures that might escalate into a confrontation with the Ottoman Empire and recommended that the matter be discussed by the Defence Committee in London before any further action was taken. As for Umm Qasr, which lies on the eastern coast of Arabia, some 80 kilometres north of Kuwait, the British report said the situation remained unclear, but that in this case the Sheikh's claim to ownership was weak, so that it would be difficult to take up a firm position. From this, it would appear that Britain had as yet no clear idea of the exact line of Kuwait's frontiers. This also emerges from a memorandum written by Lord Landsdowne in 1902, in which he explained the ambiguity of the borders.

In early 1904, to rectify the situation, Britain conducted the first comprehensive survey of the borders of Kuwait and its coastline. In April that year, Major S. G. Knox, as Political Agent, carried out a tour of southern Kuwait, reaching Al-Hafar on the borders between Kuwait and Arabia. In addition, a marine survey of the Gulf of Kuwait was conducted. In December, a group of British officers carried out a comprehensive survey in the border area between Basra and Kuwait on the basis of the surveys already carried out by the Political Agent and the Royal Navy. The borderline drawn by the British 'went through Khor Al-Sabiyya, passed south of Umm Qasr heading towards Jabal Sinam and from there to Wadi Al-Batin'. Decisions were also reached on sovereignty over the islands, except for Bubyan and Warba, which were both occupied by Ottoman troops. Sheikh Mubarak rejected the borders for Kuwait proposed by this survey, as they took no account of the land occupied by the Ottomans in Umm Qasr and Sifwan. He was also concerned that they did not deal with Kuwait's marine borders, which he regarded as including all the islands and the coastline from the island of Failaka to the Shatt Al-Arab.[37]

Sheikh Mubarak sought to create a conflict between the Ottomans and the British in order to further his demands. In July 1905, he wrote to the Political Agent insisting that the island of Bubyan belonged to Kuwait and that the Ottoman base there had been established by force, adding that he was unable, on his own, to fight the Ottoman Empire. However, if the British Government were to agree to use this location to build a coaling station to service its ships in the Gulf, then he was prepared to attempt to use force to remove the Ottoman base. Although Britain attempted to conclude a lease on the island of Warba to prevent any other power from building a base there or establishing a port in Khor Abdullah,[38] nothing in fact happened. It must therefore be concluded that whatever Sheikh Mubarak's interests may have been, Britain did not wish at that juncture to escalate its confrontation with the Ottomans.

For his part, Mubarak continued to protest against the Ottoman presence in the occupied areas on the basis that they were within the borders of Kuwait. There was some justification for this view. The palace after which Umm Qasr is named was built during the reign of Sheikh Jaber Al-Sabah, and a population with ties to Kuwait had lived in this area since the reign of his grandfather, Sheikh Jaber. The historic mud-built fort bears witness to this. As for Bubyan, Kuwaitis had long ago installed fishing equipment there and Kuwaiti fishermen were well established, while Kuwaiti families loyal to Kuwait and its Sheikh had lived at Sifwan, a way station for Kuwaiti mercantile caravans, for about 40 years.

In due course, the British changed their mind about the borders of Kuwait. Major Knox conducted further studies and reached the conclusion that the coastline from Umm Qasr to Al-Sabiyya was inhabited by Kuwaiti Arabs who recognized Sheikh Mubarak's authority. With regard to Bubyan, despite there being an Ottoman garrison there, the local inhabitants were the Kuwaiti tribes of Al-Awazim, who had fished there for several decades with the approval of the sheikhs of Kuwait. The Ottoman authorities had never previously questioned the authority of the sheikhs of Kuwait to give fishing rights to these tribes. As to the island of Warba, the British Resident noted that Sheikh Mubarak claimed to own it as his personal property and possessed a title deed.[39] Whatever the truth might have been, it seems that Britain was still reluctant to take a clear or decisive stand, but in terms of securing its own interests was content to deal with the issue of the frontiers of Kuwait as one on which a compromise could be reached.

In 1907, the British Government of India established a technical committee to resolve the outstanding issues pertaining to the borders of Kuwait. This committee concluded that the two islands of Warba and Bubyan belonged to Kuwait, but as for Kuwait's claim to the coastline between the island of Failaka and the Shatt Al-Arab, the matter remained unresolved until 1913.[40]

The British position developed during talks with the Ottomans held during the period between February 1911 and July 1913 concerning the borders of Kuwait and other matters pertaining to the Gulf.[41] The Ottoman negotiating committee was headed by Tawfik Pasha, the Ottoman ambassador to London, and the British negotiators were headed by the British Foreign Secretary, Sir Edward Grey. The British position had traditionally been based on the report written by Colonel Bailey in 1866 on the future of Kuwait, which emphasized that the British Government should not recognize Ottoman suzerainty over Kuwait because this was against British interests. In mid-January 1912, in a departure from this view, Lord Hardinge, the Viceroy of India, agreed to the possibility that Britain could recognize Ottoman suzerainty over Kuwait on condition that it should be accepted as an autonomous province. Its status would be similar to that of Egypt, which was also nominally part of the Ottoman Empire but was in practice ruled by a local sovereign with the advice of the British.[42]

Britain and the Ottoman administration exchanged memoranda on the legal and political position of Kuwait. Grey reminded the Ottomans of their agreement with the British made in 1901 that the Ottomans would continue to recognize the status quo, which included the agreements signed between Britain and the Sheikh of Kuwait, and that the two islands of Bubyan and Warba should be within the borders of Kuwait. The memorandum added that as soon as this was agreed, the British Government was ready to recognize Ottoman suzerainty over Kuwait. On 15 April 1912, the Ottoman negotiator, Tawfik Pasha, asked the British for a clarification of their use of the term 'status quo'. He enquired whether the expression was intended to refer to the status of Kuwait before the 1899 agreement, which the Ottoman Government did not recognize, or the status after that date. The Ottoman memorandum pointed out that Kuwait was, in practice, a dependency of the Ottoman Empire, since the Al-Sabah family had consistently recognized this dependent relationship and had accepted the Ottoman title of *qaimaqam*. Sheikh Abdullah Al-Sabah had fought on the Ottoman side in Midhat Pasha's campaign in Al-Hasa and the Ottoman flag flew over Kuwait. The Ottomans rejected the British proposal that the borders of Kuwait should include the islands of Warba and Bubyan, maintaining that the borders within which the Sheikh exercised control did not extend further north than Kadhima and Al-Jahra.

On 18 July 1912 Grey sent a memorandum in which he accepted that Kuwait was under Ottoman suzerainty, but reaffirmed both that Kuwait was autonomous and that the islands of Bubyan and Warba were within Kuwait's borders. Grey's memorandum stipulated that the Ottoman garrisons should withdraw from both islands. The matter was resolved with both sides agreeing to a nominal Ottoman suzerainty over Kuwait, which would not imply any practical consequences. In addition, the two sides reached an accommodation over the borders of Kuwait. This formed part of an agreement that was signed by both parties on 29 July 1913. For the Ottomans, the document was signed by the Grand Vizier, Ibrahim Haqqi Pasha, and for the British by the Foreign Secretary, Sir Edward Grey. The aim was to end the Anglo-Ottoman struggle over the region and to divide up their areas of influence, agreeing over the mutual interests of the two powers in the Gulf region.

Clauses 5 and 7 of the agreement fixed the borders of Kuwait with a demarcation regarded as the first official map of Kuwait's territory.[43] In a concession to Ottoman demands, Umm Qasr and Sifwan were excluded from Kuwait. Clause 5 fixed the area of the Sheikh's power in a rough semicircle, with Kuwait in the middle. Its northern border was to be Khor Al-Zubayr and the southern limit Al-Qurin. The islands of Warba, Bubyan, Miskan, Failaka, Awha, Kubbar, Qarruh, Umm Al-Namil, Al-Maradim and the territorial waters of these areas would belong to Kuwait. Clause 5 limited the full authority of the Sheikh to what lay in the defined area, which was marked with a red line on the map appended to the agreement.

Clause 6 of the agreement gave the Sheikh of Kuwait sovereignty over the tribes who lived in the areas defined in Clause 7, but not full political authority over the territory. It accorded him the right to impose a tithe and to levy it, and to exercise administrative authority over the areas. The Ottoman Government would not attempt to carry out any administrative activities independently of the Sheikh of Kuwait in this area.

Clause 7 defined an area roughly comprising an outer circle, with a line from the coast at the outlet to Khan Al-Zubayr, across to the south-west, passing to the south of Umm Qasr (which is 55 kilometres west of Basra), Sifwan and Jabal Sinam (but leaving these areas and their wells to the governorate of Basra). When the line reached Al-Batin (a dry wadi, about 180 feet deep between Al-Hafr and Jabal Sinam) it turned to the south-east to include the wells of Al-Safa, Al-Qira, Al-Hiba, Bara and Anta' within the borders of Kuwait and came eventually to the sea near Jabal Manifa.[44]

With Britain recognizing Ottoman suzerainty over Kuwait, it began to prepare to persuade the Sheikh to accept this outcome. Shakespear met with the Sheikh on 28 May 1913, and he wrote a report in which he said he had explained to the Sheikh the efforts Britain had made to guarantee the independence of Kuwait and maintain its special relationship with Britain. Britain had also done its utmost to impose the borders the Sheikh had demanded and had also sought to ensure there would be no Ottoman interference in Kuwait's internal or external affairs. When the Sheikh asked about what the new measures would mean in practice, Shakespear replied that the situation would be similar to Egypt's relationship with the Turks and the British.

Sheikh Mubarak continued to totally reject the idea that there should be an Ottoman representative in Kuwait. According to the Sheikh, such an official would seek to interfere in every sphere of affairs and would also be a focus for internal and external conspiracy. The result would be to weaken Sheikh Mubarak's authority over his own subjects. He asked Shakespear to inform the British Government that he was unable to accept this request, suggesting that it was not necessary for Britain to agree to it, since the Turks were presently weak and defeated. The Sheikh also implied that Britain had failed to honour the agreement it had made with Kuwait in 1899, suggesting that the intention of this agreement had been to prevent precisely what seemed now to be taking place. He added that in 1907, an explicit agreement had been made to lease the area of Al-Shuwaykh, and repeated that no Ottoman foothold would be allowed in Kuwait.

On 6 July 1913, the Sheikh wrote again to Shakespear, expressing his fears over the agreement. He said that he continued to have confidence in Britain's protection, but raised three concerns. First, he sought a guarantee that power should be inherited by his sons. He pointed out that in his previous agreements with the British Government the expression 'my sons' was used, specifying them to be his heirs. The newly drafted Anglo-Ottoman agreement, however, used the word 'successors', a term that could include both his sons and others. Second, he noted that the existing Anglo-Kuwaiti Agreement of 1907 stipulated that no agent of a foreign power should be permitted in Kuwait. In accepting the presence of an Ottoman representative, therefore, he contended that Britain had breached this agreement. His third point related to the proposal that taxes should be jointly collected by the Sheikh's government and the Ottoman Empire. The Sheikh noted that the 1907 agreement with the British Government had clearly provided that tax collection should be the Sheikh's unique right.[45]

Shakespear's reply, which was formal and couched in legal terms, came the following day. He said the agreement of 1907 debarred the Sheikh from receiving a foreign representative except with the agreement of the British Government. On the other hand, the British Government had the power to accept such a representative and had in this instance agreed to the presence of an Ottoman official. Regarding the use of the term 'successors' instead of 'sons', Shakespear assured the Sheikh that there was nothing to fear, since the Ottoman Government's sole role would be to ratify the process of succession without interfering in it. On the issue of joint tax collection, the British official expressed no view, claiming that he did not have the text of the 1907 agreement at hand.[46]

In practice, Britain disregarded the Sheikh's reservations, since Britain's interests in the Gulf were served by the Anglo-Ottoman Agreement. The agreement left Kuwait as an independent province under Ottoman suzerainty. The Sheikh of Kuwait was obliged to continue to fly the Ottoman flag, adding the word 'Kuwait' to it if he wished to do so. He would enjoy the independent internal administration of his country, with the Ottoman Government refraining from interfering in Kuwait's internal affairs, and from any military action on its territory. This also applied to the role of the Ottoman Empire when a new ruler assumed power in Kuwait. The Sublime Porte would restrict itself to the simple issue of a *firman* of succession giving its approval to whoever was chosen to succeed the Sheikh. In confirmation of the 1901 agreement to preserve the status quo in Kuwait, the Ottoman Government undertook not to seek to alter this situation, while Britain undertook not to turn Kuwait into a British protectorate.

The agreement confirmed that the tribes who fell within the borders of Kuwait were to be considered as subjects (*taabi'a*) of the Sheikh, from whom he could collect the tithe as he had done in the past. The Ottoman Government agreed not to attempt to undertake any independent administrative activity in the country. The agreement also guaranteed the right of the Sheikh to benefit from his private properties in the province of Basra, on condition that they be subject to taxation and duties according to Ottoman law. In return, the Ottomans now enjoyed the right to place a resident agent in Kuwait. A final benefit for the Ottomans was that they gained unchallenged rights over Sifwan and Umm Qasr, which were now agreed to be outside the borders of Kuwait.

From a legal point of view, the agreement contained contradictions. It defined Kuwait as an Ottoman province while at the same time specifying that Kuwait's administration should be independent from the Ottoman authorities and forbidding the Ottoman Empire from sending military forces into Kuwait to carry out any military operation within its agreed territories. A further surprise was that though the Ottoman Government had not had any role in choosing the ruler of Kuwait in the past, it was now formally excluded from doing so. Its role was defined as the simple issue of a *firman* from the Sultan to whoever was chosen to succeed to power, without any interference on the part of the Ottoman Empire, thus adding an Ottoman dimension to a process in which, however, Istanbul had no real part to play.

On the positive side for Kuwait, the addition of the word 'Kuwait' to the Ottoman flag was a demonstration of Kuwait's administrative freedom and independence from the Ottoman authorities. It may be concluded that the agreement between

Britain and the Ottoman Empire conceded only formal and nominal rights to the Ottomans. Real and practical authority over Kuwait's administration was to remain in the hands of the Sheikh. The agreement reiterated the independent political existence of Kuwait and the right of its rulers to administer its affairs independently. It also contained a definite confirmation that the islands of Bubyan and Warba formed part of Kuwait's territories.

In the event, ratification of this agreement was postponed. The two parties had agreed that the treaty confirming the agreement should be ratified by 31 October 1914. Owing to the outbreak of World War I, however, ratification never took place. When the Ottoman Empire took the decision to side with Germany against Britain and its allies, an entirely new situation arose. The result was to inaugurate a new phase in the relations between Britain and the Ottoman Empire, and in the history of Kuwait.

~3~

Social Development and the Outside World

In his time, Kuwait expanded and flourished. His era was one of strength and security.

Saif Marzuq Shamlan, *Min Ta'rikh al-Kuwait* [From the History of Kuwait]

Under Sheikh Mubarak, Kuwait underwent a wide-ranging process of social change. Developments in the system of government and administration led to enhanced security and safety for Kuwait's people, and a formal justice system was established. The first state school was founded, inaugurating modern education in the country, the first national welfare society was created and the first hospital was established to provide healthcare for all. The period also saw the flourishing of intellectual life, with visits to Kuwait by Arab thinkers and men of culture. In addition, elements of modern technology also made their first appearance in Kuwait.

Government and administration

In common with the other Gulf sheikhdoms, the traditional form of government in Kuwait was based on respect for tribal customs and a simple system of administration. This reflected the nature of society at the end of the nineteenth century. It was to Sheikh Mubarak that complaints were brought and it was he who made the decisions. He was responsible for justice, and in the last resort he was the guarantee it would be delivered. He did not regard himself as all-wise, however. For example, if a religious matter was brought before him he would refer it to an appropriate religious authority, after which he would implement the decision made. Similarly, although the Sheikh himself acted as the judge in simple commercial matters, he did not fear to take advice: 'If he could not find a solution, he would refer the matter to one, two or three of the experienced merchants and what they decided would be the last word.'[1] Sheikh Mubarak adjudicated over cases at his *majlis*, or tribunal, in the heart of Kuwait, where he issued rulings in disputes between his subjects. The Sheikh's daily *majlis* took place at the Al-Seif Palace, which he had constructed from local small burnt bricks. This was known as Al-Saray Al-Mubarakiyya. Later, he installed a second *majlis* for his son, Jaber. The Sheikh dispensed justice in public so that any person who had a grievance or dispute could come to him directly.

Kuwaiti society was made up of an agglomeration of tribes, each of which owed its loyalty to the Sheikh. Each tribe also had its own local sheikh who led it and dealt with its internal affairs, so that the ruler or emir was the leader of the sheikhs of the country. Speaking of the Sheikh of Kuwait, the missionary Dr Stanley Mylrea said, 'The country was headed by the great old man, Sheikh Mubarak Al-Sabah.'[2] In Mylrea's account of Sheikh Mubarak's style of government, he comments that the Sheikh was not isolated from the man in the street or from the ordinary nomad in the desert. Any citizen with a lawsuit to argue or a problem to solve could meet with him face to face without difficulty.[3] The Danish traveller Barclay Raunkiær, who visited Kuwait at the end of January 1912, reported that the Sheikh and his entourage would sometimes process 'through the longest street in the market, whose roof was covered with palm leaves, with the sun breaking through a little. At such moments, all work in the market would come to a halt so that people could greet the Sheikh.'[4] Foreigners who visited Kuwait during the reign of Sheikh Mubarak, or who lived there, have given descriptions of his *majlis* and the way he administered justice. Mylrea recalls that,

> He would sit on the balcony, with the sea to his left and the city's notables to his right, with their guards in front of them.[5]

Raunkiær also described the scene at the Sheikh's *majlis*:

> Next to the Sheikh you would always find his diamond inlaid cigarette box, which holds his long Baghdad cigarettes, as well as his binoculars with which he likes to watch the ships as they set sail over the Gulf waters, or to keep a lookout for the mail boat.[6]

The Sheikh oversaw Kuwait as an independent ruler. H. V. F. Winstone, the author of the biography *Captain Shakespear*, described the situation thus:

> Kuwait was nominally part of the Ottoman Empire, and the British official position was that the Sheikh was no more than a *qaimaqam*, or a local ruler. However, during Captain Shakespear's time, the Sheikh of Kuwait, Mubarak Al-Sabah, was already very different from that image.[7]

The Sheikh, in fact, conducted himself with great style, very much playing the part of a sovereign and not a provincial governor. His son, Sheikh Hamad, was married with positively regal ceremony at Al-Saray Al-Mubarakiyya. Other major celebrations were in general enacted in front of the Al-Seif Palace. Raunkiær locates it close to the beach and describes it as being made up of a number of different buildings and annexes, built at different times:

a huge building, like a castle, in the middle of which was a square courtyard. Its high walls had no windows, just small apertures in different places in the walls. It is connected with the outside world through a small door which opens on to a small corridor between the two upper wings of the palace, which are the living quarters and the servants' quarters. About five or six metres above the corridor there is an arch which has no windows and connects the two parts. Finally, there is a balcony, with carved wooden slats that overlooks the beach and the city and connects the rest of the palace with the part that holds the official quarters (the *saray*). It hangs above a wide street which separates the two sections.[8]

In his description of the palace, Abd Al-Massih Antaki adds that, when Sheikh Mubarak was building his palace, 'he wanted to preserve the customs of his people, so he built it in the Arabic style, with two sections, one for the harem and the other for guests'. Antaki describes the palace as having two storeys. The first storey was occupied by various official departments, of which,

> The most important one was that of the guards, where they lived. It was a bare room, its walls covered with weapons. After that there was the department of the affairs of the Emirate, made up of three rooms. One room belonged to the *bashkateb* [the chief scribe], or the confidential secretary. He is the noble writer Izzatlou Abdul Aziz Efendi Al-Salem ... Then there are a great number of other scribes, such as the scribe for foreign letters, the accounts scribe, the benefaction scribe, tax scribes ... and so on.

Antaki adds that beyond the department of affairs, there was Sheikh Jaber's *majlis* and beyond that the *majlis* of Sheikh Mubarak. According to his description, these departments gave on to the great courtyard of the palace, at one end of which stood the stables for the famous Najdi horses used by Sheikh Mubarak, his sons and assistants. On the second storey, some 30 steps up, was found the great reception room, which consisted of a large hall furnished with European-style sofas made in India. On the floor were some luxurious Persian carpets. Hanging in prime position in the hall was a portrait in oils of the Sheikh, together with a number of portraits of various kings and emperors. Next to this hall there were several smaller rooms to receive guests.[9]

Sheikh Mubarak was careful to choose appropriate people to work for him, identifying suitable individuals as best he could from those he encountered. There is a story, for example, about how the Sheikh met Saleh Al-Askar, who later became one of his officials. Saleh Al-Askar, the father of the Kuwaiti poet Fahd Al-Askar, was moody and volatile. He quarrelled with his wife and his father and quit his earlier positions as imam of a mosque and as a teacher, which left him with no income. The Sheikh was told the story by his land agent, Abdullah Al-Atiqi, and asked for Saleh to be brought to him. When Saleh arrived,

> Mubarak asked him, 'How could you take back your wife whom you divorced? According to Sheikh Muhammad Al-Farsi, she is forbidden to you.' Saleh Al-Askar immediately replied, 'Why did the Sheikh's government make Sheikh Khaled Al-Adasani the religious judge of Kuwait?' [This was a controversial issue of the day]. Mubarak Al-Sabah remained silent after Saleh Al-Askar's remark and its critical implications. Afterwards, however, he appointed him to the staff of the customs office.[10]

This account reveals several things. It reflects Saleh Al-Askar's intelligence and quick wit and his courage to speak his mind in the presence of the Sheikh. It also shows Mubarak's detailed awareness of the affairs of his subjects and his respect for anyone determined enough to express his opinion honestly.

According to the system that then prevailed, customs duties collected were handed over to the sovereign's office on a daily basis. When Saleh Al-Askar began to work in customs, or *al-makkus* as it was known then, he went to the office the next morning with what he had collected, which was a substantial sum. He was met by the land agent, Abdullah Al-Atiqi, who asked him what he was carrying. When Saleh replied that it was the customs money collected the day before, Abdullah Al-Atiqi advised him that if he were to give that sum to Mubarak, the Sheikh would expect a similar amount every day, and advised Saleh to hand over half the amount and keep the other half. This he did. However, although Saleh had not given him the entire sum collected, the Sheikh still found the amount quite high and this intrigued him, as he had never received such a large amount from anyone who had worked for him at the customs office before. He began to say to people, 'We lost a lot of money before Saleh started work.' The Sheikh rewarded Saleh with a monthly salary of 20 riyals in return for his effort and loyalty. This was a large sum in those days, so Saleh decided to buy the house he was renting for 100 riyals, to be paid in monthly instalments out of his salary. When Sheikh Mubarak discovered this, he paid for the house out of his own pocket and registered it in Saleh's name. Sheikh Mubarak's trust in Saleh continued to grow until he became the general agent for the Sheikh's property.[11]

The Sheikh rarely interfered directly in the affairs of the tribes, which were organized according to tribal custom. The tribes of Kuwait were in general related to one another by marriage. The Sheikh was keen to maintain this tradition and was himself married into the major tribes to confirm the blood relationship between the ruling family and the tribes as a whole, and thereby to guarantee their continued support for him. Though insurgency and disobedience were routine events among the tribes, Lorimer comments that during Mubarak's reign the tribal situation was so stable that nothing was heard from them, and opposition to Sheikh Mubarak from the tribes under his authority was insignificant.[12]

Inside the city, the Sheikh's representatives governed under his authority and carried out his instructions. These officials were not paid salaries but depended on what the locals gave them as gifts in return for services rendered, such as the approval of deeds of sale or the issue of birth or marriage certificates. They also took a share of the profits from pearl diving, hunting and trade. They sat as judges, resolving disputes between the people of the town, and issued judgements on legal matters such as inheritance, alimony and matters of personal status, according to Islamic law. They frequently sought the assistance of experts in the customs and traditions pertaining to disputes relating to business activities.

The judiciary grew in importance during Mubarak's reign. The Sheikh shared his authority with a religious judge and with the court of customary practices that dealt with commercial disputes in the marketplace, and which was made up of a number of experienced merchants. The majority of the religious judges came from the Al-Adasani family. The Sheikh exercised the authority to impose punishments on those who broke the law, which might be either lashes or time in prison, according to the type of crime and its severity. Sheikh Mubarak was careful to punish anyone who threatened the security and safety of the people. He made no distinction between the powerful and the weak, applying the law to all without exception. In particular, he was careful not to favour those close to him and would allow no transgression against citizens of Kuwait by any member of the Al-Sabah family.

In an interview reported by Antaki, the Sheikh is reported to have said:

> Crimes and transgressions rarely happen here because we pursue the criminal and punish him quickly, with tolerance but strictly according to undiluted Islamic law. We are strict in carrying out punishment and we accept no intercession. This is why our Emirate, praise be to God, is so safe. The strong and the weak live together like twin brothers. What makes it easier for us to establish security is that the people are Bedouin and are good Muslims. Very few lie, bear false witness or resort to deception or treachery.[13]

Abdul Aziz Al-Rashid records that the Sheikh punished anyone who committed religious transgressions with particular severity:

How many times did we hear him reprimanding a person who had drunk wine? How many times did we hear him punish a man who had harassed respectable women? People praised him for exiling from the city some who falsely pretended to be modest.[14]

Punishments were carried out at Kuwait's prison. This was formerly a large shop in the centre of the marketplace, close to the Grand Market Mosque and the traders' section, known as the shop of Abdul Aziz Al-Qindi. During the reign of Sheikh Mubarak, the jail was moved to a location by the sea, south of the Al-Seif Palace.[15]

The Sheikh dealt personally with any serious problem that the population of Kuwait might face. In March 1914, a large swarm of locusts descended on the city. They destroyed textiles, including canopies, tents and ropes. The Sheikh was in the desert at the time but returned to the city to deal with the danger himself as soon as he heard the news. He organized the people to bang drums and tin cans to drive the insects away until the situation was under control. Happily, nature provided a helping hand when stormy winds blew up, forcing the locusts to move on.[16]

As social life developed in the country, Sheikh Mubarak agreed in 1913 to the establishment of the first civil benevolent association, known as the Islamic Charitable Society, which soon became popular with the people of Kuwait. This was a project conceived by Farhan bin Fahd Al-Khaled Al-Khudayr who set it up to promote reform. The society was founded in March that year with the support of the notables of Kuwait.[17] Its initial purpose was educational, according to publicity distributed at the time, and its goal was to,

> send students of religious studies to Islamic universities in the more advanced Arab countries such as Egypt, Beirut, Damascus and other important Arab cities, where their expenses will be paid by the society during their period of study, and in addition, to employ a worthy expert in Hadith,

to preach to the people and guide them to the right path. Also to provide an able Muslim doctor and pharmacist to care for the poor and needy without the payment of fees. Another objective is to assure the distribution of water, the most important necessity in our country. And finally, to prepare the bodies of dead Muslims who are poor or foreign, and to provide them with shrouds.[18]

Sheikh Mubarak donated 5,000 rupees in support of the society, to encourage others to follow suit.

Alongside these declared aims, it would appear that the society was also established for a reason that was not explicitly disclosed, namely to compete with the Christian missionaries who had begun to make their appearance in Kuwait and the Gulf. Some researchers have linked the establishment of the Islamic Charitable Society to a call made by Muhammad Rashid Rida in 1912, for the establishment of Islamic organizations to serve the Muslims and counter the rise of the missionaries. The arrival of the American mission in Kuwait in 1910 was an early manifestation of this phenomenon, followed by the opening of the American Hospital in 1912. Some see a link between the Islamic Charitable Society and the establishment of the Mubarakiyya School two years earlier, viewing the two events as illustrative of a trend to develop Kuwait and to open it up to the spirit of the age. Others point to ties between Farhan Al-Khaled Al-Khudayr and the Egyptian political figure, Mustafa Kamel, maintaining that Al-Khaled was an admirer of Mustafa Kamel with his forward-looking Islamic outlook.[19]

A permanent administration for the Islamic Charitable Society was soon set up. Mishari Abdul Aziz Al-Kulayb was appointed as secretary, with the duty of informing members about meetings and activities. The headquarters was a two-storey building, with the upper floor serving as the medical clinic and the lower for religious preaching and guidance. There was also a library. The society furnished the premises and equipped them. A Turkish doctor named Dr Asaad Efendi was brought from Basra. The clinic continued its work until the outbreak of World War I in 1914, when, the Ottoman Empire having declared its support for the Germans, the Sheikh had to ask the doctor, who was an Ottoman citizen, to leave the country. The society also appointed Sheikh Muhammad Al-Shanqiti from Al-Zubayr to preach and teach. He was later obliged to leave Kuwait for political reasons.[20] With the departure of these two men, the society ceased its activities. Its benevolent founder, Farhan bin Fahd Al-Khaled Al-Khudayr, sadly died while sailing from India to Kuwait, and was buried in Bandar Abbas in Iran in 1914.

Education and literary life

During the later nineteenth and early twentieth centuries, Kuwait's education system was rooted in tradition, as was the case elsewhere in the Arab and Islamic world. Education was based on small schools in which children would learn rudimentary reading, writing and arithmetic. Most pupils were boys. The *mullah*, or religious teacher, would administer corporal punishment without hesitation if the children fell behind in their studies, using the stick, the whip, the rope and the chain. Fear was induced by curses, threats and promises of chastisements such as being locked up in a dark room. This was not at the time atypical in Arab society. When a child's father handed over his son to the *mullah* he would say, 'You have the meat and we have the bones', the meaning being, 'Do what you wish to discipline the child'. Woe to the child who failed to learn his lesson or made mistakes in it. Children paid the *mullah* an anna every Thursday, on pain of being beaten and expelled. The *mullah's* monthly salary was usually never more than a rupee, which was the equivalent of 75 Ottoman fils. According to tradition, the *mullah* also received a share of the meat distributed at the Eid festivals, and a proportion of the so-called *fitra* in Ramadan, which was a charitable donation to pay for poor people to break their fast.

When a child completed his education, he would be known as a *khatim*, and would be obliged to pay the *mullah* a *khitama* fee, generally an agreed amount. If the child came from a rich family, he would simply pay the required amount. But if he was poor, he had to collect the money from charitable donors. His parents would borrow a golden sword, a golden gown and a head cloth for him to wear, and thus dressed he and his classmates would then go about, accompanied by their mothers or other female relatives, visiting wealthier people's houses to recite the *khitma*, a speech composed for the purpose, in exchange for a donation. They would visit houses until they had gathered the required sum to pay their dues to the *mullah*. The child's education was then considered complete.

At the end of 1911, two factors came together to create a climate for the establishment of the first modern state school in Kuwait. The first was the demand created by the increase of commercial activity in the country, which had the consequence that merchants wanted there to be a school to produce scribes and employees who could both write competently and perform arithmetic. The second factor was the impetus given by social reformers. The new reformist ideas were critical of the under-development of the Islamic world, and laid some of the blame at the door of inadequate education. There was a call for change to help the Muslim world keep up with the West, and a demand that what was seen as backwardness and superstition should be ousted from the educational sphere. The result, as far as Kuwait was concerned, was the establishment of a new school where modern subjects were taught in a scientific way. It was known as the Al-Mubarakiyya School, in honour of Sheikh Mubarak.

The idea of opening the school first took root in April 1910. At a celebration of the Prophet's birthday at the *diwan*, or reception room, of Youssef bin Issa Al-Qinai, Yassin Al-Tabtabai gave a speech in which he paid homage to tradition by emphasizing the importance of taking one's lead from the life of the Prophet, but added that this should be achieved through systematic education. He added that schools must be opened to save the nation from ignorance. This idea greatly exercised Al-Qinai, who wrote an article setting out the benefits of knowledge and education and calling for the establishment of a modern school in Kuwait.[21] The merchant class in Kuwait contributed willingly towards the establishment of the new school, and 80,000 rupees were collected over a short period. The largest of these donations was given by the Al-Ibrahim family, with Qassim bin Muhammad Al-Ibrahim (who died in Mumbai in 1957) donating 30,000 rupees, and his nephew Abdul Rahman bin Abdul Aziz Al-Ibrahim (who passed away in Basra in 1960) providing 20,000 rupees. The Al-Khaled family made available a large house, in which the school was opened. The merchants imposed a voluntary levy on themselves of 1 per cent of their profits to underwrite the school's expenses. This was popularly known as the 'knowledge tax'. All this was accomplished with the support and encouragement of Sheikh Mubarak, who appointed his son, Sheikh Nasser, as the head of the committee supervising the school's establishment.[22]

In 1911 the school building was made ready for use, under the supervision of Sheikh Youssef bin Issa Al-Qinai. Sheikh Muhammad Rida, the founder of *Al-Manar*, wrote an article in the magazine's issue of 12 March 1911 entitled 'A Scientific School in Kuwait' in which he reported that he had been asked by Sheikh Qassim bin Muhammad Al-Ibrahim to devise a curriculum for the school and to help select qualified teachers to work in it.[23] Rashid Rida replied to Sheikh Qassim, enquiring about the date of the school's opening, the anticipated number of students, what the initial level of their knowledge would be and other such matters related to the fulfilment of the request.

On 22 December 1911 the school opened its doors. A financial committee was appointed that included Hamad Al-Khaled Al-Khudayr, Shimlan bin Ali bin Sayf and Ahmad Muhammad Saleh Al-Humaydi. The committee oversaw the school's budget and the use of its resources. The first headmaster of the school was Sheikh Youssef bin Issa Al-Qinai, who remained in his post until 1914, when he was succeeded by Sheikh Youssef bin Hammoud. The school's administrator was Omar Assem Al-Izmiri, and the teachers included Sheikh Youssef bin Hammoud, Sheikh Abdul Aziz Al-Rashid, Sheikh Abdul Aziz bin Hamad Al-Mubarak Al-Hasai, Sheikh Hafez Wahbah Al-Masri[24] and Sheikh Muhammad Karashi Al-Azhari Al-Masri among others.[25]

The students were assigned to various classes, with a basic curriculum of reading and writing in the classical Arabic language. Amongst other things, pupils were taught grammar, dictation, composition and handwriting and were introduced to Arabic literature. In addition, mathematics and geography were taught, together with some basic ideas about engineering. In deference to tradition, the curriculum also featured religious sciences, which included the study of the Qur'an and its exegesis, Islamic jurisprudence and an introduction to Islamic doctrine. Islamic history was also part of the curriculum, with an emphasis on the life of the Prophet and the history of the Rightly Guided Caliphs.[26] The Mubarakiyya School was considered a success, and it continued to function until 1956.[27]

Meanwhile, in early 1912, the American mission in Kuwait also opened a small school to teach English and various modern subjects. In an interview given to the mission's magazine for the January 1912 issue, Reverend Edwin Calverley said that the school had opened with nine or ten Muslim students and three Jews. The school was not considered a great success, and most of its pupils were withdrawn after a short period, which forced it to close down. Calverley believed this was because parents had been encouraged to fear that their sons would absorb the missionaries' religious ideas. Another factor may have been the success of the Mubarakiyya School, whose timely appearance may have attracted the students away from the missionaries.[28]

The establishment of the Mubarakiyya School was a manifestation of the onset of an era of intellectual enlightenment in Kuwait and the success of the call for reform. Some of the school's teachers also came to play a prominent role in the cultural and intellectual life of Kuwait, including, for instance, Sheikh

Abdul Aziz Al-Rashid and Sheikh Youssef Al-Qinai,[29] who were drawn together by the desire for reform and the wish to capture the spirit of the age. The literary endeavours of the day make this spirit clear. For example, Abdul Aziz Al-Rashid sent a letter to Ibrahim bin Muhammad Al-Khalifa (1850–1933), known as the leading man of letters in Bahrain, asking him for help in writing a book about the history of Kuwait in order to improve the knowledge of citizens about their own society. Sheikh Abdul Aziz Al-Rashid's energetic role in this period also took other forms. In 1928 he published the first magazine in the Gulf region, under the title *Kuwait*. At the time he wrote to his friend Ibrahim Al-Khalifa, telling him of the magazine's foundation and urging him to contribute to it and help in its production.[30] Later, there was also a dialogue between Sheikh Abdul Aziz Al-Rashid and another of Bahrain's leading writers, Abdullah Al-Zayed (1894–1945).[31]

Mubarak's reign saw a growing number of those with intellectual inclinations take up the call for reform, including Sheikh Muhammad bin Amin Al-Shanqiti, the founder of the Al-Najat School in Al-Zubayr. Another enthusiast was Sheikh Abdul Aziz Al-Tha'alibi, originally from Tunisia, who was a disciple of the ideas of Jamal Al-Din Al-Afghani and Muhammad Abduh. He called for the rejection of superstition and a renewal of religious thought, in order to be in a position to draw benefit from the West and its achievements. In addition, Sheikh Rashid Rida, the publisher of the magazine *Al-Manar* in Cairo, was invited by Mubarak Al-Sabah to visit Kuwait.

Sheikh Rashid Rida left an account of the week he spent in Kuwait as a guest at the palace of Sheikh Mubarak. He describes his day thus:

> Every day, apart from the day of the mail boat's departure, I would deliver a sermon in the great mosque, attracting a good-sized audience. Every night, I held a salon attended by the notables of the country. These were pious men who loved

knowledge and questioned me about whatever was troubling them in their faith.[32]

The person designated to be Rashid Rida's companion was Sheikh Nasser bin Mubarak, the head of the school committee in Kuwait, about whom Rida commented:

> He is a man who dedicates his time to reading and the pursuit of knowledge and is able to engage well on Islamic sciences ... He asks detailed questions about doctrinal study, theology, jurisprudence and other issues. He did not acquire his learning from teachers, but is a singular example of Arab intelligence.

The talks given by Sheikh Rida had a huge and positive effect on the people of Kuwait. He was described by Abdul Aziz Al-Rashid as 'causing an upheaval among its people'.[33]

The Kuwaiti intellectuals kept the people of Kuwait very effectively informed of developments in Arab and Islamic countries, and indeed in the whole world, by way of their lectures and through conversations in their gatherings, where their lesson was that Islam was the religion of progress and reform. Progress was not problem-free and without tension, however. There were also those who stirred up dissent, encouraging hatred and violence. Nothing could be easier than for them to accuse those who disagreed with them of betraying their religion. One such figure, Abdul Aziz bin Saleh Al-Alaji Al-Hasai, who had come to Kuwait from Al-Hasa, set about spreading reactionary ideas. According to Abdul Aziz Al-Rashid, some people were impressed by him. He and others denounced Sheikh Rashid Rida as a heretic and declared that the shedding of his blood was permissible. The result was,

> that someone tried to kill Rashid Rida during the year he visited Kuwait, lying in wait for him on his usual road. Fortunately, however, fate stepped in and he did not pass on that particular road on that day.

When Sheikh Mubarak heard about this incident, he instructed the Kuwaitis who had invited Abdul Aziz bin Saleh Al-Alaji Al-Hasai to ask him to leave, saying:

> Give your friend what is owed to him and let him go back to his country. We do not need men such as him to promote strife and to accuse scholars of heresy and deviation. Ask him swiftly to leave the country or we will expel him by force.[34]

This attitude displays Sheikh Mubarak's concern to permit the reformists the latitude to explain their ideas without fear for their lives. This did not imply, on the other hand, that the Sheikh necessarily welcomed the political positions adopted by certain of the intellectuals, which sometimes contradicted his own, especially in the sphere of foreign policy. The clearest example of this was the position of the intellectuals regarding the Ottoman Empire. Certain of them were entirely favourable to the Ottoman position regarding events in the Gulf, which brought them into direct confrontation with the Sheikh, whose relationship with Istanbul could be said in general to be tense. For this reason, both Hafez Wahbah and Al-Shanqiti eventually left Kuwait.

What lay behind their expulsion were the consequences of the outbreak of World War I in 1914. When Sheikh Khaz'al bin Jaber, the Emir of Al-Muhammara, declared his support for Britain, some of the tribes owing him allegiance rebelled against him. This led Sheikh Khaz'al to ask for help from his ally, Sheikh Mubarak. However, when the population of Kuwait appeared to be unresponsive to this request, as will be explained in more detail later, Al-Shanqiti and Wahbah were accused of exhorting the Kuwaiti people to take this view. Sheikh Mubarak summoned them to his palace in the presence of Colonel Grey, the Political Agent. He told them that a good Muslim did not interfere in what did not concern them, and went on to say:

> I am an Ottoman Muslim: I am protective of my religion and my country, and I am hostile to whoever causes them harm.

But I have come to an agreement with the British on a matter that is of benefit to myself and the country. This is why I cannot accept it if someone speaks against the British, even though I have no love for them and my religion is different from theirs.[35]

He informed the two men about intelligence that had come to him about their role in inciting the population to disobey his orders. Both denied they were in the habit of speaking about political matters, insisting that they were concerned only with preaching and religious guidance, and involving themselves solely with education and teaching. The Sheikh asked them to leave his *majlis*. Grey said he was convinced by Wahbah, but that he was still suspicious of Al-Shanqiti. When the Sheikh asked Grey what he should do with the two men, Grey replied that he would let him know in three days. It is likely that the Agent wanted this time to inform the Political Resident in the Gulf of what had transpired and to take his advice on the matter.

Before the three days had elapsed, however, Al-Shanqiti left Kuwait for Al-Zubayr. Abdul Aziz Al-Rashid records that he did not flee Kuwait voluntarily but was prompted by Sheikh Mubarak himself. Abdullah Al-Abdul Al-Muhsin Al-Assaf, an agent of the Sheikh and one of his close companions, told the story thus:

> Sheikh Mubarak summoned me. When I arrived in his *majlis*, he immediately rose and walked with me outside to tell me things that he did not want the people to hear. He told me to go at once and prepare a camel for Shanqiti, pay him 20 riyals, and ask him to leave Kuwait before sunrise. He told me not to tell anyone. I did what he asked me and Al-Shanqiti left Kuwait for Al-Zubayr.[36]

The question arises of why the British Political Agent was present at this meeting. This does indicate that the meeting may possibly have been held at the request of the British, whose objective was to silence voices supporting the Ottoman Empire in Kuwait and in other Gulf sheikhdoms. It would also appear that Sheikh Mubarak urged Al-Shanqiti's departure from Kuwait, while covering his necessary expenses, in order to protect him from the possibility that the British would seek his arrest. There is no indication from the manner of Al-Shanqiti's departure that the Sheikh himself was angry at him.

During Mubarak's reign, three important poets made their appearance in Kuwait. One of these was Abdullah Al-Faraj, whose sophisticated use of language was close to that of classical Arabic. For this reason, Abdul Aziz Al-Rashid regarded him as Kuwait's leading poet. Another was Khaled bin Abdullah Al-Adasani, described by Dr Khalifa Al-Waqyan in his book on the Arab cause in Kuwaiti poetry as follows:

> We find in his poetry a true reflection of the nature of the problem and the simple concerns of the people in this small plot of land.[37]

In general, Al-Faraj and Al-Adasani are considered to represent the true beginning of poetry in Kuwait. Al-Adasani died in 1898 and Al-Faraj died three years later in 1901. The third Kuwaiti poet of this period was Hammud Al-Nasser Al-Badr. Al-Badr was close to Sheikh Mubarak, who asked him to write a poem about the battle of Al-Sarif. Sheikh Mubarak's use of poetry as a 'psychological weapon', to encourage his friends and dishearten his enemies, is an illustration of the esteem in which poetry was held. At the time, poetry still served as a way of exhorting one's own men to give their best in battle and to instil fear in the enemy lines. Al-Badr died in 1915, the same year as Sheikh Mubarak.[38]

All of these developments indicate the extent to which the people of Kuwait were open to the political and social ideas that were being expressed in the Egyptian press. The Al Khaled family were the first to subscribe to Rashid Rida's magazine, *Al-Manar*, and began to call for reform in the circumstances of Kuwait's Muslims. They were also first to subscribe to the newspaper *Al-Mu'ayyed*, published by Sheikh Ali Youssef, which promoted Ottoman policy.[39] *Al-Manar* became more popular in Kuwait after

Rashid Rida's visit, which gave the Kuwaiti people the opportunity to hear his ideas and opinions.

Healthcare and the American Hospital

The population of Kuwait, in common with the people of the other Arab sheikhdoms and emirates in the Gulf, customarily relied on popular medicines and remedies to treat their illnesses. From time to time, a doctor would visit Kuwait, offering his medical services while he was there. An example of this was Hajj Hassan Al-Hakim, the so-called 'doctor' who came to Kuwait in March 1900 with his son, his wife and his servant. Hajj Hassan Al-Hakim rented a house to live in and to receive patients but it seems his sojourn in Kuwait was not particularly successful. As the British Agent, Ali Gholoum Rida, reported, since his arrival 'none of his patients have become well, and those who visit him are very few'.[40] After some time, no doubt for this reason, he departed from Kuwait and went to Basra.

The origins of a modern health service in Kuwait can be traced back to 1904. On 13 September of that year, Sheikh Mubarak wrote to Major Knox, the Political Agent in Kuwait, asking him to send 'a British doctor ... who knows about medicine, wounds and ailments', adding that 'this would be good for us and for our subjects'. The extent to which the Sheikh was involved in this is revealed in a further letter he sent Knox, on 1 November, enquiring how best to prepare the doctor's house, the cost of the medicines to be dispensed to the people and whether Britain would cover the cost, or patients would have to pay. The Sheikh proposed that healthcare for the poor should be free, within the surgery's working hours, while the better off could pay for their own treatment. Two days later, on 3 November 1904, Major Knox replied that the doctor would give free treatment to all poor people who came to his surgery and would treat the rich for agreed fees. As for medicines, they could be made available but restrictions would need to be placed on their distribution so that no patient could obtain medicine without the knowledge of the doctor.[41]

On 30 October 1904, the surgery was opened at the British Agency headquarters near the beach, in the building now known as the Dickson House Cultural Centre. The first doctor to work at the clinic was Daoud Al-Rahman, an Indian Muslim. He prepared the first report on health conditions in Kuwait, including an account of the diseases then prevalent. The report, dated 2 April 1905, was entitled 'A Brief Account of Health in Kuwait, 1904–1905'. According to the report, in the period between 30 October 1904 and 31 March 1905, 3,976 patients were treated, of whom 2,316 were men, 1,127 women and 533 children. In addition, 186 surgical operations were carried out. As well as the work in his clinic, the doctor supervised the quarantine procedure for ships entering the harbour in Kuwait. In 1907 Dr Daoud Al-Rahman's period of office came to an end, and on 12 August 1907 Sheikh Mubarak wrote to Knox expressing his appreciation and his gratitude to Dr Daoud Al-Rahman 'for his stay in Kuwait, with special gratitude from me personally and from the public for the treatment of the patients who came to his place of work and asked him to go to their homes. He did all he was supposed to and more, looking after poor and rich alike.'[42]

Doctor Al-Rahman was succeeded by Rustum Ji Ardishi Dadi Mastir, who worked from April to June 1908. Although Rustum stayed in Kuwait for only a short period, he enjoyed a good reputation. On 2 May 1909, Sheikh Mubarak sent a letter to Major Knox in praise of him and thanking him for his services.[43] The next doctor was Dr Nur Muhammad Rahmatullah, who was in charge of the clinic from 1908 to 1912. Just as with the previous two doctors, Sheikh Mubarak sent a letter to the Political Agent, William Shakespear, on 16 May 1912, thanking Dr Nur. After that came Dr S. S. Kelly, who worked at the clinic from 1912 to 1918. The clinic closed on 23 May 1921. Once reopened, the clinic continued to offer its free services to the employees of the Agency and to the people of Kuwait until 1951. In more recent times, the clinic was open from early morning until 1 pm, on every day except Friday.

The doctors compiled regular annual reports, of which the majority indicate that health conditions in Kuwait were good and that the city was free of diseases. In 1906, for example, general health was said to have been good throughout the year and the work of the clinic had apparently enjoyed the approval of the public. The 1907 report recorded the deaths of two of Sheikh Mubarak's sons. The 1909 report noted that health conditions had not been good in that year. Smallpox had spread, causing a number of deaths, especially among children. Despite this, only 185 vaccinations had been administered because of a lack of health awareness among the people. The report also noted that observance of quarantine requirements was less than desirable. In May, Sheikh Mubarak had been informed of the spread of plague in Bahrain and was told it was necessary to be very strict in implementing the quarantine procedures. The Sheikh gave orders that the procedures were to be applied to all ships coming into Kuwait port without exception and that all should be monitored.

It seems that there was a similar laxity in the application of quarantine rules in 1908. On 7 June 1908, a letter from Political Resident Major Cox to the Sheikh draws his attention to the fact that the basic principles for protecting the people's health, contrary to the Sheikh's own orders, were no longer being applied, with vessels arriving in the port of Kuwait, and their crews and passengers not being subjected to the agreed quarantine procedures. The letter also indicated that the British Government had appointed a doctor to Kuwait to be placed at the service of the Sheikh, specifically to improve the application of quarantine. The objective was to keep the port of Kuwait free of diseases and illness.[44] In the 1910 report the same observation is repeated, particularly the lack of attention to quarantine procedures, despite Sheikh Mubarak's instructions that they should be strictly applied. However, there seems to have been some improvement. When the port of Bushire was afflicted by the plague, quarantine procedures were applied to all ships coming from there. When Muscat, Al-Muhammara and Basra experienced cholera, ships were subjected to the same procedures. The difficulty, it seems, was in applying these procedures to Kuwaiti ships.

The 1911 report indicates that fewer people had visited the clinic that year, owing to the opening of a clinic at the American mission, with an American doctor in attendance. The report in 1913 indicates that smallpox had been prevalent in Kuwait between September and December, and that quarantine had been applied to all boats and ships coming from Bushire after an outbreak of the plague there in April. The 1914 report gives an account of the activities of the American mission's clinic, which it was observed had begun to enjoy the appreciation and patronage of the Sheikh. It was noted that Sheikh Mubarak had donated land to the mission as a gift, in addition to the land that had already been purchased for the clinic's construction.

In parallel with the improvements in health services, a number of pharmacies were opened. Sheikh Hafez Wahbah's pharmacy and that of Abdul Ilah Al-Qinai both opened in 1914. Though these pharmacies began modestly, they reflected, in common with the clinics, a general will to provide better healthcare for the people of Kuwait.[45] The 1915 report, in the year Sheikh Mubarak died, indicated that health conditions were excellent, that there were no epidemics and that quarantine had operated without any problems. The report noted a reduction in the number of patients visiting the clinic because of the work of the American Hospital.[46] The Arab–American mission, set up by the Dutch Protestant Church from the United States, had established itself in Basra in 1891 in order to set up missionary centres in the Gulf and to offer both health services and education to those who chose to visit them. They also sought to establish other centres in the Gulf.

Representatives of the Arab–American mission paid repeated visits to Kuwait. The first recorded missionary visit was by Revd Dr Samuel Zwemer in 1896, the year Mubarak became ruler. The

Sheikh suspected him of proselytization and asked him to leave. Zwemer returned in February 1903, however, to inspect the work of the bookshop, whose opening the Sheikh had permitted the previous year to sell the mission's books to Christians resident in Kuwait. Zwemer met the Sheikh during this visit, apparently to discuss with him the issue of opening a hospital.[47] In 1904, Dr James Moerdyk was received by the Sheikh when he visited Kuwait to seek permission for the establishment of a hospital by the American mission. On this occasion, the Sheikh rejected the idea and asked Moerdyk to leave. In 1905, when Dr Wells Thoms came to Kuwait to discuss the same issue, the Sheikh refused to allow him even to disembark from the ship on which he arrived, and his feet never touched Kuwaiti soil. The notion of establishing a mission hospital in Kuwait originated with the mission's central office in New York; money that had already been donated had been earmarked for this purpose. In 1909, because it was proving difficult to establish the hospital, one of the participants at the annual mission meeting said it might be best to contact the donor to ask whether the money allocated to Kuwait could be used in a different country. This was rejected and the mission continued its efforts to build the hospital in Kuwait.

It was in 1909, however, that the idea began to bear fruit. Doctor Arthur Bennett, head of the medical unit in Basra, visited Al-Muhammara to treat Sheikh Khaz'al, the ruler. It happened that at the same time, Sheikh Mubarak was paying a visit to Sheikh Khaz'al, and that the Naqib Al-Ashraf of Basra was also present. Both Sheikh Khaz'al and the Naqib were admirers of Bennett's efforts, and praised him to Sheikh Mubarak. This prompted the Sheikh to ask Dr Bennett to visit his yacht to examine one of his daughters who was complaining of pain in her eyes. The doctor treated her successfully and the girl recovered. It was this fortuitous event that at last convinced Sheikh Mubarak to permit the establishment of a missionary hospital in Kuwait.

In 1910, Dr Bennett visited Kuwait several times and during his time there he established a temporary clinic at a building belonging to a Kuwaiti in the centre of the city, where he treated a number of patients and gave a positive impression. Abdullah Khaled Al-Hatem and Sayf Marzouq Al-Shamlan believe it is most likely that that house was the *diwan* of the Al-Boudi family, near the inner market, and this is therefore regarded as the site of the first American mission clinic in Kuwait. Bennett was assisted by a Christian nurse from Iraq, whom he left behind when he left Kuwait for Basra so that she could continue to give first aid to patients at the clinic.[48]

In 1911, Sheikh Mubarak formally asked the American mission to set up a hospital, on condition that its purpose would be entirely medical and that it would not be involved in missionary activities. The mission sent a commission to Kuwait to select a suitable location. When a site had been acquired, Sheikh Mubarak demanded that a resident doctor be sent to provide his services all year round. In fact, during 1911, three doctors shared this job. These were Drs Bennett, Harrison and Mylrea. The clinic was open every day except Sundays.

According to Dr Mylrea's memoirs, while the Sheikh welcomed the idea of establishing the hospital, the majority of the population, including the notable families, continued to oppose the presence of Christian missionaries in their country. According to Mylrea,

> It was acceptable to call a doctor from Basra to treat an important personality, but the establishment of a hospital by Christian missionaries in the city was not acceptable at all.

Despite their reservations, however, people did begin to attend the clinic for medical tests or surgical operations if they were in pain or suffering from illness. In 1911 the number of cases treated reached 387. This figure included residents of Kuwait, some patients from Faw and Bedouin patients from outside the territory of Kuwait.[49] In the same year, Sheikh Mubarak agreed that the mission could purchase the plot of land necessary for the building of the hospital. The area chosen was Tell Al-Saghir, near the coast on the western side of the city. The mission bought the land from Sheikh

Mubarak for a very small sum. He presented the mission with the title deeds as his own donation for the building of the hospital.

At the beginning of 1912, Dr Mylrea left Kuwait on holiday. In his absence, he was replaced by Dr Paul Harrison and Dr Eleanor Calverley, who later gave herself the name 'Khatoun Halima' to make it easier for people to speak to her. The mission had originally intended to build a single hospital for both men and women. However, it was soon realized that it would be necessary to build a hospital solely for women in order to adapt to the reality of the situation in Kuwait, where there would be reluctance for women to receive treatment in a men's hospital and at the hands of male doctors. This was the reason for the arrival of women doctors, of whom Dr Eleanor Calverley was the first.[50] Later, Dr Mary Ellis was to join the staff. Just as Dr Calverley had taken the name 'Khatoun Halima', Dr Ellis became known as 'Khatoun Shafiqa'. In the diaries Dr Calverley kept, she records that she began her work on 1 January 1912. She prepared and equipped the women's clinic, which was made up of two consulting rooms and a reception area, which had an independent entrance from the street. In severe cases, Dr Calverley would make home visits to patients. She also successfully oversaw difficult births, which made her famous among the women in the city.[51]

Mylrea records that determining the boundaries of the hospital's site was a difficult task, as it was defined by irregularly placed piles of stones, with the result that, 'instead of being rectangular, it appeared to have seven sides'.[52] The mission sent two American engineers from Michigan, who happened to be in Basra for professional reasons, to Kuwait to build the hospital. When they arrived, they discovered that, according to the deeds, the plot of land was supposed to be rectangular, and the stones placed by the Sheikh's men bore no relation to the intended boundaries. Their first task was to carefully mark out a rectangular plot according to the deeds and to place cement markers in the four corners. This later resulted in a confrontation with the Sheikh. The building was then constructed on the site, in reinforced concrete. This was the first time that concrete, which had to be specially imported, had been used for construction in Kuwait.

Delays to construction irritated the Sheikh, especially after the engineers left Kuwait on completion of the foundations and the basic structure, having completed their contractual responsibilities, leaving Drs Mylrea and Calverley to supervise the completion of the building, which they were scarcely qualified to do. Meanwhile, rumours spread that the mission had taken more land than the Sheikh had intended to give. Not realizing how fraught the situation had become, Mylrea remarked that he had always dreamed of building a doctor's house on the high hill next to the hospital and asked his colleague Dr Calverley whether she thought Sheikh Mubarak might also like to donate this plot of land, which was of no other obvious utility, to the hospital. Dr Calverley replied that in her view dealing with Sheikh Mubarak had already become difficult enough, as he had come to believe that the missionaries had let him down and was reluctant to offer any further assistance.

Mylrea nevertheless went to visit the Sheikh the same day to ask him if he might give the land to the mission. He discovered that the Sheikh was indeed not favourably disposed. He was irritated that the boundaries of the plot, as his men had fixed them, had been changed and said his patience had run out. The Sheikh responded:

> It has been more than three years since I sold this land to your mission, and at that time you promised to build a hospital and send a doctor. The hospital has not been built yet and only God knows when it will be finished. As for the doctors, they come and go and I do not know how long you will stay. And now you come to me and tell me that my boundaries have been changed. I am thinking seriously of cancelling the privileges I have granted you and of expelling you from Kuwait.

After this, Mylrea quickly took his leave.

Later, in the hope of a reconciliation, Mylrea invited the Sheikh to visit the site to verify the boundaries and reassure himself that the mission had not taken land to which it was not entitled. On 9 February 1914, a rainy day, the Sheikh, together with his eldest son and the British Resident, as well as a number of Kuwaiti notables, paid a ceremonial visit. The land was measured and, fortunately for the mission, it emerged that the area of the land sold to it by the Sheikh had not been exceeded. According to Mylrea, the Sheikh gave a speech to those present intended to reassure the Kuwaiti people about the nature of the hospital's work, in which he said:

> I ask myself every day, who are these people to whom I sold the piece of land we are standing on now? Are they politicians? No. Are they a commercial company? No. Why have they come here? They have come to educate us and God knows that we are in need of education. They have come to build a hospital and look after our sick. They have come to do us a service.

While this positive mood prevailed, Mylrea asked the Sheikh to agree to the addition of the plot of land on the small hill close to the hospital, so that a house for the doctors could be built there. The Sheikh agreed to the request and said that his men would come the following day to draw the new boundaries of the land, which the Sheikh gave to the hospital for no payment.[53]

This story is significant in more than one way. First, it shows that Sheikh Mubarak was essentially keen to establish the hospital. He had asked for it to be built, provided the necessary land and kept an eye on its construction. Second, it shows that the Sheikh had respect for the prevalent customs of Kuwait. He became angry when he thought that the Americans had exceeded the boundaries of the piece of land they had been given, and went as far as to threaten to cancel the whole project were that to be the case. Third, however, it reflects the underlying wisdom of the Sheikh and his sense of justice. When it turned out that the land had been measured correctly, and that the mission had not gone beyond the agreed boundaries, his attitude changed entirely and he was willing once more to give them credit for their actions.

Construction work on the hospital, which was to be known as the American Hospital, was completed in October 1914. The final costs totalled 6,000 dollars. The completed building was distinctive, with the use of much glass, which led to its being known familiarly as the 'Glass House'. The doctor's house was also built, and Mylrea lived in it with his wife for 27 years. In an additional move to support the hospital, the Sheikh exempted the imported furniture and equipment from customs duties. The hospital continued to provide its services to the people of Kuwait until 1949, when the first state hospital, the Emiri Hospital, was constructed.[54]

In the first instance, the Kuwaiti people paid little attention to the American Hospital, and made only limited use of it. Gradually, their confidence in the health services it provided increased, and more people used it. Meanwhile, the hospital's activities began to extend beyond its walls. In 1914, Emir Abdul Aziz ibn Saud came over from Al-Hasa with his fighters, many of whom were suffering from malaria. He asked Mubarak to send a doctor to where they were camped, west of Kuwait City. They were treated by the doctors from the American Hospital, and Dr Harrison subsequently made several visits to Riyadh and Najd.

The American Hospital, despite the vicissitudes of its construction and it slow start, eventually became a symbol of progress in Kuwait of which Sheikh Mubarak was proud. In January 1915 the Sheikh visited the hospital and expressed his admiration of the scientific equipment that had been installed. Mylrea recalled the visit as follows:

> In my private office, the Sheikh asked me about the microscope. When I found it difficult to explain without a practical demonstration, I produced a flea, placed it under the

microscope and asked him to view it, with its size multiplied many times ... The Sheikh never forgot that flea. Over the next few days, many people came to us asking to see the flea. They enjoyed seeing it magnified many times under the microscope, just as the Sheikh had done. This one little flea became the talk of Kuwait and made the hospital famous.[55]

Many of the prominent personalities who visited Kuwait also toured the hospital, including Al-Sayyed Rajab the Naqib of Basra, Sheikh Khaz'al the Emir of Al-Muhammara and Lord Hardinge the Viceroy of India.

Introducing modern technology

The reign of Sheikh Mubarak witnessed the introduction of elements of European technology into Kuwait, including a number of modern European inventions that were the products of scientific advancement in the West. During the Sheikh's reign, electricity, cars, voice recorders, cameras, radios, mechanical fans, ice-making machines, sewing machines and water-purification machines were all introduced in Kuwait. Many of these represented major advances. For example, before that time, when electricity had not yet arrived in Kuwait, light at night was customarily provided by a lamp known as a *kindayri*. This consisted of a small cylindrical box, filled with flammable oil, such as animal grease, whose cover would be pierced and a wick of cotton thread or cloth placed in it. After the wick was soaked in the oil, it would then be lit. After kerosene was introduced, this was used instead of grease.[56]

Kuwait's first electric generator was brought from India by Sheikh Mubarak, for his own use in the Al-Seif Palace. It was run by an Indian technician and his assistant, who were brought to Kuwait for that purpose. Later, the Sheikh also wanted to use electricity to light his personal yacht. Sheikh Mubarak wrote to Major Knox to ask him to investigate the details of what would be necessary to install electric light aboard the yacht. The Political

Agent informed the Sheikh that he would arrange for a technician to provide the necessary information.[57] On 27 April 1914, apparently at Knox's suggestion, an engineer named Muhammad bin Salem Al-Sidrawi wrote to Sheikh Mubarak that he would hire two qualified technicians, one to work on the generator and the other on the electric machinery, who would work for the Sheikh for a salary and living expenses.[58]

Sheikh Mubarak's reign apparently also saw the introduction of photography. According to Abdullah Al-Hatem, who has searched for evidence to the contrary, there appear to be no photographs in existence of rulers or other personalities before Sheikh Mubarak's time, leading to the conclusion that cameras had not been brought to Kuwait before then. Anecdotally, it is said that the first camera was brought to Kuwait in 1909 by William Shakespear, during his tenure as British Political Agent; he was said to have been a skilled photographer.[59]

It was also during Sheikh Mubarak's reign that the first car was brought to Kuwait. This was a gift to Sheikh Mubarak from Sheikh Qassim bin Muhammad Al-Ibrahim, a well-known merchant from the Al-Ibrahim family who was one of the owners of the Al-Dawra estate. Sadly, the Sheikh was seldom able to use the car because the emirate's roads were narrow and uneven, and therefore unsuitable for motoring. It was of course a car of its era, less sophisticated than later vehicles, but when it first arrived in Kuwait the population regarded it as almost supernatural. When people saw it coming, they were terrified, even fearing the noise of its engine. There is a story that a man called Mubarak bin Abdullah Abu Jarwa once bribed the Sheikh's chauffeur, Ali Hussein Abu Khanfar, with a gold lira to allow him to ride in it through the merchant quarters. When the car passed through, with its horn sounding, people came out of their shops and stood by respectfully, as was their custom when Sheikh Mubarak's convoy passed through, thinking it was him.

In 1912, the first ice-making plant opened, owned by a Jewish citizen of Kuwait, Khawaja Saleh Muhlib. His factory, which was situated on the coast near the Al-Khalifa Mosque, began production in the summer of 1912. The popular demand for the ice was great, and customers flocked to buy it. However, the factory was not destined to be a success. Soon after it opened, there was an unexpected turn of events whereby a group of religious extremists began to call for the purchase of ice from the factory to be prohibited on religious grounds. Their obstruction and the difficulties they caused led the owner to close down the factory, which he later sold.

Towards the end of Mubarak's reign, in 1915, Abdullah Al-Zaydi, who was a supporter of Al-Rashid from Al-Zubayr, placed a gramophone in a café he owned in Al-Safat Square. This was the first gramophone ever to be used in Kuwait, and as soon as the public heard about such an extraordinary machine they flocked to listen to it. Al-Zaydi saw the profit to be made, and would put on a record only if each customer paid an anna for the privilege. The machine became the talk of the town. Again, there was religious concern, with some saying the gramophone was 'a portent of the Day of Judgement', while others claimed that 'the devil was singing inside it'. Again, the obscurantists had their way, when one of the Sheikh's sons, Sheikh Salem Al-Mubarak, who was known for his religiosity, took the opportunity of his father being away at Al-Muhammara to forbid the further use of the gramophone.

All these technological developments affected people's lives, but a further innovation in Sheikh Mubarak's time that was perhaps of more far-reaching importance was the introduction of three main means of communication with the outside world: the telegraph, regular mail services and, later, the telephone.[60] The telegraph was first proposed to Sheikh Mubarak by the Ottoman authorities. On 13 July 1910, Sheikh Mubarak wrote to the British Political Resident in Bushire informing the Resident that the Ottoman Governor of Basra had suggested that a telegraph cable be laid to Kuwait. Mubarak's letter informed the British official that he had refused, on the grounds that his subjects would not want it. The question remained unresolved for two more years.[61] On 2 July

1912, however, Major Cox, in his capacity as British Political Resident, went to the Sheikh and explained the advantages of laying a telegraph cable to Kuwait to make it easier to communicate with the outside world. This time, the Sheikh agreed in principle. On 13 July, Cox confirmed that the British Government's desire to lay the cable was serious, and that Shakespear would keep him informed of the details and planned date for when construction would begin.[62] In a letter to Cox on 26 July 1912, the Sheikh confirmed his agreement, and said he would provide all necessary facilities. As the Sheikh put it in his letter, 'having the telegraph would afford our government and people convenience and ease'. Despite his agreement, however, the project was only completed after the death of Sheikh Mubarak. In 1917 Britain constructed an overground telegraph line from Basra to Kuwait. In familiar Kuwaiti Arabic, the telegraph became known as the *tele*.

During his reign, the Sheikh was still obliged to send cables from the telegraph offices in Faw or Bushire, through which he also received telegrams. He communicated with Faw and Bushire by letter. For instance, on 9 May 1910, William Shakespear informed Sheikh Mubarak that a telegram had been received by the director of the telegraph office in Faw reporting the death of King Edward VII, the King of Britain and Emperor of India, on the morning of 7 May. The Sheikh replied by letter on 12 May, asking for a cable to be sent expressing his deepest sorrow at the death of the King and wishing the new King, George V, every success.[63]

The mail system gradually developed under Sheikh Mubarak. Initially, in order to use the postal system, people would bring their letters to an agency at Al-Mazid and place them in a special bag. Indian postage stamps were used. The mail would then be taken by hand to Basra, were it would be passed on to the Ottoman post office there to be sent on its way. If senders had packages and letters that they did not wish to send by this route, they could be entrusted to travellers and the captains of ships passing through the port of Kuwait to be taken to Bushire or elsewhere. Sheikh Mubarak and his close family would send their letters through the British Agency, which transported them through diplomatic channels.[64] On 28 February 1904, the Sheikh announced he had made an agreement with the British Government to open an official post office to facilitate trade and the affairs of Kuwait's citizens, declaring that, 'The British government has agreed, according to my wishes and for the interest of trade, to establish a post office in Kuwait.'[65] On 21 January 1915, the first official post office was opened in Kuwait. It was located in the British Agency building and was administered by the Indian Postal Service. Instead of the stamp of the Indian post office in Bushire, the stamp now carried the name of Kuwait in Roman script,[66] spelled 'Koweit' in the way favoured by the British.[67] Indian stamps also continued to be used. The post office remained in this location until 1929, when Colonel Dickson, newly appointed as Political Agent, took a lease on another location to use as a post office. The new office was in use until 1941.[68] Colonel Dickson, incidentally, was the most attached to Kuwait of all the British officials who served there. After his retirement he settled in Kuwait and lived there until his death in 1959.

Social conditions

In the closing years of the nineteenth century, Kuwait City, which stood on the coast, was ringed round with a mud-brick wall that began in the east at Freij Al-Batti and ended in the west at Freij Saud. It passed through the Al-Abd Al-Razzaq gate at the midpoint of the city and the other gates that surrounded Kuwait. The wall enclosed an area some 3 kilometres in circumference along the coast, and the city extended on average about 1 kilometre inland from the coast. Abdul Massih Antaki describes his first view of the city on arriving by sea: 'The buildings of Kuwait were getting closer ... They were spread over great distances along the coast.'[69] Most of the city's residences were on the coast or only slightly inland. They were built from mud or rocks taken from the sea. A single house would accommodate a number of families over more than one generation. Antaki describes the city as it was in 1907:

> Built in the Arab style, its streets are narrow and it is rectangular. Its population is about 50,000 and during festival days, when the Bedouins of Najd come into town to buy and sell, there could be as many as 80,000 people in the city.[70]

Bennett's report of his visit to Kuwait in 1910 describes the houses in the city as built from pebbles and mud, noting that its streets and side alleys were remarkably clean. The cleanliness of the city was the achievement of Sheikh Mubarak, who inaugurated the use of carts to collect rubbish and take it outside the city. Visitors to the city also reported that there was nothing green within it. Trees were rare, because of the extreme heat and the paucity of water. The few palm trees that stood on the coast served as direction markers towards which sailors could guide their boats as they came towards the shore.

Bennett describes the people of Kuwait as,

> friendlier and more polite than other people in the region. Everyone here is well-mannered and civil, which I believe is because they have a just and benevolent ruler. We found that the people were well treated, and the city prides itself as being the cleanest in the Gulf.

Bennett also noted the generosity of the people of Kuwait, remarking that,

> for those who live in harsh conditions life is a struggle ... But they are simple folk. Some of them might bargain when buying or selling to gain a few pennies, but they will slaughter their last sheep if you arrive as a guest at their tent.[71]

He also noted that the Kuwaitis were very devout, and reported their adherence to the precepts of Islam. In 1915 he wrote:

> First of all, it must be said that Islam in Kuwait is a fortress
> for the Kuwaiti people. If you are enjoying the sunset by the
> coast on any day, you will surely see that all the men on boats
> are praying. I have even seen children performing their
> prayers with a care and reverence I have never seen before.
> The mosques are full at every time of prayer.

He also noted that he would hear religious recitations from the
schools. On a visit to a house in Kuwait, he found a little school
where small girls were learning the Qur'an.[72]

In Sheikh Mubarak's time, there were three major mosques: the
Al-Khalifa Mosque, the Ibn Bahr Mosque and the Al-Adasani
Mosque. Abdul Aziz Al-Rashid notes that their origins are lost in
history and that it is uncertain which of the three is the oldest. The
Al-Khalifa Mosque, named after the Al-Khalifa family, the rulers
of Bahrain, lay on the coast. It was originally a small mosque but
Sheikh Mubarak rebuilt it and greatly increased its area. He re-
named it the Al-Hamidi Mosque, after Sultan Abdul Hamid.
Another well-known mosque was the Al-Badr Mosque, built by
Hajj Nasser Al-Badr in 1897 in the Qibla quarter. In 1910,
Sheikh Mubarak also had this mosque enlarged. The Al-Saqr
Mosque was built between 1907 and 1911 in Freij Al-Fallah
by Muhammad bin Abdullah Al-Saqr, the celebrated date mer-
chant, together with his brother Saqr. In 1921 Muhammad bin
Abdullah Al-Saqr became the head of the first Shura Council in
Kuwait. There were also the Hilal and the Al-Nisf mosques in the
market area.[73]

Kuwait was known for its religious tolerance. Sunni Muslims
lived in an atmosphere of friendship and co-operation as
neighbours of the Shi'ites who had come to Kuwait from Iraq,
Bahrain and Iran. In 1906, the Shi'ite Al-Ma'rafi family built what
became known as the Ma'rafi Husseiniyya, which was the first
husseiniyya in Kuwait. A husseiniyya is a Shi'ite religious and social
meeting place where religious instruction is offered by preachers
and religious scholars, and where Shi'ites can gather during their
religious festivals. The husseiniyya would welcome visitors in the

months of Muharram, Safar and Ramadan. A second *husseiniyya* was established in 1918, located in Mubarak Al-Kabir Street in the central commercial area. This was known as the Al-Husseiniyya Al-Khaz'aliyya because Sheikh Khaz'al had given 10,000 rupees for its construction. Before he died, Sheikh Mubarak donated the necessary wood for the building. This *husseiniyya* continued to function until the mid-twentieth century.[74]

Christian and Jewish communities also lived in the tolerant climate of Kuwait. This was confirmed by Dr Samuel Zwemer, who opened a bookshop during his first visit to Kuwait in 1903. He records that the Sheikh allowed Salim Antoun, a Christian from Mosul, to take a year's lease on a house, where he lived with his wife and five children, and to open a bookshop in the main market of the city to sell the Christian mission's books. Zwemer adds that upon his arrival in Kuwait, Antoun came on board his ship to greet him and then welcomed him to his own house. The American visitor said that he 'felt completely comfortable, and found that his host's family were not harassed for being Christians living near Muslim families'. He records that he met many of Antoun's visitors, among them a Jewish rabbi and a Sufi Muslim, and that he discussed various religious issues with them.[75]

The meeting places known as *diwaniyyas*, maintained by private individuals, were venues where groups of people were able to meet on a regular basis, as well as on feast days and other important occasions. Local issues and world affairs were discussed, and merchants could exchange news and information about the prices of commodities in the marketplace. In the holy month of Ramadan, they would remain open all night. The Qu'ran would be recited, and food to break their fast would be offered to the poor of the area. In the *diwaniyya*, people sat according to their social status. The status and wealth of a family could be judged from the size of their *diwaniyya*. They long continued to play the role of club, café and social centre. Some *diwaniyya* owners were intellectuals, religious scholars and literary men who encouraged intellectual talk. They would gather to read books and poetry, and lectures and classes would be given in their *diwaniyyas*. This kind of *diwaniyya* became a magnet for those who wished to acquire knowledge, and it was there that libraries of books on religion, language and literature would be found.[76]

The various 'eids', or religious festivals, were important occasions in the lives of Kuwaitis. Abdul Aziz Al-Rashid maintains that in Mubarak's reign, Kuwaitis used to,

> stop working for the whole week of an Eid, and play war games all day. Each area of the city would line up a group of men like the beads on a rosary, dancing, playing, and chanting thrilling military songs. They would play their tambourines and bang their drums, filling the skies with bullets from their rifles. All eyes would be enchanted by their shining swords.

Sheikh Mubarak fostered all these activities and encouraged Kuwaitis to celebrate such occasions.[77]

The people of Kuwait were used to receiving visitors and migrants from the tribes of Najd, Iraq, Iran and even from India, but Europeans, when they first appeared, with their strange white skins sometimes reddened by the sun, were not a familiar sight on Kuwait's streets. In 1911, Stanley Mylrea records that they were considered a strange phenomenon in Kuwait. He says that children used to follow them, and that they would 'call out harsh words at us, and every once in a while throw stones too'. The Kuwaiti upper classes, however, were conservative and proud, and 'maintained their good manners, politeness and kindness to Europeans as to other strangers'.[78]

His wife wrote of her experience with the women of Kuwait in 1915, reporting that Kuwaiti women were fascinated by her clothes, which appeared strange to them. The children would scream and laugh when they saw her because her clothes were so unfamiliar. She says that she changed her impression of Kuwaiti women after she got to know them and realized how unaggressive, well-mannered and generous they were.[79]

A major social problem for the people of Kuwait was the lack of fresh water. For everyday life, they had traditionally relied on the fresh water from wells outside the city walls. The water from these wells, in the areas of Al-Shamiyya, Hawalli, Keifan and Al-Nogra, was transported into the city on the backs of donkeys. When the water carriers reached the city and entered the *freij*, the residential area, they would call out the name of the well from which the water had been brought, naming it as Hawalli water, Al-Shamiyya water or Muruq water. When their containers were empty, they would go out through the city gates to refill them and bring more. There were no restrictions on the amount of water an individual could take, whether for personal use or to sell.

In 1904 a Christian priest, Anastase Al-Karmali, wrote a study of Kuwait in the Lebanese magazine *Al-Mashriq*. In it, he noted that,

> there is not a single river in Kuwait. They drink from pools and wells. The wells are plentiful and their water is drinkable. The Sheikh, the upper classes and the merchants bring their water from an island close to Kuwait, called Failaka (which they pronounce Failaja), which has sweet water, and has vegetation.[80] The wells fill with rain water and if it chances there has been no rain for more than a year, they dry up. If this happens there is famine and drought and the people find themselves in a crisis that can only be solved by rainfall. People call for help in the mosque and fervent prayers are performed, beseeching God to bring rain so that well-being and comfort can return.[81]

There was a water market close to the Al-Kishk building in the centre of the old city where water sellers would gather waiting for buyers. The average price for a small container of fresh water was 'a piaster and a half' and the price of fresh water contained in it was 'half a piaster'. There were wells inside houses in the city that provided partially saline water, but this water was used for bathing and cleaning, not for drinking or cooking. The people of Kuwait also built water reservoirs in their houses to collect rainwater, and there were various other ingenious ways of collecting water.[82]

As the population of the city increased, so did the demand for fresh water. In 1909, there was an initial effort to bring water to Kuwait from the Shatt Al-Arab. A merchant named Muhammad Al-Yaqoub transported water from Faw in wooden barrels on board his boat to sell to Kuwait. The profits exceeded his expectations, and others began to engage in the same trade. The boats used were sailing boats, specially adapted for transporting fresh water, with well-made wooden reservoirs. The water sellers would cluster round each boat as it arrived in Kuwait to fill their containers, which were made of goatskin or were tin cans. They would carry their containers on donkeys, or even on their own backs, and hasten to hawk the water round the streets of the residential areas. At this stage, the professional water sellers known as kanadira (singular kindar) made their appearance. They were Persian migrants from across the Gulf who came to Kuwait to work in the water business using 'a kindar, a wooden spear the length of a man that was balanced across their backs so that two containers could be carried, one on each side'.[83] Despite all the expansion in the trade, however, the people's demand for water remained unsatisfied.

The existing water boats, which were propelled by sail, were able to ply between Faw and Kuwait only on an irregular basis, owing to their dependence on the weather and the tides. Sheikh Mubarak therefore purchased a steam ship to ensure regular deliveries. A large ship fitted out with a sizeable reservoir designed specifically for water transportation was bought in India and was renamed the Sa'id. This was the first ship to be owned by the Government of Kuwait.[84] As the demand for water increased, Sheikh Mubarak took further steps. In 1914, he bought the first water-purification plant, from a British company, for 250,000 rupees. This desalinated seawater for drinking and other uses. Its tall chimney was supposed to carry the smoke it generated away from the city. His objective was to obviate the droughts that intermittently affected Kuwait, especially when the boats that brought fresh water from Faw were delayed. There was also a public health aim, namely to avert the outbreak of epidemics of disease that resulted when the population were obliged to drink stagnant water, which were responsible sometimes for widespread illness and numerous deaths.[85] Sadly, the Sheikh passed away before the machine was fully put into action in 1915, transforming saltwater from the Gulf into fresh water for drinking.[86]

A further development related to public health was the opening in 1915 of the first public bath, which was constructed in the centre of the city on a site belonging to Sheikh Mubarak close to the mosque built in 1782 by his ancestor the Beneficent Mubarak.[87] The public bath was not a success, however, and it was hard to attract people to it, in part because the freshwater supply it required was still insufficient.[88]

Until 1902, firewood was the fuel generally used for cooking and other domestic purposes in Kuwait. In that year, a British merchant named McKinsey began to import kerosene in cans from India. There were two brands, known as the Lion brand and the Sun brand. McKinsey marketed his kerosene to local merchants, explaining the benefits and attempting to convince them there were profits to be made. The local traders were cautious, so McKinsey offered a monopoly on sales to the first person to agree a deal with him. He signed a contract with Hajj Ali bin Al-Sheikh Ahmad Al-Umar, who became the sole agent for importing kerosene. Once the benefits of the fuel became clear, its use swiftly spread so that it became a virtually essential commodity.[89]

In addition to the domestic use of kerosene, it was also used for lamps on boats and to fuel signal lights on shore. Sayf Marzouq Al-Shamlan recounts how each evening a large kerosene lamp was hoisted above the house of the British Political Agent to guide the sailing boats at night as they got close to Kuwait port. The sailors could see the lamp while they were still far offshore, enabling them to steer towards it. For some time, there was only one lamp of this kind in the city.[90] In May 1901, the Russian Consul in Baghdad reported that the British had put up a high pole to light the port at night.[91] Raunkiær also noted its development when he described the house of the Political Agent as 'a prominent building, in front of which the British flag flies on a high pole over which a red lamp has been placed to guide sailors into the port'.[92]

There were of course many social events in Kuwait, some of which also began to see changes at this time. Weddings in Kuwait had been simple affairs, with local musicians providing entertainment. However, when the Sheikh's grandson, Abdullah, was married in 1908, the Sheikh organized an unprecedentedly huge celebration in the city for which musicians and singers were brought in from Iraq and Egypt. The wedding was attended by all the Kuwaiti notables as well as Sheikh Khaz'al and others from Al-Muhammara. A similarly large affair was the wedding in 1910 of Saud bin Muhammad Al-Sabah to Sheikh Mubarak's daughter.[93] It should be said that Kuwaiti women played a central role in society, perhaps more so in Kuwait than in other Arab countries, because the men were often away from Kuwait, trading or on pearl-diving expeditions, for much of the year.

In general, it can be said that the reign of Sheikh Mubarak saw the introduction of various aspects of modernity to Kuwait in the fields of education, health and technology. These changes were connected to the increase in the population of Kuwait and to the growing familiarity of the population with Western ideas and features of life by way of visitors to the country. Such change was not limited to social life, but also affected economic activity and commerce.

~4~

Economic Development

He wanted trade to grow and the fortunes of the merchants
to increase.

Abdul Aziz Al-Rashid, *Ta'rikh Al-Kuwait*

Trade and commerce

Youssef bin Issa Al-Qinai, one of the pioneers of reform in
Kuwait, in his book *Safahat Min Tarikh Al-Kuwait* [Pages
from the History of Kuwait], makes this favourable assessment:

> During Mubarak's reign Kuwait grew and urbanization
> increased. Its reputation in the Persian Gulf was high.
> Security was established in the desert; wealth increased and
> trade advanced. Ships passed through Kuwait as they went to
> and from Basra. The pearl divers grew ever more prosperous,
> with bigger boats and a growing harvest.[1]

From the outset, Kuwait was controlled by the desert and the sea.
The desert imposed the Bedouin way of life, with camel and goat

herding, as the nomads travelled to find water and new pastures. On the other side, the sea was the key to Kuwait's prosperity. Pearl diving provided a major source of income, while maritime commerce was Kuwait's outlet to the rest of the world.

Kuwait's unique geographic location made it a natural outlet for its Arabian hinterland. Its excellent harbour, the best on the eastern coast of Arabia, enabled Kuwait to achieve a key position as an entrepôt on the trade routes from east to west. According to the captain of the Russian cruiser *Varyag*, which visited Kuwait in September 1901, there was no doubt that Kuwait was,

> the best port on the Gulf coast. It is a deep wide bay, open to eastern winds only. Because of the good depth, ships can anchor relatively closer to the shore than in Bushire or Bandar Abbas. During the high tide, rowing boats can moor without difficulty, as there is a narrow deep channel, making a sort of inlet that extends across the sea ... A sufficiency of good quality provisions for ships can be obtained at relatively low prices.[2]

Goods and merchandise from around the world could be unloaded with ease in Kuwait, to be stored and shipped onward to the interior of eastern Arabia. A variety of goods were transported through Kuwait for Arabia's desert peoples. Kuwait also served as a bustling market for the people of Najd, Al-Hasa and the Syrian Desert.[3] The Saudi historian, Dr Abdullah Al-Saleh Al-Uthaymni, explains how Kuwait became the market where merchants from Najd would buy goods that had come to Kuwait from India and beyond. It was also a magnet for those seeking work, in the diving industry in particular.[4]

According to Barclay Raunkiær,

> Most trade in Arabia passes through Kuwait. It is therefore the gateway not only to Iraq, but to the heart of Arabia. It is the only country between Shatt Al-Arab and the Musandam peninsula which has natural routes.[5]

Antaki confirms this, declaring that in commercial terms the reason Kuwait was one of the most important harbours in the Gulf was as follows:

> It is the port of the Najdis. Through it they import what they need from India and export their goods, most importantly the famous Najdi horses, to Basra, Baghdad, the bays of the Persian Gulf and India.[6]

Thanks to its expansion, Kuwaiti trade began to extend even to Egypt. In a British report from 1900, it was noted that a Kuwaiti citizen, Saud Sulayman Saleh Al-Shibli, bought camels in Kuwait for export to Egypt, making much profit from the trade.[7]

In an analysis of commercial exchange for the years 1905–1906, the figures given show that 30.7 per cent of Kuwait's trade was with India, which was the main source of the majority of food commodities imported into Kuwait, such as rice, sugar, tea and flour. Meanwhile, 26.7 per cent of Kuwait's commerce was with the Ottoman Empire, 14.6 per cent with Britain and 9.21 per cent with Iran. The most important exports were pearls, animal fat from desert flocks, horses, skins, wool and dates. The chief imports were cotton and silk textiles, sugar, tea, oils, tobacco, cereals such as wheat and barley, wood, ropes for maritime use and water brought on sailing boats from the Shatt Al-Arab.[8]

The Sheikh's support for commerce

Sheikh Mubarak was well aware that commerce was the lifeblood of Kuwait and the mainstay of the Kuwaiti people. This is why he sought, in every way possible, to maintain an atmosphere conducive to a vigorous economy and to promote increased trade in Kuwait. During his reign there was a highly significant growth in trade, attributable to his efforts to foster a climate of security, suppress piracy and protect merchants from theft. He reacted with severity towards anyone who attacked Kuwait or its people, on land and sea. The Sheikh personally led many campaigns to exact retribution against tribes who attempted to plunder Kuwaiti caravans, and sent out naval expeditions to hunt down and destroy ships engaged in piracy. Once the lives and goods of merchants were secure, they became more prosperous.

The Sheikh took particular interest in the security of the land route between Kuwait and Basra. In 1911, however, in a raid by a group of Bedouin, a merchant from the town of Barida named Abdul Aziz Al-Ruwaf, who was on his way from Al-Zubayr to Kuwait, lost his life. When Sheikh Mubarak heard this, he ordered that the culprits be tracked down, and a number of them were arrested in possession of part of the stolen money. He then put the protection of caravans between Kuwait and Al-Zubayr on a regular footing, engaging a permanent force of some 40 men to guard the road between the two in future.[9]

With security in place, Kuwait became a favourite destination for craftsmen and professionals from Najd, Iran, Iraq and Al-Hasa, who began to opt to live in Kuwait and set up businesses there. Raunkiær confirms that Kuwait also became a destination for the Arabs because of their antipathy for the Ottoman Turks:

> Kuwait is the only country in the area which can be considered independent. It has made it easier for the inhabitants of central Arabia to reach the sea ... The deep hatred felt by the Arabs towards the Ottoman Turks has had a great effect on commercial activity in the areas ruled by the Turks. Furthermore, the Turks' style of rule has not helped to remedy this problem ... Another reason for the inhabitants of central Arabia to avoid Turkish customs posts is that the Turks prohibit trading in weapons ... In Kuwait, because the authority of the ruler of Kuwait is very strong, the Arabs of the interior can get hold of weapons without being stopped by anyone trying to confiscate them.[10]

Sheikh Mubarak also encouraged boat builders to construct larger vessels, enabling Kuwaiti merchants to voyage easily as far as India and beyond. The harbour at Kuwait was much better than neighbouring facilities, for instance at Al-Muhammara where larger boats faced considerable difficulties. The Sheikh was also active in promoting communications between Kuwait and India. After he signed the protection agreement with Britain in 1899, the Sheikh entered into a contract with the British-India Steam Navigation Company, under which its passenger and cargo ships would dock in Kuwait on average once a week. This meant that a merchant could now travel to India on a monthly basis with little difficulty. The Sheikh also set up an office in Bombay to help Kuwaiti merchants, offering them assistance in their dealings with merchants of other nationalities and protecting their rights. This was run by Salem Al-Sidrawi, and later by his son, Muhammad. Mubarak also encouraged Kuwaiti merchants to open their own businesses in India to carry out import and export activities. The result was that increasing numbers of Kuwaiti merchants began trading in India, as well as in Iran and elsewhere in the Gulf.[11]

As well as ensuring security for external trade, the Sheikh also kept a careful watch on commercial activity inside Kuwait, and severely punished any criminal actions. For this reason, theft was rare in Kuwait. While he was walking in one of the markets in Kuwait in 1907, Antaki observed the money changers:

> Each one had a short desk in front of him with various currencies, such as the various denominations of Ottoman, Iranian and Indian coinage. I discovered that when evening came, these merchants are able to close up their offices, leaving their money inside, and to go home feeling that their money is safe.[12]

Sheikh Mubarak's officials would also mediate between merchants and others involved in trade, to ensure transactions were honoured and debts paid, especially in cases where the repayment of a loan was overdue. Merchants would sometimes attempt to gain the Sheikh's attention by contacting the British Political Agent about such matters. For example, on 20 March 1909, Captain Knox wrote to Sheikh Jaber, Sheikh Mubarak's eldest son, asking him to assist a merchant named Khalaf bin Ghisan to recover a debt of 27 riyals owed to him by one Ali Abdullah bin Fayez Al-Qassab. In another incident, William Shakespear wrote to the Sheikh on 10 October 1909 about the problems of one Mirza Ja'far, of Bushire, evidently a British subject, who had been unable to recover debts owed to him by various Kuwaitis. It became a long-drawn-out affair.

On this occasion, Shakespear asked Sheikh Mubarak to recover these debts according to a list supplied by Mirza Ja'far, which he attached to the letter. The Sheikh sent an agent to find the debtors and to collect what was owed, charging them first to verify that the complaints were genuine. On 4 March 1910, however, when Mirza Ja'far next arrived in Kuwait, he still had not been able to recover all the debts owed to him. Once more, he approached Shakespear, who asked the Sheikh if he would intervene in accordance with what he called 'justice and fairness' if the debtors continued to refuse to pay. On 14 March, Shakespear informed the Sheikh that Mirza Ja'far had found out that some of those who owed him money were out of the country, while others had simply refused to pay and others again had denied that they owed anything. Mirza Ja'far once more returned to Bushire. On 16 March, Sheikh Mubarak replied saying that everything possible had been done to investigate, but no proof could be found of Mirza Ja'far's claims, despite his willingness to assist British subjects 'on the path of justice'.[13]

Meanwhile, on occasion, the Sheikh also asked the British authorities for their good offices. For example, on 29 September 1908, the Sheikh wrote to Captain Knox about a difficulty he was having in relation to a pearl merchant, Abdul Razzaq bin Salem bin Sultan. The problem was that this man, whose business was the sale of pearls in India on behalf of Kuwaiti merchants, had borrowed 5,000 rupees in 1907 from a Kuwaiti named Muhammad bin Abdul Wahhab Al-Mishari, while the latter was visiting Bombay, and had entrusted the pearls he held on behalf of various Kuwaiti merchants to Al-Mishari for sale. Sultan had then travelled to Basra, where he unfortunately died. Meanwhile, it seems that Al-Mishari had delayed selling the pearls. Sheikh Mubarak asked Knox to request the British authorities in India to intervene, confiscating the pearls and putting them on sale as soon as possible, since the price of pearls was falling. He requested that after the debt owed to Al-Mishari was settled, the remainder of the proceeds from selling the pearls be divided fairly among the pearl merchants in Kuwait who owned them, so that any loss incurred would be born equitably by all. Knox informed the Sheikh that he would ask Major Cox, the Political Resident in Bushire, to take action as soon as possible.

After the outbreak of World War I, the British authorities forbade ships from leaving India without a permit, and the movement of money out of the country was also prohibited. A number of Kuwaiti vessels that were in Indian ports at the time were not allowed to set sail with foodstuffs and other goods on board. Sheikh Mubarak intervened with the British authorities, asking them to grant the necessary permits for these boats to sail with their cargoes. In addition, as the voyage to Kuwait would be lengthy for these sailing boats, the Sheikh asked the British Political Agent in Kuwait to help ensure there would be no shortage of commodities in the markets in Kuwait by asking the British Government to permit a steamship to travel to Kuwait every two weeks.[14]

Other measures were taken from time to time by Sheikh Mubarak to protect the merchants of Kuwait and their property when they were outside the country. On 29 March 1910, the Sheikh wrote to Faisal bin Turki, the Sultan of Oman, asking him to arrest one Muhammad Saleh, a Kuwaiti subject who was a member of the crew of a Kuwaiti-owned boat that flew the Kuwaiti flag. This individual had deserted the ship and fled to Muscat.[15] In similar vein, the Sheikh wrote to William Shakespear on 4 November 1912, asking him to intervene on behalf of Saud Al-Mutairi, the captain and owner of a Kuwaiti-registered vessel, one of whose crew had jumped ship in Calcutta owing 460 rupees to the captain. The Sheikh asked Shakespear to draft a letter on the captain's behalf to the British authorities in Calcutta to help him recover his money. Shakespear replied on the same day, informing him that his request had been acted upon.[16]

In the same year, the Sheikh also intervened in the case of Abdul Rahman Al-Ibrahim, a pearl merchant in Bombay who had suffered business losses that had left him unable to pay his debts to a number of Kuwaiti merchants. When the creditors asked the Sheikh to intervene to guarantee they would get their money, the Sheikh undertook that Qassim Al-Ibrahim, who was Abdul Rahman Al-Ibrahim's cousin and one of Kuwait's richest men, would pay the debts, telling the Al-Ibrahim family that he would confiscate their farms in the Al-Jura region if Qassim did not settle the debts. In the event, Qassim Al-Ibrahim settled the debts in annual instalments. He later appeared to develop a close relationship with the Sheikh. In 1913 the Sheikh sent a boat to Bombay to bring Qassim Al-Ibrahim back to Kuwait, and when he arrived he was ceremonially welcomed with a four-gun salute. Qassim was a guest in Sheikh Mubarak's house, and then travelled on from Kuwait to Al-Filiya on one of the Sheikh's own boats, accompanied by the Sheikh's son, Sheikh Jaber. Qassim Al-Ibrahim continued to make the payments by instalment as he had agreed until Sheikh Mubarak's death, but ceased to do so thereafter.[17]

On 16 May 1912, the Sheikh complained to the Political Resident about the excessive zeal of British naval vessels searching Kuwaiti boats sailing in the Gulf to ascertain that they were not carrying unlicensed weapons. The Sheikh wrote that although he had committed himself to the agreement prohibiting illegal trading in weapons, and had agreed that British boats could conduct searches, it was unacceptable for searches to be carried out on boats owned by those he called 'the most notable Kuwaitis, including prominent men and my own neighbours'. The Sheikh named Khalifa bin Shaheen Al-Ghanem, his uncle Ahmad bin Muhammad Al-Ghanem, Abdul Latif bin Issa and Nasser Al-Badr as the owners of boats that had been searched in what he said was an unseemly manner, humiliating the crew and preventing them from working for three days.

The Sheikh wrote that the British boats had unloaded the cargo in order to carry out their search, stripping the boats down to the bare wood of the decks, which had led to the loss of much of the cargo in the sea, and that the captains themselves had been obliged to pay for the lost cargo and the damage to the boats. He commented that this reflected an unfounded distrust of the Kuwaiti people, adding that 'we seek good treatment as is our right and to safeguard our honour'. He emphasized that his subjects did not carry or transport unlicensed weapons. 'As I myself safeguard my honour,' he said, 'so they also safeguard their own. Whilst obeying my orders.'[18]

In order to be able to certify the identity of the merchants and boats under his patronage, the Sheikh began to provide documentation for the merchants. On 2 August 1911, such papers were issued, for example, to Abdullah bin Muhammad Al-Khalil, certifying that he was a Kuwaiti subject, 'through his father and grandfather, both of whom were born and lived in Kuwait, and that his profession was that of a trader'. The certificate carries the official seal of Mubarak Al-Sabah, in his capacity as ruler of Kuwait.[19] The Sheikh similarly certified the Kuwaiti origin of boats from the port of Kuwait with a document addressed to 'such seafarers and city dwellers of all great and leading friendly countries to whom is presented this order issued by ourselves'. On 7 October 1911 a similar certificate was issued to,

> a sailing boat named the *Al-Salimi* owned by Abdul Latif bin Issa bin Hajji, who is a man of Kuwait and our subject. We expect that those in authority in the friendly powers if they see him or stop him will treat him well according to the principles, laws, conditions and ties between friendly nations.[20]

The Sheikh also issued certificates for boats that carried weapons for their own defence, in order, as he put it, to 'preserve their souls' in case of attack at sea. These certificates specify the variety of boat, the name of the owner and of his father, that the owner is the Sheikh's subject, the name of the captain and his father, the number of the crew and the quantity and variety of weapons held on the boat.[21]

Economic activities of the people of Kuwait

Sheikh Mubarak's stewardship and patronage of the commercial and economic life of the country resulted in growing prosperity in Kuwait, with increasing wealth in the country and the expansion of its economy. Kuwait's economic and commercial fortunes were always intimately linked with the sea. Aside from hunting and some handicrafts, the principal economic activities of the Kuwaiti people were essentially maritime and included diving for pearls and the pearl trade, maritime commerce, trades connected with ships and also fishing. Over time, these activities fell within organized structures, and regulatory systems developed in Kuwait within which they were controlled.[22] We shall examine each trade individually.

Pearl diving
Pearl diving and the trade in pearls constituted one of the most important sources of income not just for Kuwait but for the Gulf in general. In each Gulf city there was a market for the sale and purchase of pearls, some of which were justly renowned. In the seventeenth and eighteenth centuries, pearls from the cities of the Gulf found their way to markets in Basra and Baghdad, some were exported to Damascus and Istanbul and in due course some even went onwards to Europe. After the introduction of commercial steamships, the market for pearls moved from Iraq to India. The pearl-diving season was in the summer, from May to September.

During Sheikh Mubarak's reign the pearl trade expanded until the number of Kuwaiti boats diving for pearls exceeded 800, each with an average crew of some 70 men. According to estimates by

Sheikh Youssef bin Issa Al-Qinai, the income from pearl diving reached about 6 million rupees.[23] Towards the end of Sheikh Mubarak's reign, the pearl trade had grown to such an extent that 1913 was known as the year of the 'bounty', as production in that year went far beyond the normal harvest. In the last years of Sheikh Mubarak's time, however, Ramadan fell in the summer, so the divers were not able to work. The diving season was limited to the months before and after Ramadan, with divers able to work only up to the beginning of the fast and returning to work on the Eid al-Fitr, as soon as they had held their feast. At that time, the season was effectively regarded as having two parts rather than one. Because of the difficulty caused by the occurrence of Ramadan in the middle of the diving season, the captain of one pearling vessel wrote to the religious scholars in Mecca and at Al-Azhar in Cairo asking them to issue a *fatwa* that would rule definitively whether diving was permitted during the fasting period. The response was, however, that diving was not permitted during Ramadan and that breaking the fast in order to dive was also not permissible.[24]

Pearl diving, with all the other activities and maritime activity linked to it, was the principal occupation for Kuwaitis and many of the population were involved either directly or indirectly. Several kinds of fishing boat were in use, each with its own characteristics and designation, for example the *batil* and the *baqqara*. The names of the former included the *Sa'id* and the *Musa'id*, while names of the latter included *Al-Mayyasa* and *Al-Humr*. Another smaller variety of boat was the *sunbuk*. There were also other types such as the *shu'i*, the *jalyut* and the *bum*. Among these were boats named *Marzouq*, *Mansour*, *Mashour* and *Al-Mustalaha*.

There is a tale about the construction of *baghla* sailing boats in Kuwait, which were the variety mainly used by Kuwaitis to travel to India and the eastern coast of Africa before the advent of steam. In the early days, while Sheikh Muhammad was still in power, Abdul Rahman Al-As'usi commissioned a *baghla* from Muhammad Jarouf, who began his work and completed the outside frame. Meanwhile, Sheikh Mubarak came to power, with the result that Jarouf took fright and fled to Kufa. When the Sheikh found out, he laughed and said, 'May God disappoint him'. He ordered that the boat be completed by someone else. The work was done by Saleh bin Rashed and the boat became known as the *Mirdawiyya*, after its owner Sheikh Khaz'al Al-Mirdawi, the ruler of Al-Muhammara.[25]

Those engaged in the diving business were known as the *tawwashin*. They would take their boats to the pearl-diving sites in the waters of Kuwait, as well as to Al-Hasa, Bahrain, Qatar and sometimes even to distant diving sites off the coast of Oman. They would also go to Bahrain, regarded as the centre of the pearl trade in the Gulf, to buy and sell pearls and to replenish their supplies. The two best-known *tawwashin* in that period were Hilal Al-Mutayri and Issa Al-Qattami, who were regarded as the most renowned Kuwaiti captains. Another was an Egyptian named Hafez Wahbah, who also worked as a teacher in the Al-Mubarakiyya School.

The seamen working on board the pearl-diving boats were classified into five categories, according to their jobs and ranks, each taking a share of the profits of the dive in proportion to his status. The highest category was of course that of captain, the master of the ship. His job was to sail the boat, keep it on course and ensure its well-being until it arrived safely at port. The second category was accorded to the pearl divers, who swam down to bring up the oysters that contained the pearls, which they did with great skill without any of the technical equipment that would be used today. The third category was the *suyub*, those who looked after the safety of the divers and pulled them up from the bottom of the sea when the divers indicated. The fourth group were the *radif*, the men who worked on the boat and helped the *suyub*; they owned the smallest share of the profits. The fifth and lowest category was the *tabbab*. These were the boys who would perform simple duties such as making tea and coffee and ensuring that the others had what they needed. Usually they would work for no pay, apart from food or gratuities given to them by the captain and the crew.[26]

So many Kuwaiti men were engaged in this profession that Kuwait City sometimes seemed to have no men amongst its population during the summer season when diving was taking place. The return of the boats to Kuwait was a major public event, and people would gather on the shore to witness it. Yaqoub Youssef Al-Hajji describes the occasion:

> There is no more marvellous sight in old Kuwait than the return of the divers to the city at the end of the diving season. When the boats arrive in the city with their white sails raised, they look like seagulls covering the sea. All across the shore, men, women and children line up waiting for the arrival of these boats and to welcome their loved ones, who would have been away for four months on the arduous venture of diving for pearls.[27]

Sadly, with the cultivation of artificial pearls in Japan and elsewhere, the curtailment of the resources of wealthy Indian princes, who had been among the main buyers of pearls, and the discovery of oil in Kuwait, which offered an alternative and more lucrative way of life, pearl diving gradually diminished until it came to a complete halt. Diving as an activity declined until, by 1955, the number of pearl-diving boats that remained was probably less than 20.

Commercial shipping

In the early decades of the twentieth century, the maritime trade was an important source of income for Kuwaitis, second only to pearl diving. A fleet of sailing boats had been built, using wood imported from India. They plied between ports on both the Persian and Arab sides of the Gulf, also venturing further afield to the ports of Baluchistan in Pakistan, India, East Africa, the Arabian coast and the Red Sea. They were used to transport goods and commodities such as dates, grains, wood and textiles. With the introduction of steamships, however, the number of these boats gradually declined until they disappeared altogether.[28]

The outbreak of World War I provided a lucrative opportunity for the Kuwaiti fleet. The British military had commandeered all the large freight ships owned by the British-India Steam Navigation Company and by the other commercial sea companies that operated in the area, in order to use them for the war effort. This meant that the larger and more modern ships were no longer available to transport goods between the ports around the Gulf, and the demand for sailing boats returned. The profits to be made from shipping increased, and merchants raced to build more boats in the ports of Kuwait and in Calcutta, which at the time was known in Kuwait as the port of Faliqot or Caliqot. Three of the most celebrated of these boats were the *Nur al-Bahr*, *Al-Muhammadi* and the *Samhan*.[29] In general, the boat-building industry was given a fillip. Sailing boats of the *bum* and *baghla* types were constructed out of Indian teak. The boat builders were masters of their trade. Some of the most celebrated boat builders were Hajj Salman, with his son Ahmad, Saleh bin Rashid, who worked with his brothers Jassem and Abdullah, and Hajj Hammud bin Badr.

Fishing

Fishing was the third most important maritime occupation in Kuwait in terms of its rank as a source of income. The fishing fleet consisted originally of small rowing boats. Later, sailing boats were used, though because of their small size these vessels were still unable to stray too far away from the shore. There were a number of fishing techniques in use.[30] Fishing with nets was most common, but another method was the *qarqur*, which was a kind of large woven metal cage with sides more than a metre long and with an open door on one side for fish to enter it. Bait was placed inside and a rope tied to the top of the *qarqur* so it could be pulled up. Lanterns were also used at night to attract fish, which could then be speared.

In the course of a visit to Kuwait in 1902, the captain of the Russian cruiser *Askold* noted that there were many boats whose crews still used simple fishing rods. Fish, it seems, were very plentiful:

> The captain of one boat was simply pulling out one fish after the other. Fishing on the shores of Kuwait was done with very simple methods. Along the whole coast, before reaching the city, you can see walls made of bamboo stakes in great numbers. Fish would enter them during the high tide and would become trapped inside them during low tide.[31]

Handicrafts

During Sheikh Mubarak's reign, Kuwait saw the rise of local industries connected to supplying materials needed for common economic activities and people's daily needs, including boat building, the manufacture of fishing equipment, tent-making and tailoring clothes, including traditional dress for men and women. All these were activities for the manufacture of previously imported goods. Markets grew up named for the craft whose products were sold, such as the jewellers' market, the *bisht* market (a *bisht* was a cloak often made of fabric woven from camel hair), the gun market and so on.[32]

Of course, the most celebrated industry was boat building. Pearl diving, fishing and maritime commerce all depended on these craft. There was little or no wood in Kuwait, and the boat builders imported their wood from India and East Africa. The boats varied in size and design depending on their use, and on whether they were going to sail close to shore or travel farther away, to the Red Sea or the Indian Ocean. The British Political Agent William Shakespear commented on the boat-building skills to be found in Kuwait:

> The wood brought in by Kuwaiti merchants from Africa on sailboats was very carefully cut so that each panel fitted exactly in place next to the other. This is how a boat would be shaped. They are so wonderful that they truly appear to be a work of nature and not man made.[33]

Kuwaitis also practised other small manufacturing trades linked to their daily lives, such as ironmongery, where artisans produced nails, knives, hammers and building equipment. Brass founders made pots for cooking, utensils to eat with and tea and coffee pots. Goldsmiths created ornamental pieces, gunsmiths made traditional weapons, and skins were cured for carrying water and milk. Straw mats were woven and traditional textiles were made, and there were workshops milling grain and making soap.[34] There was also the skill of making straw mats, while traditional textiles were handwoven from yarn spun by the Bedouin. In the city the construction industry was prevalent.

There was also, of course, agriculture, which flourished in locations surrounding Kuwait, notably at Al-Jahra and Failaka. At the oasis of Al-Jahra, wells provided water for orchards and date palms. The oasis was the site of two palatial villas, one of which, known as the Red Palace, was the property of Sheikh Mubarak, while the other was the country house of Khalaf Pasha Al-Naqib. Failaka was an island with fresh water in shallow wells. In Sheikh Mubarak's day, the farms and orchards there were said to be delightful.[35] Most desert dwellers around Kuwait were shepherds, many of whom also worked intermittently in the caravan trade.[36]

Markets and commercial activity

Sheikh Mubarak carefully fostered the prosperity of Kuwait's markets. He watched over mercantile activity and introduced judicious measures in terms of taxation and customs, which meant that commercial activity became an important source of Kuwait's wealth.[37]

Markets

It was Sheikh Mubarak's habit to tour the markets each afternoon in an open Victoria carriage, lacquered in black and drawn by two black horses. He would fall into conversation with the men who sat at an old café in the heart of the market area, asking them about their affairs.[38] He took steps when necessary to ensure that prices remained within acceptable limits and did not exceed the ability of the people of Kuwait to pay. The Sheikh dealt with each case according to its circumstances. Sometimes, he used his authority as a ruler to lower prices, but most of the time, with his good understanding of the mechanisms of trade and commercial life, he would manipulate the market.

For instance, there were protests on one occasion about the excessive price of meat, which had risen from 10 annas an ounce to 12 annas (there were 16 annas to a rupee). Members of the public complained to Sheikh Mubarak, who reassured them. He summoned all the butchers to come to see him and issued strict orders that an ounce of meat should be one rupee and eight annas, threatening anyone who charged a different price with stern punishment. The next morning, the people of Kuwait were startled to discover the new price and were furious with Sheikh Mubarak. As soon as news of the price rise spread outside Kuwait, however, thousands of cattle were brought to Kuwait from every direction for slaughter and sale. With the sudden excess in supply, the Sheikh permitted the new fixed price to be abandoned and prices fell to less than they had been before. The people perceived what the point of raising the price of meat had been, and understood the saying, 'an expensive market increases supply'.[39]

As a result of the Sheikh's concern to suppress fraud and cheating in commerce, and of his direct supervision, traders felt secure in doing business in Kuwait, and consequently the markets prospered. Abd Al-Massih Antaki describes the markets in Kuwait during Mubarak's reign:

> Kuwait imports and exports goods, like other major ports, and many of its people are engaged in commerce. As for the level of activity in the markets, I saw them to be prosperous and developed. The markets were full of people and a guide told me that the time I was there was not even one of the high seasons.[40]

Raunkiær adds that the markets in Kuwait were not only places of business, but also the starting point for caravans going to and from Kuwait. When a caravan was preparing to set off, the camel herders and their camels would gather on the southern side of the market area. It was from there that the merchants sent their goods into the desert. Raunkiær described the marketplace as he saw it in 1913, noting that it was crowded with people and goods. The booths where goods were sold consisted of tents woven from straw and palm leaves, built on wooden platforms. Vendors sat in the shade within to exhibit their wares. On the outskirts of the market area there were the black tents of the nomadic Bedouin. The marketplace was patrolled by the Sheikh's men, who collected the taxes due on goods. Close to the main market there was a market for coal, which was in general imported from Iran and served as an additional fuel.[41]

Bennett also gives a description of the centre of the city and of its sprawling market area, frequented by Arabs from various cities. He observed that a booming trade was carried on, with deals sometimes settled in cash and sometimes through barter. The merchants would generally give Bedouin traders goods to sell on credit, accepting a promise of repayment on the nomadic trader's next visit.[42]

Currencies

Multiple currencies were used in the markets and elsewhere in Kuwait during Sheikh Mubarak's reign. One of these was known at the time as the so-called 'French riyal', which was in fact the famous 'Maria Theresa dollar'. This was originally an Austrian silver coin, known in German as a 'thaler', which bore the portrait of Maria Theresa, Holy Roman Empress from 1740 to 1780. By the time of Sheikh Mubarak it was no longer used in Austria, but was minted there and elsewhere for circulation abroad. It was equivalent in weight to about two-and-a-half silver rupees. This coin was the most valuable silver currency used in Kuwait in terms of purchasing power, and the most sought-after currency. It continued in use until after World War II, when Britain agreed with Austria that the coin should no longer be minted.

A coin known as 'the second rupee' was also used in the Sheikh's time. The Kuwaitis called it 'the one with the girl', because it had Queen Victoria's image on it. A so-called 'third rupee' was also used. This was struck during the reign of Edward VII, and the Kuwaitis called it 'the bald one' because the King was depicted as bald in the coin's image of him. This currency included coins valued at half a rupee, four annas, two annas and one anna. This last coin was known in Kuwait as *al-metlik*, which was derived from the English word 'metal'. The quantity of one anna coins of this type in circulation was small, which made it rare. It was distinguished by an image of King Edward VII wearing a crown. The so-called 'fourth rupee' was known by the Kuwaitis as 'the old man's rupee' because a portrait of King George V in old age, with a moustache and beard, appeared on the coin. In addition to these silver coins, paper bank notes began to be used in Kuwait in 1913.[43]

In 1918, after the British occupation of Basra in November which followed World War I, British gold guineas began to be used in Iraq. The British authorities, however, feared that these gold coins might be smuggled into Ottoman territory, where they would be used to swell the Ottoman coffers, and therefore insisted that the Indian rupee continue to be used for transactions in Kuwait. Political Resident in Bushire, Colonel Cox, as he now was, wrote to Sheikh Mubarak to tell him that the rupee should continue to be used in Kuwait, and asked him to help fight the smuggling of gold coins. The Sheikh replied:

> Our transactions side are linked to India and are all denominated in rupees and riyals, just as they would be in India. There is definitely no one here sending gold outside.[44]

Taxes and customs duties
Before the time of Sheikh Mubarak, the sheikhs of Kuwait had few sources of monetary income to speak of. There was only the *zakat*

collected from the desert tribes (i.e. the alms tax levied on all Muslims for charitable purposes) and the limited amount of money that came from a 3 per cent customs duty levied on certain activities. In reality, none of the sheikhs sought to enforce this duty, but the merchants chose to pay it on a voluntary basis to support the Sheikh, who would not otherwise have had sufficient income to be able to run the country's administration. In addition, in the period before Mubarak there was a tax imposed on shops but this was paid directly to the guards who kept watch over the city at night.

During Mubarak's reign, Kuwait's trade increased and its merchants became wealthier. In addition, Mubarak faced the increased costs of the larger army he established and of his military campaigns. The Sheikh therefore imposed various additional taxes and duties, including an increase in customs duties. He attempted to convince the merchants that this was in their interests, and that the money was being used to protect commerce and secure trade routes.[45] The Sheikh and the merchants, however, had different points of view on this. For example, after the battle of Hadiyya, when the Sheikh needed money to purchase weapons, he levied further taxes on the merchants of Kuwait, and in particular on the pearl traders. In 1911, however, when some of them refused to pay these taxes, the Sheikh took draconian action, prohibiting pearl diving, the sole source of their income, in order to put pressure on them to pay. Naturally, the merchants in the pearl trade objected strongly to this, and in a meeting with the Sheikh they told him how big the financial losses would be, not just for them personally but for Kuwait as a whole. Pearl diving, they insisted, was the principal source of Kuwait's wealth and the basis of its commerce. Nevertheless, when the Sheikh continued to insist on his ban, they swiftly relented and most of the merchants paid the taxes due.

Three of them, however, held out against the Sheikh. These were Hilal bin Fajhan Al-Mutayri, Ibrahim bin Mudaf and Shamlan bin Ali. The Sheikh summoned them and reprimanded them for not paying the taxes due. Fearing further action on the part of the Sheikh, the three left Kuwait and went to Bahrain.

Sheikh Mubarak had not expected this, and reacted with concern, as he knew how valuable such merchants were to the economy of Kuwait. He sent a delegation to persuade them to return, which failed to achieve its objective. The Sheikh then sent his son, Sheikh Salem, with a letter urging them to return, offering them reassurance and asking them to forget what had happened. Two of them returned, but Hilal Al-Mutayri did not. The merchant community of Kuwait advised Sheikh Mubarak that he should go personally to persuade Hilal Al-Mutayri to return. So the Sheikh travelled to Bahrain on his yacht, *Mishrif*, with Ibrahim bin Mudaf and Shamlan bin Ali on board. At last, Hilal Al-Mutayri allowed himself to be reconciled to the Sheikh and agreed to return, thus resolving the problem.

Sheikh Mubarak also imposed a property tax. The tax arose when a house was sold, at which time a third of its sale value was due to the treasury.[46] The Sheikh's objective here was not only to raise revenue but also to prevent the misuse of a concession he had granted to the people of Kuwait. His practice had been to donate land free to Kuwaitis who wished to build houses for themselves and their families, according to their needs. The purpose of the tax was to prevent this grant of land, whose intention was benevolent, being used for commercial gain.

The Sheikh also reorganized the administration of customs duties. In May 1899 he established a formal customs department, just a few months after he signed a protection agreement with Britain. Until 1921, this remained the only official government department. The location of the customs office was opposite the Nayef Gate in Kuwait's old city wall, and the customs men were stationed just inside the gate. Work at the department would begin at 6.30 or 7.00 am and continue until midday, later resuming work from 2.00 pm until sunset. Customs duties were levied on imports such as camels, goats, skins and goods from Iraq.

In May 1899, the Sheikh imposed a duty of 5 per cent on all goods imported into Kuwait, including those coming in from Ottoman ports, which until then had been totally exempt from paying customs duties. This new duty gradually rose until it reached 10 per cent on some goods. The Ottoman reaction came on 25 August 1899, when Hamdi Pasha, the Governor of Basra, wrote to Sheikh Mubarak to inform him of the appointment of an Ottoman official as director of the port in Kuwait. This official's duties would be 'to supervise the boats that frequented the port'. Hamdi Pasha's letter went on to inform Sheikh Mubarak that, 'The present director of the port of Basra, Hassan Efendi, has been appointed as the director of the port of Kuwait.'

On 2 September, when Hassan Efendi arrived, accompanied by five soldiers, Sheikh Mubarak wrote to Hamdi Pasha contending that, 'vessels entering Kuwait had always been under the supervision of the port authorities in the port of Basra, and that there was therefore no need to change the existing system'.[47] Meanwhile, he refused to receive Hassan Efendi and his men, and ordered them to leave Kuwait the next day. This action demonstrated the Sheikh's confidence in himself, as well as his awareness that if necessary the British authorities would support him.

Import and export duties were also levied on goods transported by land. Additionally, the Sheikh levied customs duties on caravans entering Kuwait. These were imposed according to the size of the caravan, rising until it reached 10 per cent in some cases. However, the Sheikh also offered improved facilities for the merchants, including a large stone-built warehouse where they could store their goods after they had been unloaded and until they were sold. He also provided the guards necessary for the protection of the warehouse.[48]

In 1904 he imposed a specific tax on imported rifles at an average of one Maria Theresa dollar on each rifle, which was raised in 1907 to six dollars. In 1909, taxes on imports were once again increased, particularly those on tea and coffee.

The date farms in Faw
In addition to the interest he took in commerce, the Sheikh was also keen to develop the date farms that had been owned by the

Al-Sabah family in the Faw area of Iraq for some time. He wished to use the income from these as additional revenue for Kuwait, to enable him to continue carrying out his administrative duties. The orchards were situated in Faw and Al-Sufiyya, close to the Shatt Al-Arab. There were also some areas on the island of Qut Al-Zain, close to Al-Muhammara, as well as on the island of Al-Ujairawiyya and in the areas of Kurdlan and Al-Dawasir.

In 1907, Abd Al-Massih Antaki was invited by the Sheikh to go with him to visit one of the farms in Faw, and what he told Antaki on that occasion clarifies his motivation. His explanations to Antaki included a disquisition:

> [on] how date palms are cultivated, and what profits can be derived from them. The palms were of little benefit until the foreigners discovered them. Foreign merchants began to purchase the dates and pack them into boxes, sending them to Europe and America, which made this the source of great wealth for the people of the country.[49]

The Sheikh bought additional land in the area, and the income from the Faw farms became a permanent supplement to his budget. From time to time, governors of Basra attempted to use the Sheikh's ownership of the farms to bring economic pressure to bear on him. In 1901, for example, when he wished to record in his own name in the Ottoman Land Registry land he had bought from the Al-Zuhayr family in Basra and from Sa'dun Pasha, the current Governor of Basra, Abdul Rahman Hassan Bek, objected because Sheikh Mubarak did not hold Ottoman nationality. The governor knew perfectly well that in tribal areas such as Kuwait not everyone held Ottoman nationality. The Sheikh sent many letters on the issue to Istanbul, but to no avail.

In December 1901, the Basra court issued a ruling in absentia that the Sheikh had to transfer land he owned in the village of Al-Zain to his nephews. At the Sheikh's request, the Sultan ordered a commission to be set up to adjudicate on the dispute. The commission was duly established, and included Hajj Mansour representing Sheikh Mubarak, Abdul Wahhab Al-Qortas representing the Ottoman authorities and F. E. Crow, the British Consul in Basra. The committee decided that the property in Faw was the absolute private property of Sheikh Mubarak, but that the other land should be attributed to his nephews. The committee's decision was officially sent to Basra on 11 July 1904, and was adopted by the Governor of Basra and its council. The British Consul ratified it at Sheikh Mubarak's request.

On 28 May 1902, the Ottoman authorities arrested Abdul Aziz bin Salem Al-Badr, the Sheikh's agent in Basra. Al-Badr was accused of corresponding with the newspaper *Al-Khilafa*, published in Calcutta. The Ottoman authorities had banned the newspaper because it incited opposition to its policies. During a search of the agent's home, the Ottoman police took possession of the deeds to the Sheikh's lands in Iraq. When the Sheikh discovered this, he sent a cable to the governor demanding to know why his agent had been arrested. The governor replied that the arrest had been made in accordance with a decree issued by the Sultan. Al-Badr was tried and sentenced to ten years in prison, but was released in 1905 as a result of the intervention of the British authorities, who asked for his sentence to be reduced. He was allowed to go to Kuwait, and later returned to live in Iraq under supervision.[50]

In 1905, when Ottoman soldiers broke down dams forming part of the irrigation system on the farms in Faw, damaging Sheikh Mubarak's property, the Sheikh sent a letter of complaint to the Governor of Basra, Mahram Bek. The governor claimed that the date-palm plantations had been purchased by the Sheikh on behalf of the British Government and were not his property. The Political Resident, Major Cox, intervened with the governor, asking him to stop harassing the Sheikh and inciting depredations to his property.[51]

Problems between the Sheikh and the Ottoman authorities continued. In 1906, when the Sheikh bought some land in the Um Al-Gharb area from Sa'dun Pasha, the Sheikh of Al-Muntafiq, to the value of 8,000 Ottoman lire, the Ottoman authorities in Basra refused to register this land in his name at the Land Registry, on the excuse that he was not an Ottoman subject and that he did not possess Ottoman documents to prove he accepted Ottoman suzerainty. Therefore, they refused to register his ownership because he was a foreigner who had not registered himself and his family in the Ottoman General Register Office. Sheikh Mubarak refused to do so.[52] There was a similar development in December 1908, when the Sheikh asked for his agricultural property in Faw and the areas around it to be registered. The Governor of Basra again refused to register them unless and until the Sheikh agreed to take Ottoman nationality and was able to produce official papers to prove he had done so.[53]

Because of the Sheikh's continuing refusal to accept Ottoman nationality, the Ottoman authorities began to deliberately damage his land and his orchards. Some flagrant incidents took place. For example, in mid-1907 a bridge that separated the Sheikh's property in Faw from the Ottoman military fort next to it was destroyed. The Sheikh was alarmed and feared the loss of his land, so he asked the British authorities to intervene to stop the attacks on his rights and property. As a result, the Ottoman military authorities repaired the bridge and restored it to its previous condition.

In 1910 the Sheikh's troubles over land ownership continued. On 5 June 1910, Sheikh Mubarak wrote to the Political Resident in Bushire, Colonel Cox, informing him of the arrival in Kuwait of Ahmad Pasha Al-Zuhayr and Abdul Wahab Al-Qortas, and asking him to arrange the transfer of land he had bought from them in the area of Al-Fadayja. He also said that he had sent his representative, Abdul Aziz Al-Salem, to see Sulayman Nadhif, the Governor of Basra, to inform him of the purchase and to request that the land be officially measured. The governor replied that he had received orders from Istanbul to postpone the sale until further notice, and that the deal could be registered only if it was in the name of the Sheikh's sons, and on the condition that they had acquired Ottoman nationality. This had been rejected by the Sheikh, who now asked the Political Resident to intervene. The

Governor of Basra indicated his refusal to recognize the sale by insisting on asking the original owners to continue to pay the appropriate property taxes. The Sheikh reminded Cox that according to the agreement the Sheikh had made with Britain, the British had promised to safeguard his possessions.[54] On 7 June, Cox replied to say that he had telegraphed the British Government and would inform Sheikh Mubarak as soon as he received a reply.

The affair continued, with the Ottoman authorities turning up the pressure by raising more obstacles. On 12 June 1910, the Governor of Basra wrote to the Sheikh to point out that the agreement on the property in Al-Fadayja signed by the Sheikh and Mahram Pasha, the previous Governor of Basra, had confirmed that the sale was to the four eldest sons of the Sheikh, but that the Sheikh had now asked for the name of the beneficiary of the sale to be amended to his son Nasser alone. This, the governor said, he did not have the right to do, but must comply with what was specified in the original agreement. The letter also expressed the governor's displeasure with Sheikh Mubarak after certain of the Sheikh's men had been accused of harassing the inhabitants of Al-Zubayr. In a further turn for the worse, on 29 June the Sheikh's agent in Basra informed him that Ahmad Pasha Al-Zuhayr had decided after all not to sell, on the excuse that the amount the Sheikh had offered was less than realistic.[55]

Meanwhile, on 24 June, William Shakespear had sent a letter to Colonel Cox informing him that Sheikh Mubarak had shown him a letter from his agent in Basra, as well as another letter from a person whom Shakespear said he regarded as one of the most influential men in Basra, who had requested anonymity. These letters made a number of points. First, it would appear that Ahmad Pasha Al-Zuhayr's decision not to sell was apparently prompted by the Ottoman authorities. The Sheikh was rightly angry because he had already handed over the purchase price and had also spent money improving the irrigation and constructing buildings. The purpose of the Ottoman manoeuvres appeared to be to oblige Mubarak to adopt Ottoman nationality. The letters sent in confidence to the Sheikh appear to reveal that Ahmad Pasha Al-Zuhayr and others were expecting recompense from the Ottoman authorities for having taken a hostile stance towards him. Shakespear also confirmed that the Sheikh was resisting the pressure being brought to bear on him to acquire Ottoman nationality, or to register his sons as Ottoman nationals. Meanwhile, he had advised the Sheikh not to resist by force any attempt by Ahmad Pasha Al-Zuhayr to re-enter the land.

On 13 July 1910, a new element emerged. Sheikh Mubarak sent a further letter to Cox in which he informed him that, in his view, his problems in registering the land in Al-Fadayja were the result of an attempt on the part of the Ottoman authorities to blackmail him into agreeing to an Ottoman plan to build a telegraph line to Kuwait and on to the Ottoman possessions further south on the Gulf, which he had previously rejected.[56] On 13 September, Ahmad Pasha Al-Zuhayr finally backed down and recognized that his sale of the land to Sheikh Mubarak had been perfectly legal and proper, despite the refusal of the Ottoman authorities to recognize it. Ahmad Pasha Al-Zuhayr had now received a further demand for property taxes from the Ottoman authorities, which he asked Sheikh Mubarak to pay, as the land had in fact been sold. He said in his letter:

> I remain obliged to pay the Ottoman land taxes due on Al-Fadayja, which I have sold to you. I ask your excellency to send me the amount mentioned so that I can pay the land tax and also send the deeds which I will take to the government and show them that it is in your name, which is a crucial matter.[57]

The affair ended well for Sheikh Mubarak after he agreed to make the financial contributions to the Ottoman Empire on the various occasions already mentioned above. In 1912, after the Sheikh made a donation in support of the Ottoman war in Bulgaria, the Deputy Governor of Basra informed the Sheikh that he had received an instruction from the Sublime Porte allowing him to register Sheikh Mubarak's property at the Ottoman Land Registry. As a result of this, Sheikh Mubarak sent to Basra the documents necessary for the registration of his property.[58]

It was notable that the Ottoman authorities began to harass the Sheikh just as warning signs of the onset of World War I began to appear. There were rumours in Basra that Sheikh Mubarak would support the British if their forces attacked the city. According to Hussein Khalaf Al-Sheikh Khaz'al, 'the governorate of Basra sent orders to seize the property of Sheikh Mubarak in Faw, claiming that he had not paid the land taxes that were due'. The Sheikh sent a letter to the *qaimaqam* in Faw, Khaled Pasha, informing him that he had received no tax demand and that he was fully prepared to pay. Despite the apparent hostility of the Ottoman authorities in Basra, the Sheikh was careful to maintain friendly relations. For example, he sent a letter to Subhi Pasha, the Governor of Basra, congratulating him on the occasion of the Eid Al-Adha. When the Ottoman authorities asked the people of Basra to donate dates to feed the Ottoman armies, the Sheikh made a contribution.[59]

It may well be that the continuous harassment of Sheikh Mubarak by the Ottoman authorities, and Britain's awareness of it, explains the inclusion of a clause in the Anglo-Ottoman Agreement signed on 29 July 1913 that relates to the rights of the Sheikh of Kuwait to the enjoyment of his property in Basra. The clause specifies the Sheikh's rights over his lands and his freedom to act as he wishes in relation to his lands according to Ottoman law, while accepting that they were subject to Ottoman taxes and regulations.

We have seen evidence of the scale of the evolution in Kuwait's economic and commercial life during the reign of Sheikh Mubarak. This included notably the Sheikh's efforts to put Kuwait's markets on an organized footing and to stimulate their growth, invigorating the movement of trade into and out of Kuwait, as well as his concern for the interests of Kuwait's merchants at home and abroad, his protection of those interests and his actions in securing crucial land and sea trade routes. Lorimer's assessment of the situation was that, 'It was clear that no one could administer the internal affairs of Kuwait better than Sheikh Mubarak.'[60] The Sheikh was acutely aware that the growth of commerce was linked to the establishment of security and stability in Kuwait and its hinterland. In the interests of the secure environment he sought to achieve, he adopted an active role in regional affairs.

~5~

Regional Relations and the Employment of Political Resources

Nominally he was a subject of Turkey; but he was determined to keep Kuwait independent and for himself.

H. C. Armstrong, *Lord of Arabia*

The period of Mubarak's rule was one of great change, with regional and international conflict and many political developments. There were clashes between the sheikhs of various Gulf Emirates, and a bitter dispute in the heart of Arabia between the Al-Rashid and the Al-Saud for control of Najd. European rivalry over the Gulf also cast its shadow on these regional conflicts.

In spite of these military conflicts Sheikh Mubarak, in contrast to the custom of the time, neither restored Kuwait City's old wall nor built a new one, despite the possible danger of attack. When Dr Mylrea was working in the American Hospital in Kuwait, he asked the Sheikh why he had not built a wall around the city. The Sheikh replied: 'I am the wall.'[1]

On 16 September 1904, the Muscat correspondent for the Egyptian newspaper *Al-Ahram* reported: 'Sheikh Mubarak, the Sheikh of Kuwait, is a close friend of all the Bedouin sheikhs operating on the Arabian and Iraqi routes. He also supplies rebel sheikhs, including those who are 50 kilometres distant, with all the weapons, ammunition and supplies they need.'

Conflict and alliance: the relationship with the emirs of Najd

In the years before Mubarak came to power, relations between Najd and Kuwait were characterized by tension and enmity. This was connected to the conflict between the Al-Saud and the Al-Rashid over control of Najd. When Abdul Aziz bin Mut'ab Al-Rashid succeeded in undermining the foundations of the second Saudi state, defeating Al-Saud in the battle of Al-Malida in 1891 and occupying the Saudi capital, Riyadh, Imam Abdul Rahman Al-Faisal was obliged to flee from Najd. For some time he lived in Qatar, then went on to Kuwait, to wait there for a chance to return to power. With him was his son, Abdul Aziz, who was just eight years old at the time. Thus, the Emir Abdul Aziz grew up in Kuwait, under the patronage of Sheikh Mubarak, who took a personal interest in him and included him in affairs of state. This offered the young emir a unique experience and developed his skills. Khair Al-Din Al-Zarakli maintains that Kuwait was the first school for Abdul Aziz, where he learned the art of practical politics. He comments:

> Sheikh Mubarak's days were full of manoeuvres and negotiations, how he would start to make a deal and how he reached his goal were imprinted on the mind of Abdul Aziz. He even participated in some discussions, and Mubarak sensed in him a natural bent for diplomacy. He kept Abdul Aziz near him and permitted him to attend his *majlis*, where he heard Mubarak's discussions with the representatives of the British, Russian, German and Turkish governments.[2]

Another author notes that:

> The reception rooms of the Sheikh were like a school for the young Abdul Aziz, and the discussions carried out there gave him experience and skill in how to deal with Arabs and foreigners.[3]

And in Sheikh Mubarak's *majlis* Abdul Aziz met

> men from various countries and religions, merchants and investors in companies, stockbrokers, money changers and employees, politicians and adventurers, as well as agents of the big powers.[4]

In his book on the history of Kuwait, Dickson maintains that it was Sheikh Mubarak's patronage above all other influences that helped Abdul Aziz to become politically mature.[5] It was in Kuwait that he learned about local and international politics, and in Sheikh Mubarak's *majlis* he became familiar both with British policies in the Gulf and the policies of its rival powers.

Tension and conflict also arose from the attitude of the Al-Rashid. They supported Sheikh Mubarak's adversary Yusuf Al-Ibrahim and, in turn, Yusuf Al-Ibrahim exploited this relationship to encourage the Al-Rashid and co-operate with them in their plans to invade Kuwait. In 1897, Muhammad bin Abdullah Al-Rashid and Sheikh Jassem Al-Thani, the Emir of Qatar, planned to join forces to attack Kuwait. In this situation, Mubarak sought to exploit the differences between those who opposed him and encourage their rivalry. He made approaches to the Ottoman *mutasarrif* of Al-Hasa, attempting to turn him against the Qatari ruler, whom he accused of being disloyal to the Ottoman Empire. This strategy bore fruit, when the Ottoman Governor of Basra sent a gunboat to quell the ruler of Qatar. However, after Muhammad bin Abdullah Al-Rashid's death in late 1897, the collaboration envisaged between the Al-Rashid and Qatar failed to come to fruition.

Nevertheless, the animosity between Sheikh Mubarak and the Al-Rashid continued. The Sheikh was therefore obliged to develop a strategy once and for all to dispose of the constant threat to his country. In the long term, a key element of Sheikh Mubarak's strategy proved to be the lasting alliance he struck up with the Al-Saud, the Al-Rashid's sworn enemy. The years between 1897 and 1906, however, continued to be marked by an ongoing bitter enmity between Mubarak and the Emir Abdul Aziz bin Mut'ab Al-Rashid, the nephew of Muhammad bin Abdullah Al-Rashid, and his successor as the Emir of Ha'il. The Ottomans encouraged Ibn Al-Rashid to oppose the Sheikh, and further encouragement came from Yusuf Al-Ibrahim, who continued to use all the means at his disposal to undermine Mubarak.

In 1899, at a moment of tense relations between Sheikh Mubarak and the Ottomans, Ibn Al-Rashid realized that if he showed himself as hostile towards Kuwait, he could gain the backing and endorsement of Istanbul. The Ottoman Empire could grant him control over the port of Kuwait, so that Najd could have an outlet onto the sea, through which it could build up its trade.[6] Ibn Al-Rashid began once more to prepare for the invasion of Kuwait in 1900, exploiting as a pretext an incident in which Mubarak's men had clashed with a number of merchants from Ha'il, in which some of the merchants had lost their lives. However, the Kuwaiti Army, led by Sheikh Hommoud Al-Sabah and Sheikh Salem Al-Sabah, was already stationed on the Kuwaiti-Najd borders. Before Abdul Aziz bin Rashid's army could make a move, the Kuwaiti Army fell on them and won a resounding victory. The result was that Ibn Al-Rashid thought better of attacking Kuwait and instead marched on the Sheikh of Al-Muntafiq, Sa'dun Pasha Al-Mansour, supposedly in revenge for transgressions committed by Sheikh Sa'dun's tribe, but also because of Sa'dun's support for Kuwait. Ibn Al-Rashid overcame Sa'dun's forces and took booty.

Sa'dun Pasha turned to Sheikh Mubarak for help. In support of Sa'dun, Sheikh Mubarak sent a force towards Al-Samawa in Iraq, led by Sheikh Hommoud and his own son, Salim. Sheikh Mubarak marched on the Al-Zubayr road at the head of another contingent, accompanied by Emir Abdul Aziz bin Saud and his brother, Emir Saud. When he reached Al-Khamisiyya, he received a letter from the Governor of Basra, Muhsin Pasha, asking him to cease his campaign against Ibn Al-Rashid and to come to parley at Al-Zubayr. Sheikh Mubarak could not ignore the Governor of Basra's summons, which was backed up by a similar request from the Ottoman military commander in Baghdad. When he met Muhsin Pasha in Al-Zubayr he made great play of his loyalty to the Ottoman Sultan. At the same time, however, he had sent his army to pursue Ibn Al-Rashid and continued engaging his troops. When the Kuwaiti force caught up with Ibn Al-Rashid's men there was a short battle, in which Ibn Al-Rashid's force was defeated.[7]

When Hamdi Pasha became Governor of Basra again, in late 1899, he once more urged Ibn Al-Rashid to attack Kuwait, offering him financial and military support and promising him the throne of Kuwait if he were to succeed in capturing it. Hamdi Pasha assured Ibn Rashid that Britain would not interfere in an internal conflict in areas subject to the Ottoman Sultan. For his part, Ibn Al-Rashid's ambition was to add Kuwait to his territory because it was the channel through which trade passed from Najd and the rest of Arabia. His plan was to increase the income flowing into his treasury with the proceeds from Kuwait's customs duties. In addition, were he to hold Kuwait, the Al-Saud, his implacable enemies, would lose all hope of retrieving their throne.

Hostility between Mubarak and Ibn Al-Rashid continued. The Shammar tribes began to harass the border areas of Kuwait, intending to raid caravans leaving the country. In 1901, Sheikh Mubarak prepared an army, led by his brother, Sheikh Hommoud, and his son, Salim, to halt these attacks. The Kuwaiti force was victorious in an engagement in the area of Al-Rukhayma against tribesmen who backed Ibn Al-Rashid. Sheikh Mubarak an-nounced the victory to his friend Sheikh Khaz'al, the ruler of

Al-Muhammara, remarking that, 'There is no doubt that God wreaks vengeance against all aggressors. With God's praise, they will be destroyed.'[8] Sheikh Khaz'al was quick to reply, warning Sheikh Mubarak that Emir Abdul Aziz Al-Rashid was planning something, and that the Sheikh should be careful and prepare for the next round of fighting. He sent him two heavy guns and some rifles and ammunition. Meanwhile, Imam Abdul Rahman Al-Faisal Al-Saud had taken Sheikh Mubarak's advice on the recapture of Riyadh from the Al-Rashid. The Sheikh had told him to wait and be patient because he himself was 'determined to march soon to destroy the power of Ibn Al-Rashid in all of Najd'.

Mubarak was aware that Ibn Al-Rashid was preparing to invade Kuwait, so he decided to frustrate his plans by striking a pre-emptive blow. He began to make preparations, first meeting with the leaders of all his forces in Al-Jahra. He wrote to Sa'dun Pasha informing him of his intention to fight Ibn Al-Rashid and asking him to bring his own troops to join his army. In due course, Sa'dun's forces joined the Sheikh's forces at Al-Jahra. The Sheikh then sent emissaries to ask the tribes loyal to him to join the war. When the moment came, Sheikh Mubarak marched at the head of the army he had assembled. He captured Al-Aarid without fighting, and designated Emir Abdul Aziz bin Saud to administer it. Next, he captured the cities of Unayza and Barida, virtually without a fight. Meanwhile, a contingent led by Ibn Saud marched on Riyadh with the intention of capturing it. Ibn Saud succeeded in entering the city, but could not capture the ruler's palace.

When the news of these victories reached Ibn Al-Rashid, he judged that the principal danger facing him continued to be the army led by Sheikh Mubarak, rather than the presence of Ibn Saud's force inside Riyadh. He therefore gathered his own forces, who belonged to the Shammar tribes, to confront Mubarak's army. The two sides met in the area of Al-Sarif in March 1901.[9] Unfortunately for Sheikh Mubarak, the battle ended in Ibn Al-Rashid's favour, leading to a grave defeat for the Kuwaiti forces. Among the dead were Hommoud, Sheikh Mubarak's brother, and his cousin, Khalifa bin Abdullah Al-Sabah. In the wake of the defeat, an atmosphere of mourning prevailed in Kuwait, which prompted Sheikh Mubarak to attempt to bring solace to his people by reassuring them that he would strive to inflict defeat on Ibn Al-Rashid as soon as possible.

A number of explanations have been advanced for the defeat of the Kuwaiti forces. The historian Abdul Aziz Al-Rashid argues that Ibn Al-Rashid's true power had been underestimated before the conflict, while Sheikh Mubarak had relied on what were described as 'Bedouins, who were not fighting for a national cause or principle'. Others contended that the principal reason for the defeat had been a tactical one, and that Sheikh Mubarak's troops had been unwisely divided into two separate columns, representing the Al-Sabah and the Al-Saud, between which coordination had not been perfect.[10]

Grigori Bondarevsky, basing his account on Russian documents, adds that Mubarak's defeat

> was principally because several of his allies, most of whom were tribes from Najd, decided at the last minute not to engage in the fighting. From the point of view of the Bedouins of the central area of Najd, the war had gone on longer than they had expected, and with the advent of the drought they were obliged to leave the area immediately with their livestock ... Also, representatives of Ibn Al-Rashid succeeded in bribing some of the leaders of the tribes just before the battle, so they withdrew their men ... Three thousand fighters from the Shayban tribe deserted and joined Ibn Al-Rashid in the middle of the battle. They attacked Mubarak's troops from behind and caused fear and chaos among their ranks. This caused them great damage.[11]

A rumour spread that Sheikh Mubarak had been killed in battle. Britain therefore sent a military ship to Kuwait to control the instability that they feared would result from the Sheikh's death. On 18 April, Colonel C. A. Kemball, the British Resident in the

Gulf, personally visited Kuwait to verify that the Sheikh was still alive. An amusing anecdote reported by Kemball was that Sheikh Mubarak never mentioned the battle of Al-Sarif, which left Colonel Kemball himself reluctant to raise the issue with the Sheikh or indeed even to mention it.[12]

Meanwhile, Ibn Al-Rashid did not hesitate to exploit the outcome of the battle. In the summer of 1901 he laid siege to Kuwait City, terrifying and intimidating its people. He failed in his bid to take the city because he was opposed by an alliance made up not only of Sheikh Mubarak's army but also of the Al-Muntafiq tribe, led by Pasha Al-Sa'dun, and the Al-Mutayr and the Banu Murra tribes, as well as the Al-Saud. A further deterrent to any advance by Ibn Al-Rashid was the presence of British warships in Kuwait City's harbour.

Nevertheless, Ibn Al-Rashid imagined that his victory at Al-Sarif would throw open the door for further military advances and enable him to extend his political influence over Kuwait. The reason this did not happen in practice was that the conflict between the Sheikh of Kuwait and the Emir of Najd prompted agreement between the British and the Ottoman Empire on the desirability of preserving the status quo. The Ottoman authorities undertook not to occupy Kuwait and to do what they could to prevent the Emir of Najd from attacking it. In return, Britain promised not to occupy Kuwait or declare it to be a British protectorate, and to discourage Sheikh Mubarak from attacking Najd. In August 1901, Lord Curzon sent Kemball back to Kuwait with the task of establishing peace, or at least some kind of truce, between Sheikh Mubarak and Ibn Al-Rashid. Mubarak proposed that Sheikh Khaz'al should represent him, and the British Consul in Basra was asked to facilitate contact between Sheikh Khaz'al and the agent of Emir Abdul Aziz Al-Rashid in that city.

British diplomatic efforts continued. London took steps to ensure that the Ottomans did what had been agreed. On 31 December 1901, the Grand Vizier, Sa'id Pasha, wrote to the Sultan to inform him of a meeting between the British ambassador in Istanbul and the Ottoman Foreign Minister in which the British diplomat had asked the Foreign Minister to intervene with Ibn Al-Rashid and induce him to withdraw the troops surrounding Kuwait. He also reported that the German ambassador had told the Foreign Minister that if Ibn Al-Rashid remained in these areas, it might lead to dire consequences.[13] The Sultan agreed to Ottoman intervention to persuade Ibn Al-Rashid to withdraw his troops from the areas around Kuwait. On 1 January 1902, a telegram sent by the Ottoman embassy in London to the foreign ministry in Istanbul included the text of a memorandum from Lord Landsdowne, the British Foreign Secretary, in which he indicated 'Britain's desire to preserve the balance of power in Kuwait' and undertook that Britain would 'withdraw its guns, which are now positioned on land in Kuwait, as soon as the Emir of Najd's troops withdraw'.[14]

As a result of these interventions, Ibn Al-Rashid withdrew without gaining any benefit from his success at Al-Sarif. A further factor that disposed him to withdraw his troops to Riyadh was his receipt of information about a rebellion against him by some tribes that had profited from his absence and his preoccupation with the campaign against Sheikh Mubarak. Ibn Al-Rashid was furious with what he saw as the weakness of Ottoman policy. When his patience with the Ottomans ran out, he met the British Consul in Basra to suggest that Najd be declared a British protectorate. The British Foreign Office, however, did not agree.[15] Meanwhile, the Al-Saud asked for British protection in their conflict against Al-Rashid. On 18 August 1904, Abdul Rahman Al-Faisal Al-Saud sent a letter to Captain Knox, the Political Resident in Kuwait, informing him of Al-Rashid's growing friendship with the Ottoman Empire and telling him that there were plans to deploy Turkish troops against the Al-Saud. He said that his troops could not fight such a force and asked for Britain's support. As he put it: 'We are asking your imperial glorious country to protect our kingdoms and we will be at your service.'[16]

On the basis of his prior experience, Sheikh Mubarak concluded that the only way to put an end to such threats was to strike a fatal blow against Ibn Al-Rashid on his own territory. His plan was to engage Al-Rashid's troops while Abdul Rahman's son, Abdul Aziz ibn Saud, invaded Riyadh. Sheikh Mubarak marched out to Al-Jahra, at the head of his army, in order to oblige Ibn Al-Rashid to remain in the area and defend the tribes loyal to him there. At the same time, the Sheikh supplied Abdul Aziz ibn Saud with the men and weapons he would need to enter Riyadh and re-establish the Saudi state. This was the second attempt to invade Riyadh by the Al-Saud, after their initial bid in early 1901.

Ibn Saud marched out of Kuwait at the end of 1901, Sheikh Mubarak having supplied him with camels, weapons, money and supplies. On 15 January 1902, when he occupied Riyadh, he hastened to send messengers to Kuwait to inform Sheikh Mubarak, and his father, Imam Abdul Rahman Al-Faisal Al-Saud, of the victory. The British documents clearly illustrate the extent of Sheikh Mubarak's support for Ibn Saud. Albert Charles Wratislaw, the British Consul in Basra, wrote to his ambassador in Istanbul as follows: 'Mubarak is helping Ibn Saud and pushing him ... [Ibn Saud] would not have been able to accomplish anything without his help.' The concern Wratislaw expressed was that Kuwait would become further embroiled in the affairs of Najd. For this reason, London warned Sheikh Mubarak to avoid further involvement, and to refrain from anything that could lead to any direct confrontation with the Turks.

This was not the first time that British diplomacy had taken such a position. The British had constantly warned the Sheikh against interfering with matters outside the borders of his emirate. The most unambiguous of these warnings had been sent some time earlier by Kemball to the Sheikh, when, on 10 December 1900, he forthrightly offered the Sheikh the following advice: 'I hope that no steps are taken which will force others to make more forceful interventions in your country. It seems to me that you are following a perilous policy by continuing to provoke the Emir of

Najd. I advise you again to refrain from doing so and to seek security and stability.'[17]

Nevertheless, Sheikh Mubarak continued to support Ibn Saud in military terms, with weapons and ammunition, and logistically, with supplies and goods necessary for the maintenance of his troops. In addition, he also gave political support to Ibn Saud in his dealings with the Ottoman Empire, approaching Sheikh Mustafa Nuri Pasha, the Governor of Basra, to report Ibn Saud's capture of the city of Riyadh, asking him to inform the Sublime Porte of this development and offering his advice that Ottoman recognition should be extended to Ibn Saud's rule at an early date. British and other diplomats closely observed the positions adopted by the Sheikh. On 2 April 1902, the Russian Consul in Basra reported that Ibn Saud's successes 'are principally because of the help given to him by the Sheikh of Kuwait.'[18] In August 1902, Wratislaw wrote in a report to the British ambassador in Istanbul: 'It is well-known that Mubarak has been supporting and encouraging Ibn Saud for a long time. Without his help, the latter would not have been able to achieve these victories.'[19]

Arab and other historians concur on the centrality of Sheikh Mubarak's support for Ibn Saud's efforts to restore the rule of his grandfathers. Abdul Aziz Al-Rashid described Sheikh Mubarak as, 'The major pillar on which Ibn Saud depends ... [Mubarak] sends him supplies with generosity and benevolence. He sends him military units, one after the other, and despatches successive caravans carrying food or ammunition. More than that, when Ibn Saud was in Kuwait, Mubarak helped him formulate his military strategy.'[20] When Ibn Rashid sought to block Ibn Saud's advance though Najd, Sheikh Mubarak immediately supplied Ibn Saud with weapons, ammunition and supplies, sending off successive supply columns. Knox reported as follows: 'Ibn Saud cannot install himself without outside help. As he cannot seek help from the Turks, who are allied to Ibn Al-Rashid, his only source is Sheikh Mubarak.'[21] In addition, Sheikh Mubarak had long since gone further than merely providing logistical support to Ibn Saud; he

also committed his own troops. When Sheikh Mubarak heard that
Ibn Al-Rashid had enlisted the support of the Al Zafir tribe
against Ibn Saud's attack on Riyadh, and that Ibn Saud had
already begun his siege of the city, the Sheikh sent an army from
Kuwait on 5 October, under the leadership of Saqr Al-Ghanim.
Looking back on the period, Stanley Mylrea said, in a speech he
gave in Kuwait in 1949 as he was recalling his memories of
Mubarak's reign:

> In those days, when I came to Kuwait, Kuwait was the main
> port for the Arabian interior. Anything sent to Najd had to
> pass through Kuwait, which at the time was ruled by one of
> history's greatest Arab men. As I shall explain to you, it is to
> Sheikh Mubarak that Ibn Saud owes his power today. He
> learned from Sheikh Mubarak the art of ruling an Arab
> country and Arab ambitions.[22]

With Emir Abdul Aziz's entry into Riyadh on 15 October 1902,
Mubarak's plan, to assist the Al-Saud in ousting the Al-Rashid and
regain their erstwhile supremacy in Riyadh, was fulfilled. The
restoration of the Al-Saud to power in Riyadh inaugurated a
period of alliance between Kuwait and Najd that manifested itself
in close military, political and personal relations. The personal
relationship between the Sheikh and Emir Abdul Aziz played a
large part in all this. Sheikh Mubarak would call Abdul Aziz 'my
son' and the latter would respond with 'my father'. Nothing,
however, is permanent in politics, and it was perhaps inevitable
that differences between the two would later begin to emerge as a
result of their divergent political and economic agendas. On the
other hand, such differences of view never came to the point of
overt dispute or conflict.

After 1902, co-operation between the Sheikh and the Emir
continued. In 1903 Sheikh Mubarak launched a campaign against
Sultan Al-Dawish, the Sheikh of Mutayr, which was led by Abdul
Aziz bin Saud and the Sheik's son, Sheikh Jaber bin Mubarak. Al-
Dawish had allied himself with Ibn Al-Rashid and had stationed

his forces in the area of Julaban, near the border of Kuwait, ready to launch an attack. Mubarak's plan was to regain the initiative before Al-Dawish had finished his preparations. The Kuwaiti force, with support from the Al-Saud, attacked Al-Dawish first, inflicting great losses at the battle of Julaban. Meanwhile, while Abdul Aziz bin Saud was preoccupied with this campaign, Ibn Al-Rashid began to prepare a counter attack on Riyadh. Ibn Saud quickly returned to Kuwait City, and Sheikh Mubarak came to his aid. The Sheikh ordered his army, which was returning to Kuwait, to march on to Riyadh. When news of this reached Ibn Al-Rashid, he withdrew his forces and refrained from attacking the city.[23]

By the late spring of 1904, Abdul Aziz Al-Saud had regained all his ancestors' lands and had brought Najd once more under his control. He would become, in due course, one of the most prominent Arab leaders and one of the most confident, primarily because of the political and material significance of Najd in the Arabian Peninsula. It was perhaps inevitable that the relationship between the experienced Sheikh and the young Emir would cool down. One researcher has described this as a change from the phase of 'absolute alliance' to one of 'differences within the framework of the alliance'.[24] In 1905, Ibn Saud took a step that resulted in a real chill in his relations with Sheikh Mubarak. The Najdi caravans, which had formerly bought their goods from Kuwait, had hitherto avoided payment of duties on goods they imported into Najd, having taken devious routes through the desert. The Emir ordered his inspectors to accompany these caravans and enforce the payment of duty before they even left Kuwait. However, he took this step without informing Sheikh Mubarak and without prior consultation. Sheikh Mubarak did not receive the news well, not merely because it came as a surprise, but more importantly because it meant that an authority other than his own was being exercised on his territory. The Sheikh instructed his agents to prevent this order from being carried out.

In response, Ibn Saud placed a ban on trade between Najd and the people of Kuwait, which he stated he would rescind if one of three conditions were met. These were (1) that he be granted an annual stipend in lieu of payment of the duty, (2) that a Saudi employee be allowed to collect the duties in Kuwait or (3) that Kuwaiti officials collect these taxes and remit them to Riyadh. In addition to this there were other clashes between the Sheikh and Ibn Saud, of which the historian Abdul Aziz Al-Rashid gives a detailed account.[25] In response, Sheikh Mubarak made overtures to Ibn Al-Rashid. His intention was to exert pressure on Ibn Saud with the aim of restoring his relationship with the Al-Saud to its previous level. He also hoped to disrupt Ibn Al-Rashid's alliance with Yusuf Al-Ibrahim. This, incidentally, was to improve the Sheikh's relations with the Ottomans, who still regarded Ibn Al-Rashid as their ally of choice in Arabia.

Later in 1905, Ibn Saud contacted Sheikh Mubarak to ask for his mediation in reaching an understanding with the Ottoman authorities. Ibn Saud had indicated that he was prepared to reach an agreement with the Ottomans that would include his recognition of Ottoman suzerainty and his acceptance of the title of *qaimaqam*, as well as his agreement to accept Ottoman troops being stationed in Unayza and Barida. However, events were to develop very quickly, and Ibn Saud abandoned his policy of seeking reconciliation with the Ottomans. Owing to the constant raids by the tribes against the Ottoman forces in Al-Qasim, the Ottomans decided by the end of the year to withdraw their troops so that they no longer represented a challenge to Ibn Saud's power in Najd.[26] The alliance between Sheikh Mubarak and Ibn Saud continued on its prior footing, however, and in 1906 Sheikh Mubarak supplied the Al-Saud's forces with 3,000 rifles, estimated at the time to be worth 150,000 dollars.[27]

In April 1913, Ibn Saud's occupation of Al-Hasa raised his standing, and it was at this time that he was able to initiate direct contact with Britain. He told Captain Shakespear, who had by then become the British emissary to the Al-Saud, that he no longer dealt with any of the Arab emirs. As Ibn Saud's ambitions grew, he informed the British that his condition for signing an agreement with them would be that they agree to him occupying Qatar, Muscat and Oman, and that Sheikh Mubarak must return to his original borders. All this aggravated the Sheikh's suspicion of Ibn Saud's intentions. Sheikh Mubarak, who was now over 70 years old and whose energy had begun to flag, felt that Ibn Saud's growing influence would conflict with the role he had for so long fought to establish for himself in Kuwait. However, Abdul Aziz Ibn Saud's view was that the time had come for him to shake off Sheikh Mubarak's influence and lay down his own diplomatic policy. The Sheikh's response was increasingly to play off Ibn Saud and Ibn Al-Rashid against each other, in order to benefit from the hostility between them and so that each would weaken the other. In a further move, when the Ottomans wanted to negotiate with Ibn Saud, Sheikh Mubarak sought to ensure that any such talks would be held in Kuwait. The Sheikh's purpose was to enhance his regional role and influence. Ibn Saud agreed to hold the conference in Al-Sabiha, a Kuwaiti-administered area that lay between Najd and Kuwait. The Sheikh's position was given a boost by the attendance at the meeting of a Kuwaiti delegation.

Despite all the differences between the Sheikh and the Emir, each had his own reasons to preserve their alliance. In 1914, an agreement was signed to draw up fixed borders between Najd and Kuwait, with the implication that the Al-Saud recognized the situation of Kuwait and its borders. The two sides also co-operated during World War I. In October 1914 the Sheikh sent a letter to Ibn Saud asking him to declare his support for Britain, because they were, as he put it, the 'Empire of Peace', while the Turks on the other hand were the enemies of the Arabs. Ibn Saud replied confirming his co-operation with Britain and averring that his position was the same as that of Sheikh Mubarak.[28]

Sheikh Mubarak never hesitated before offering his support to Ibn Saud whenever the latter was under threat. This became evident after the forces of Ibn Al-Rashid defeated Ibn Saud at the battle of Jirab in 1915, which undermined Ibn Saud's standing and led to a deterioration in his position. As a result, the tribes of Al-

Ajman rebelled against Ibn Saud, besieging him in Al-Hufuf. Mubarak sent an army to help Abdul Aziz and his men, under the leadership of his son, Salem, and his grandson Ahmad Al-Jaber. The Kuwaitis succeeded in breaking the siege and defeated the forces of Al-Ajman close to Al-Qatif.

Alliance and co-operation: relations with the Sheikh of Al-Muhammara

There was a relationship of very long standing between the sheikhs of Kuwait and the emirs of Al-Muhammara. The port of Muhammara, now known as Khorramshahr, lies on the east bank of the Shatt Al-Arab in the area known then as Arabistan. In theory it belonged to the Persian Empire, but Persia did not have the necessary military ability to impose its rule there and for this reason the emirs of Al-Muhammara were able to enjoy internal independence. Until the early seventeenth century, the area east of the Shatt Al-Arab was an Arab emirate ruled by Sheikh Mubarak Abdul Muttalib. He ruled his emirate independently of both the Persian and Ottoman Empires. A later ruler, Sheikh Mansour, resisted Shah Abbas I's attempts to interfere in his affairs. He also rejected the Shah's call to join the Persian forces besieging Baghdad in 1623. In the middle of the seventeenth century, groups of Arab Bani Ka'b immigrated from Iraq and Kuwait to Arabistan, reinforcing its Arab character.

In the eighteenth century Arabistan enjoyed autonomy from the Persian Government. The Ottoman authorities, however, in co-operation with the British, sought to weaken the Bani Ka'b tribes and a joint Anglo-Ottoman campaign marched on the emirate in 1763. This culminated in victory for the Arab tribes. Two years later, Persia launched a violent and destructive military campaign that led the Arab inhabitants of Arabistan to abandon their capital in Qabban and seek refuge in the village of Al-Fallahiyya (now known as Shadegan). Because of this, Arabistan became fragmented and it divided into scattered tribal groups, the most prominent of which was the Al-Muhaysin group, ruled over by Sheikh Jaber from 1819 to 1881, who was succeeded by his sons Miz'al (who ruled from 1881 to 1897) and Khaz'al (from 1897 to 1925).

In due course, the capital of Arabistan moved again from the village of Al-Fallahiyya to the city of Al-Muhammara, which had been built by the Bani Ka'b Arabs near the mouth of the river Karun on the Shatt Al-Arab, and continued to be Arabistan's capital until 1925. Al-Muhammara was given its name because its soil was red. It became known as Khorramshahr when it was absorbed into modern Iran. In 1827, Sheikh Ghayth, the Emir of Arabistan, asked Sultan Said bin Sultan, the ruler of Muscat and Oman, for military support to counter the Persian pressure that was threatening the independence of his country. This aspiration towards independence became stronger under Sheikh Jabir, who up to his death in 1881 refused to open up the river Karun for British ships to pass.

The period of Sheikh Khaz'al's rule in Al-Muhammara, from June 1897 to April 1925, was a highly significant period in the history of Arabistan, in terms of its relations both with the Ottoman Empire and with Kuwait.[29] Sheikh Mubarak and Sheikh Khaz'al clearly took a similar stand on many issues and were linked by strong ties. First, they were united by the desire to preserve the independence of their countries and safeguard their freedom to administer their internal affairs without outside interference. One of the features of this independence is highlighted in the Egyptian newspaper *Al-Mu'ayyed* in an article published on 19 May 1910 relating to Sheikh Khaz'al's refusal to hand over a number of accused men wanted by the Ottoman Government. This caused Istanbul to ask the Persian Government to take the measures in its support.[30] Second, as maritime states, they were linked by the sense of threat that both Kuwaiti shipping and that of Muhammara itself faced from the new Belgian-administered customs regime introduced by Persia in 1900, as well as by the activity of pirates, who were very active around the mouth of Shatt

Al-Arab and the coasts of Arabistan. The situation was further exacerbated by an intensification of the rivalries between Britain, Russia and Germany, and to a lesser extent France, all of which aimed to spread their influence and if possible impose their hegemony in the region. Thirdly, they were brought together by their shared Arab sentiment, and the desire for Arab provinces to become independent, of the Ottoman Empire in the case of Kuwait, and of the Persian Empire in the case of Al-Muhammara.[31] This will be touched on further below.

One indication of the closeness of the links between the two was the fact that Mubarak built a residence for Sheikh Khaz'al in Kuwait, while he in turn built a similar residence for Mubarak adjacent to his own in the port of Al-Fayliyya, a small port that he had designated as his residence and seat of government, which lay in his territory on the Shatt Al-Arab to the north of Al-Muhammara itself. The sheikhs exchanged visits and went on hunting trips together. Another sign of the depth of the relationship was the fact that Hussein Khalaf Al-Sheikh Khaz'al (the son of Sheikh Khaz'al) wrote a five-volume book on Kuwait's political history, which included the text of letters exchanged between his father and Sheikh Mubarak. One more indication of the closeness between the two rulers came in an incident in 1900 when Sheikh Khaz'al agreed to accept the intercession of Sheikh Mubarak in favour of a would-be assassin, one Muhammad Al-Yaqoub. There had been a conspiracy to take the life of Sheikh Khaz'al, and one of the conspirators, Muhammad Al-Yaqoub, had fled to Basra. His friends there told him to throw himself on the mercy of the Sheikh of Kuwait because he was the only person whose mediation Sheikh Khaz'al would accept. Sheikh Khaz'al reproached Sheikh Mubarak for protecting a person who had conspired to kill him, but Sheikh Mubarak replied that he had ascertained that the man had genuinely repented and had therefore forgiven him because of his certainty that Sheikh Khaz'al would have done likewise.[32] When Sheikh Khaz'al read this letter, he accepted what Mubarak had done.

On another occasion, Sheikh Khaz'al accepted Sheikh Mubarak as a mediator in relation to a dispute concerning the tribe of Al-Nassar. In 1903, the members of this tribe ceased to pay their taxes, preparing instead for rebellion. Sheikh Khaz'al began to ready his forces for a military campaign against them in order to impose discipline. Sheikh Mubarak interceded on their behalf, and Sheikh Khaz'al acceded on condition that the instigators removed themselves to Kuwait. He promised to pay them annual stipends, and on this condition they agreed. Similarly, in the other direction, Sheikh Mubarak was receptive to intercession on the part of Sheikh Khaz'al. When Sheikh Mubarak signed the protection agreement with Britain in 1899, a member of his family, Sheikh Hommoud Al-Sabah, was not in agreement with the move and left Kuwait with his family for Al-Dawasir in Iraq. When Hommoud died, his sons expelled their brother Sulayman and his family. To avoid destitution, Sulayman decided that his only recourse was to return to Kuwait, but the only person he could find to intercede on his behalf with Sheikh Mubarak was Sheikh Khaz'al. Mubarak accepted Sheikh Khaz'al's intercession, and when Ibn Hommoud returned to Kuwait, the Sheikh was generous to him and brought him into his circle.

It was not unusual, therefore, for either Mubarak or Khaz'al to offer support to the other in the case of a problem or crisis. In 1901, when the Russian Consul in Bushire visited Sheikh Mubarak to offer him closer relations with Russia, one reason why Mubarak rejected the offer was Russia's support for the Persian imposition of a Belgian-administered customs office in Al-Muhammara. To the Russian Consul's argument that this was no more than what was happening in all other Iranian cities, Mubarak replied that Al-Muhammara was different from the other Iranian cities as it had hitherto not been regarded as part of Persia but had been autonomously ruled by the Bani Ka'b. He pointed out to the Russian Consul that Sheikh Khaz'al was his close friend, and that 'he could not make an agreement with any country if he was not part of that agreement, because they are one country and one hand, nothing can apply to one if it does not include the other'.³³ The Russian Consul promised to seek further advice on the matter. In the same year, Sheikh Khaz'al interceded to effect a reconciliation between Sheikh Mubarak and Abdul Aziz Al-Saud on the one hand and the Ottoman Government on the other.³⁴

Another feature of the close relationship between the two rulers may be seen in what took place in 1902, when a Kuwaiti ship was attacked by pirates near the island of Bubyan while sailing from Basra to Kuwait. All its cargo was stolen and some of the crew were killed. When Sheikh Mubarak heard of this, he hastened to the region of Al-Qasaba to identify the culprits. He telegraphed Hajj Abdul Aziz Al-Salem, his agent in Basra, asking him to raise the matter with Governor Mustafa Nuri Pasha with a view to persuading the Ottomans to take action, though without result. When Sheikh Khaz'al heard of these events, he met with Sheikh Mubarak as soon as he could. He was later able to find out who the guilty parties were, and to arrest them and hand them to Mubarak.

In 1907 a boat from Muscat landed in Al-Muhammara harbour, part of whose cargo was the property of a group of Kuwaiti merchants. The head of the Persian customs asked for the cargo to be offloaded for inspection, but the captain refused and returned to Muscat. When Mubarak heard of this, he was furious. He sent a letter of protest to Colonel Knox, the British Agent. He also informed Sheikh Khaz'al. The latter warned the Belgian official in charge of the customs never to do anything similar again, and insisted that he should apologize to Sheikh Mubarak, which he did. Later, in 1910, after Kuwaiti forces had suffered serious losses at the hands of the Al-Muntafiq tribes at the battle of Hadiyya, Sheikh Mubarak needed to buy a large amount of weapons and ammunitions. Khaz'al offered to support Mubarak with whatever money, men and weapons were at his disposal. In response, not wishing to deplete Sheikh Khaz'al's resources, Mubarak asked for this support to be given in the form of a consignment of dates to be sold in India to buy the required weapons. Sheikh Khaz'al did this through his agent in Al-Qasaba, Hajj Sultan.

With the outbreak of World War I in 1914, Sheikh Khaz'al declared his support for the British. In response, the Ottomans sent a military force, led by Muhammad Fadel Al-Daghistani, with a number of religious men in attendance, to take up a position on the borders of Arabistan in order to rouse the tribes against Sheikh Khaz'al. The Ottoman authorities alleged that his anti-Ottoman stand amounted to heresy. The result was an outbreak of uprisings by the tribes, which the Ottoman forces supported. Even some of the tribes of the Bani Ka'b revolted, under the leadership of Jaber bin Al-Sayyed Mish'al, with the assistance of some Bedouins. Sheikh Khaz'al sent a force of his own against them under the leadership of his son, Jasib, which successfully crushed the rebellion.

Sheikh Mubarak, who was at the time at his palace in Al-Fayliyya, was concerned that Sheikh Khaz'al might not be able to quell these tribal rebellions on his own, and wrote to his son Jaber asking for troops to be sent from Kuwait to support Sheikh Khaz'al. The Sheikh's decision, however, was not widely popular in Kuwait, where many had been swayed by Ottoman propaganda and by the religious arguments of Shaykh Muhammad Amin Al-Shanqiti and Shaykh Hafez Wahbah, both of whom were supporters of the Ottoman Empire. These two had issued a *fatwa* declaring that failure to support the Ottoman Empire, which was the home of the Caliphate and therefore the heart of Islam, would be an act of apostasy. When Sheikh Jaber wrote to his father explaining the situation, Sheikh Mubarak became very irate. A delegation of Kuwaiti notables led by Hajj Ibrahim bin Mudaf sought an audience with him to attempt to calm his anger. The Sheikh reproached them for not explaining the situation correctly to the people of Kuwait, saying, 'I did not ask my son Jaber to send me an army to fight alongside Khaz'al, what I asked for was to send a few empty boats to be ready to transport Khaz'al's furniture and wealth if need be.' He ordered them to return to Kuwait and to prepare these boats immediately. After persuading people that this was all Sheikh Mubarak wanted to do on behalf of Sheikh Khaz'al, six boats with 180 men on board were despatched and moored in front of Sheikh Khaz'al's palace in Al-Fayliyya. Sheikh Khaz'al was able to quell the rebellion, and the situation did not require any direct Kuwaiti participation. Sheikh Khaz'al's forces helped to support the British military effort in Basra, which was occupied by British forces in 1915.[35]

With the death of Sheikh Mubarak in 1915, Sheikh Khaz'al lost a strong ally. His relationship with Britain deteriorated after the British began to back Reza Shah and lent their support to his policy of exerting Persian sovereignty over Arabistan. Gradually, Sheikh Khaz'al's authority over his tribes waned, and he did not have the military resources to restore it in the face of the support Iran was giving them. Inevitably, the authority of his agents to collect taxes and duties in the emirate weakened, and the Iranians imposed their administrative system on the region. A permanent Iranian garrison was established in Ahwaz and then Tehran issued an order to change the emirate's name from Arabistan to its modern name of Khuzestan. Finally, on 19 April 1925, an Iranian military force arrested Sheikh Khaz'al and took him to Tehran, where he lived in exile until his death on 30 June 1936 at the age of 75.[36]

Rivalry and military clashes: relations with the Sheikh of Qatar

In the second half of the nineteenth century, the relationship between the sheikhs of Kuwait and Qatar may be described as one of consistent enmity and hostility. Each had taken the part of the other's enemies in regional clashes. In the period before Mubarak's accession, the Sheikh of Kuwait had co-operated with the Ottomans against the Sheikh of Qatar. During Sheikh Mubarak's reign, Sheikh Jassem Al-Thani, the Sheikh of Qatar, supported Yusuf Al-Ibrahim's conspiracies against him. There was also direct rivalry between the two powerful sheikhs for regional influence in Arabia.

In the last decade of the nineteenth century, the Ottoman authorities sought the assistance of Sheikh Mubarak's brother and predecessor, Sheikh Muhammad Al-Sabah, the ruler of Kuwait from 1892 to 1896, in a military campaign against Qatar. He agreed, and placed Sheikh Mubarak at the head of a strong contingent of Bedouins, which reached Al-Hasa in March 1893. Some historical sources suggest that the Sheikh of Kuwait engaged in a political stratagem as regards the Ottomans, giving the appearance of taking part in the campaign against the Qataris while his troops never actually participated in any engagement. Thus, the Kuwaiti force, which travelled overland from Kuwait, was deliberately slow and reached Qatar only after military operations had ended. The outcome of the Ottoman campaign against Qatar was that the Ottoman forces, led by Hafez Pasha, the Governor of Basra, were badly defeated. The campaign failed in its purpose.[37]

However, the relationship between Mubarak and Jassem always had a mixture of hostility and rivalry. It was for this reason that Sheikh Jassem supported Yusuf Al-Ibrahim in his attempts to remove Sheikh Mubarak from power. After Yusuf Al-Ibrahim's bid to turn the Ottomans and Britain against Mubarak, Al-Ibrahim went to Sheikh Jassem in early 1897 to ask for his support, drawing Sheikh Jassem's attention to the help he had given Qatar in its war with Abu Dhabi in 1888. They agreed to carry out a joint plan to attack Kuwait by sea and by land, and that they would also seek support from the Sheikh of Ha'il and Ibn Al-Rashid and would attempt to persuade the Al-Ajman tribe not to support Sheikh Mubarak. The plan was that Ibn Al-Rashid would invade Kuwait from the north, while Jassem would invade it from the south.

This plan would have been put into effect in November 1897, had the Ottomans not opposed it and if Muhammad Ibn Al-Rashid had not passed away that year. Sheikh Mubarak had convinced Sa'id Pasha, the Ottoman *mutasarrif* of Al-Hasa, that the situation was dangerous. Sa'id Pasha wrote to the Governor of Basra warning him that the schemes in which Sheikh Jassem was involved would threaten the security of the area, and remarking in particular that the plan implied naked aggression towards Sheikh Mubarak, who as he put it, 'is the obedient subject of the Sublime Porte'. The Ottomans sent a delegation to Ibn Thani to deliver the Governor of Basra's warning not to carry out any operations against Sheikh Mubarak.

Documents in the Ottoman Archive in Istanbul show how the official position evolved. They include a report of the meeting of the military committee of the ministry of defence in 1897, headed by the minister Riza Pasha, to discuss the situation regarding Jassem Al-Thani, described as the *qaimaqam* of Qatar, and his preparations to invade Kuwait. The report said that Lieutenant General Muhsin Pasha, the Chief of Staff of the Sixth Army in Baghdad, who was seeking a settlement of the conflict between Kuwait and Qatar, had reported that the Governor of Basra had been delaying the settlement in order to obtain money and gifts for himself, and that the governor's reputation was that he never finished a job until he was paid for it. The committee's report recommended a number of measures, which included the appointment of General Muhsin Pasha as Governor of Basra, speeding up the settlement of the various rights of the heirs of Muhammad Pasha Al-Sabah, appointing Mubarak Al-Sabah to the honorary position of *qaimaqam* in Kuwait and taking such steps as might be necessary to prevent Jassem Al-Thani from attacking Kuwait.[38] Riza Pasha then sent a memorandum setting out these recommendations to the Sultan.[39]

A week later, the special committee of the Ottoman ministry of defence held a further meeting in the light of a telegram Jassem Al-Thani had sent from Bushire, which included his sentiments of loyalty to the Sultan and the Ottoman Empire. The committee decided to indicate their appreciation of Sheikh Jassem's loyal sentiments while at the same time repeating to him the injunction that he should not attack Kuwait, pointing out that this might lead to dire consequences for him. They concluded as follows: 'All that [Jassem] ... has said about Mubarak Al-Sabah has been taken into consideration by the Sublime Porte and has changed their minds about appointing [Mubarak] ... as Qaimaqam of Kuwait.'[40]

We do not know the content of Sheikh Jassem's telegram, but an analysis of these documents illustrates how exhausted the Ottoman administration had become and how indecisive its organization was. In the earlier telegram, there were direct accusations of corruption against the Governor of Basra. In this document, the ministerial committee rescinds its decision to appoint Mubarak as *qaimaqam* of Kuwait. Later in the same year, they decided after all to appoint him. The issue took three months in the corridors of Ottoman committees until it finally reached the ministerial committee of the Grand Vizier, Rifat Pasha, which recommended 'assigning to Rajab Efendi, the Naqib Al-Ashraf of Basra, the task of bringing Mubarak Al-Sabah to Basra'.[41]

In the same year, the head of the Ottoman Imperial Diwan received a telegram from the Governorate of Basra, signed by the governor and by his chief of staff, Muhsin Pasha, which said that Sheikh Jassem Al-Thani, the *qaimaqam* of Qatar, was insisting on defending the inheritance rights of Sheikh Mubarak's two brothers: 'Nothing will discourage his determination until the heirs receive their inheritance or he is ordered by the Sublime Porte to withdraw.' The Governor of Basra and its military commander recommended the appointment of Mubarak Al-Sabah as the *qaimaqam* of Kuwait, to secure the rights of the heirs and to hasten in compelling Jassem Al-Thani to, 'adhere to obedience and subjugation to the orders of the Empire and to let him know that he will be held fully responsible for every transgression he commits'.[42]

The special ministerial committee held a meeting to discuss the content of this telegram, concluding that their course of action should be, 'to send a warning to Sheikh Jassem Al-Thani against attacking Kuwait; and to send a military force to Kuwait under the leadership of General Muhsin Pasha, while concealing the true purpose of the mission and to pretending that this was part of military measures taken to prevent Jassem Al-Thani's plans which were to attack and invade Kuwait'.[43]

Sheikh Jassem continued to regard Sheikh Mubarak as his enemy. On 27 January 1898 the Sheikh of Qatar sent a telegram to the Ottoman Sultan announcing his submission to and support for His Majesty the Caliph. He accused the commander of the Sixth Army of receiving bribes from Mubarak Al-Sabah, and gave an incorrect account of developments in Kuwait. Sheikh Jassem urged the Ottoman authorities to intervene militarily in Kuwait, adding that Kuwait was 'a developed country which was independent of the policies and administration of the Ottoman state, and interests dictate that this opportunity should be seized to restrain it and bring it under control'.[44]

Mubarak did not stand idle in the face of these developments. His objective was to instil fear into Jassem's followers so that they would refrain from carrying out any attacks against Kuwait and its dependent tribes in the future. In April 1898, therefore, he attacked one of the tribes under Sheikh Jassem's protection, the Al-Huwayr, making off with the greater part of their livestock. Jassem calculated that Mubarak would never have done such a thing without Ottoman support, and therefore launched an attack on the Ottoman garrison in Qatar, with casualties on both sides.

In July of the same year, Sheikh Mubarak launched a military campaign against one of the tribes loyal to Sheikh Jassem, the Bani Hajar, alleging that they were raiding and stealing Kuwaiti property. The Sheikh of Qatar complained to the Ottomans because the booty captured by the forces of the Sheikh of Kuwait from the Bani Hajar included some of his property. At first, the Ottomans refused to intervene, indicating that Sheikh Mubarak's actions had served the Ottomans' interests in Qatar. Later, the Ottoman authorities sought once more to reconcile the two sheikhs, but without any notable success.[45] The enmity between the Sheikh of Kuwait and the Sheikh of Qatar continued. In 1908, Sheikh Mubarak supported the rebellion of the Al-Bu'aynayn tribe in Al-Wikra in Qatar. The leaders of this tribe accused Sheikh Jassem and his son, Abdul Rahman, the Sheikh of Al-Wikra, of seeking to exclude them from lands where they had lived for generations. In November of the same year, the Al-Bu'aynayn wrote to the Governor of Basra, asking him to establish an Ottoman garrison to protect their presence on their land. The British quartermaster in Basra intervened, in accordance with instructions he received on 15 December 1908 from the Foreign Secretary, Sir Edward Grey. He informed the Ottoman Government that London did not recognize the Ottoman Empire's right to intervene. Therefore, no Ottoman military garrison was established to protect the tribe.

Because of this development, the leaders of the tribe felt that they could no longer live in Qatar. They asked permission from the Sheikh of Bahrain, Issa Al Al-Khalifa, to establish themselves in his territory, but he did not respond to their request. They then made a similar request to Sheikh Mubarak, who welcomed them and settled them in the area of Qasr Al-Sabiyya. They moved there in October 1909, numbering over 1,000 men, with their dependents. After a period, they moved on to the coast of Al-Hasa, where they established the city of Al-Jubayl in 1911.[46]

The call for Arab independence

Ottoman-Kuwaiti relations, and Ottoman-Arab relations in general, were governed by the political developments that took place in the Ottoman Empire in the first years of the twentieth century. As the reform movement within the Ottoman Empire grew, the pressure from the Committee for Union and Progress advocating for reform in the Empire increased. In 1907, the Young Turks, as they were known, carried out a constitutional coup, and in 1908 they promulgated a new constitution. In 1909, Sultan

Abdul Hamid was replaced by his brother Muhammad Rashad. Arab fears and concerns began to multiply.

Previously, the Arab masses had viewed the Ottoman Empire as the seat of the Islamic Caliphate, whose moral authority prevailed over the whole Arab world. However, when the Committee for Union and Progress seized power, the Arabs realized that the Ottoman Empire had taken on a new character. This aroused their trepidation. The Empire was now following a more centralized policy, which aimed at the active control of its provinces, including the areas in the Gulf under its sovereignty. The new Ottoman authorities were no longer satisfied with legal or symbolic sovereignty. The Committee for Union and Progress, now the ruling party, also sought to destroy any non-Turkish local power which might have had the ability to limit the authority of their governors in the provinces. The relationship of the governing power with the Arabs deteriorated further when the pan-Ottoman movement turned into the so-called 'Turanian Movement', which unequivocally asserted the superiority of the Turks and sought to install Turkish as the only official language in Ottoman provinces. This outraged Arab political and intellectual leaders and increased their hostility towards the policies of the Ottoman Empire during the time of the Young Turks.

These policies led Sheikh Mubarak into direct conflict with the Ottomans, as it also did with other Arab leaders who sought Arab independence. Sheikh Mubarak's personal belief, strengthened by the political circumstances, was that the Islamic Caliphate belonged to the Arabs and that they had more right to it than all other peoples and nations. Despite this, he called for the unity of Arabs and Turks, in order to preserve solidarity within the Ottoman realms and, in his own interest, to maintain friendly relations with the imperial state. Early on, this is revealed in several articles written in April 1905 by the French arms dealer Antonin Goguyer, whose role has been discussed above, where he reveals his discussions with Sheikh Mubarak over the future of the Arabs and the Sheikh's policy as regards the limitation of both Ottoman and British interference in Kuwait.[47]

In a discussion between the Sheikh and Abd Al-Massih Antaki in 1907, Mubarak criticized the Ottoman policy of inciting internecine conflict between the various sheikhs and emirs of the Arab world. As reported by Antaki, the Sheikh said that the Turks, 'perhaps feared that the Arabs might unite and claim the Caliphate', but that these fears were baseless and were founded on 'their ignorance of the true nature of the Arabs'. The Sheikh pointed out that the Al-Saud, who fought the Turks for a long time and finally took the holy cities of Medina and Mecca, still did not claim the Caliphate. As he put it: 'it never occurred to any of them to do so. We are all aware that each era has its Empire and its men, and that the Empire and the men of this era are the Turks. Therefore, for the Turks to keep the Caliphate causes glory to accrue to Islam and champions the Word of the Muslims.'

The Sheikh went on to expand on these views. He added that union between the Arabs and the Turks, 'is not merely possible but is a definite duty. It is the duty of a true and faithful Muslim to seek harmony between the two nations.' Corruption must be expunged, he said, and reform should be in the interests of the Caliphate:

> First and foremost, there must be reform in the Ottoman Empire to remove every trace of those traitors who take bribes; who sell the rights of God's faithful; and sacrifice the interests of the Empire for their own benefits ... true reformers take over, who sacrifice their own interests for the sake of the Caliphate and Islam, then they will extend the hand of loyalty to us and we will shake it, for better or worse. Then they will see, from the Emirs of the Arabs, such unbeatable power, and bastions that can only be broken by God's permission. By God, every Emir, Sheikh, or other leader, will devote himself, his wealth and his power to the defence of the Ottoman Caliphate and of Islam.

Declaring his own position, he added: 'Here I stand: if the Empire was to extend loyalty and friendliness to me, they would have no further need for the Sixth Imperial Army in Baghdad ... I assure you that if some are less inclined towards the Empire, it is because of the injustices committed by their governors, may God reform them.'[48]

Similar sentiments were expressed by Sheikh Mubarak to Sheikh Rashid Reda when the latter visited Kuwait in 1913. The Sheikh told Rashid Reda that the Ottoman Empire had mistreated him, seeking to enforce its sovereignty over Kuwait and to expel him from the country. Sheikh Reda says that Mubarak had asked the Turks what he had done to deserve exile from his country and his tribe. He reminded them of his loyalty to the Naqib of Basra and how the Naqib must be aware of Mubarak's loyalty and of the financial support he was accustomed to provide for the Ottoman authorities, whatever might happen. He added: 'The English interference in Kuwait was not at my behest but at their instigation. They told me to choose a flag for myself to fly over the country and to declare independence under their protection, but I refused and here you can see the Ottoman flag flying over my head every day.'[49]

In 1914, in the same vein, Ibrahim Hilmi wrote a comment in the Beirut newspaper, *Fata Al-Arab*, on the past and future of Arabia. In the article, he drew attention to the tension between the Arab emirs and the Ottoman authorities. As he put it,

> there is no way out of this crisis except to follow a prudent policy in the Arab provinces and to strive to disseminate civilization in those areas, to unite the efforts of the Emirs and leaders, to tame their hearts and to seek their appeasement. When countries undergo an intellectual renaissance, and the Arab people come to know their rights and duties, then the Empire could create a wide Arab entity under their authority, uniting these Emirates. Were this proposal to be found good and to be adopted by those in charge of the Empire, then it may be said that the future of Arabia would be brilliant and prosperous.[50]

It was in this atmosphere that political and intellectual movements that called for reform in the Arab lands arose. The demand of these movements was decentralized rule and Arab autonomy, or even independence, from the Ottomans. The first reaction of the political leaders in the Gulf in the early years of the twentieth century, including Sheikh Mubarak, was to seek to conciliate the new rulers in Istanbul and to gain their trust. To this end, both Sheikh Mubarak and his neighbour Sheikh Khaz'al, as well as Sayyed Taleb Ibn Rajab Al-Naqib from Basra, the son of the Naqib of Basra, joined the Committee for Union and Progress, though the latter aligned himself later with the Arab liberals. However, faced with the reality of the actions of the successive governors of Basra under the new regime, the nearest organ of the Empire, it became clear to the two sheikhs that compromise would be impossible.[51] Sheikh Mubarak's relations with the new regime in Basra were very tense. As a result, the *Tannin* newspaper, which expressed the policies of the Committee for Union and Progress, carried vicious diatribes against him, penned by one Ismail Haqqi, who insisted that the Sheikh should be compelled to make a public declaration of loyalty to the imperial state. Not content with this, in June 1910 the unionists encouraged Sa'dun Pasha, the leader of the Al-Muntafiq tribes, to attack the Sheikh's forces at the battle of Hadiyya, where the Kuwaiti force suffered a defeat.

Most studies link the rise of unity movements in the Arab world to the takeover of power in the Ottoman Empire by the Committee of Union and Progress. Sheikh Mubarak seems himself to have been quick to make this connection. As long ago as July 1898, the Sheikh sent a letter to the British Political Resident, J. Calcott Gaskin, telling him that the Al-Sa'dun family of Al-Muntafiq wished to liberate themselves from the yoke of the Turks. Gaskin commented that it might be Sheikh Mubarak himself who was pushing for the creation of what he called 'a large Arab alliance' under British influence. He noted that Sheikh Mubarak was a very ambitious man and that, having signed the protection agreement with Britain, 'he was trying to create a union between the great Arab tribes under his power, so that it could become a strong enough force to stand up to Turkish attacks. If this is the case, he had to give these people enough reasons to believe that he had a force behind him supporting him in expelling the Turks, which would encourage them to join him.'

Sheikh Mubarak contributed to the Arab movement against Turkification. Together with Sayyed Taleb Al-Naqib and Sheikh Khaz'al, he established a branch of the Freedom and Accord Party. This defended decentralization and opposed the policies of the Committee for Union and Progress, which endorsed the policy of tightening the Ottoman grip on the Arab areas, while giving them a Turkish character. The Sheikh and his associates established their branch of the Freedom and Accord Party in August 1911. Mubarak also supported the Basra Reform Association established by Sayyed Taleb Al-Naqib in February 1912, which sought to implement administrative decentralization in Ottoman provinces. The historian Mahmoud Ali Dawoud sums up these developments thus: 'It is no exaggeration to say that the brilliant political role played so well by the two great personalities, Khaz'al and Mubarak, was highly crucial in the initiation of the appearance of modern states and Emirates, followed by the Arab nationalist movements in the Arab Gulf basin.'

In this context, Sheikh Mubarak attended many regional conferences, such as the Al-Fayliyya conference in Al-Muhammara in March 1909. It was held in Sheikh Khaz'al's palace and attended by Sheikh Khaz'al as well as Sa'dun Pasha, the leader of the Al-Muntafiq tribes, who had not yet succumbed to the influence of the Ottomans, as well as a number of leaders from the clans of Al-Amara and Al-Qurna from Iraq. It was also attended by Abdul Wahhab Al-Qortas, a member of the administrative council of Basra province, and Sayyed Rajab Al-Naqib. The aim of the conference was to formulate a common political line among the Arab leaders present, and to demand their rights in Basra province. In reaction, the Ottomans appointed a strongly anti-Arab figure,

Sulayman Bek Nadhif, as the Governor of Basra in November of the same year.

When news spread that Abbas Hilmi, the Khedive of Egypt, intended to perform the Hajj in 1909, Sheikh Mubarak was prompted to discuss with Abdul Aziz bin Saud, Sheikh Khaz'al and others among the Arab sheikhs and emirs the possibility of making contact with the khedive while he was in the Arabian Peninsula in order to consider the idea of taking the Caliphate away from the Turks and returning it to the Arabs. They also discussed between themselves the possibility of offering the Caliphate to Abbas Hilmi, in his capacity as the leader of the largest Arab country in terms of population. However, they decided that such a move would not be appropriate as Abbas Hilmi was not an Arab from Quraysh, but, as a member of the dynasty of Mohammed Ali, was himself of Turko-Circassian of Albanian descent. They therefore moved on towards considering Sherif Hussein bin Ali, the Emir of Makkah, as a candidate for the Caliphate. Sheikh Mubarak had correspondence with the sherif, and entertained feelings of friendship and respect towards him.[52]

Sheikh Mubarak also participated in the Al-Muhammara conference in 1913, which was held while the Ottomans were distracted by war in the Balkans. This meeting, the purpose of which was to discuss the future of Iraq and to demand its independence, was also attended by Sheikh Khaz'al and Sayyed Talib Al-Naqib. More broadly, the future of Arab policy also came under discussion, in the light of deterioration in Turkish-Arab relations. The Ottoman press attacked both these meetings, accusing the participants of seeking to dilute the authority of the Ottoman Empire. In any case the Ottoman authorities were undeterred by such Arab gatherings, and simply pressed on with their policies. The new law relating to the government of the provinces was ratified. This promoted centralization and implied the practical imposition of the authority of the Empire. Sayyed Talib Al-Naqib declared his opposition to the new legislation, and asked the Governor of Basra to expel anti-Arab employees from the Ottoman Government. He sent word to his two allies, Mubarak and Khaz'al, asking them to help him with weapons and supplies. Mubarak responded quickly. The security situation in Basra continued to deteriorate, leading Sayyed Talib Al-Naqib to plan for a conference in Kuwait under the Sheikh's auspices which would bring together all the leaders of Arabia to discuss the future of the Arabs and to resolve their problems.

At the beginning of 1914, invitations were extended to such a conference. Among those invited to participate were Sherif Hussein, Emir Abdul Aziz Al-Saud, Emir Saud Al-Rashid, Ajami Pasha Al-Sa'dun, Sheikh Khaz'al and Sayyed Talib Al-Naqib. However, because Abdul Aziz Al-Saud and a number of others declined their invitations, the conference was not held.[53] Nonetheless, such developments confirm that Kuwait was not isolated from the Arab movements that were appearing across the eastern Arab world, which were intended to defend the rights of the Arabs, to demand more decentralization from the Ottoman Empire and to assert the right of the Arabs to self-rule. Sheikh Mubarak had become one of the symbols of this movement.

~6~

The International Struggle for Kuwait

In his policies, Mubarak used the Anglo-Turkish, Anglo-Russian and Anglo-German conflicts with skill and expertise.
Grigori Bondarevsky[1]

The reign of Sheikh Mubarak in Kuwait represented a turning point in the history of the Gulf. On the one hand, the period saw an increase in competition between the great powers to extend their influence into the region. The diplomatic correspondence of the representatives of these countries in the Gulf reflects the frantic atmosphere of rivalry among them. On the other hand, the period also witnessed an attempt to revive Ottoman institutions under the guidance of Prime Minister Midhat Pasha. Such efforts, however, did not succeed in stemming the decay of the Ottoman Empire. They also failed to halt the efforts of the European powers to divide up its legacy, the so-called 'sick man of Europe'. Indeed, the year before the Sheikh's death saw the outbreak of World War I, which ended with the empire's disintegration.

These international changes were reflected in Kuwait. The Ottoman Empire did not have the economic or military ability to impose its power in its provinces, while those European powers that had interests in the Gulf became more prominent, particularly in Kuwait. The most significant of these was Britain, which signed a series of agreements with the sheikhs of the Gulf's western littoral. The Royal Navy controlled the waters of the Gulf, and Britain made every effort to obstruct the diplomatic efforts of Germany, France and Russia to find areas of influence in the region.

Germany finally achieved unification in 1871, and among its economic goals were the expansion of its leverage in the Ottoman regions. The German leader, Otto von Bismarck, worked to strengthen his relations with Istanbul with the aim of gaining financial and commercial privileges in the Ottoman Empire. Russia also continued its quest for access to the warm waters of the Gulf. France had succeeded in keeping Britain away from the construction of the Suez Canal and its administration after its opening in 1869, and it was keen to enlarge its share of Ottoman inheritance. In the midst of the continuing rivalry, positions changed and alternated. In the last decade of the nineteenth century, the interests of Russia and France temporarily converged, which meant that Britain lost its naval control of the Mediterranean. Another alliance of convenience was forged between Germany and the Ottoman Empire.

In this context, Kuwait's strategic position became important. All the various European projects for a railway to the Gulf envisaged a terminus in Kuwait. According to the Egyptian *Al-Ahram* newspaper's correspondent in Muscat, writing on 16 September 1904: 'Kuwait is crucially important because it is the gateway to the entire region. From Kuwait departs the only road to Iraq and Mesopotamia. The land route from Kuwait to Iraq avoids the difficulties of the Shatt Al-Arab and its tributaries.' Similarly, the Danish correspondent Raunkiær wrote in his memoirs: 'The power which controls Kuwait will also be the power that controls the Shatt Al-Arab.'[2]

Sheikh Mubarak was obliged to remain aware of all such developments, and also to keep open his lines of communication with the various rival powers, especially those with Istanbul and London. Much depended on his ability at each stage to opt for the power likely to prevail and to exploit Europe's rivalry for the Ottoman lands in order to preserve his own country's independence, fending off interference from foreign powers in Kuwait's internal affairs. The Sheikh's success was documented by Philip Perceval Graves, the author of a major biography of Sir Percy Cox, the British Political Resident in the Gulf, who noted that Sheikh Mubarak's skill as a politician, diplomat and soldier enabled him to respond to the pressures brought to bear upon him, whether by rival military powers in Arabia or by the Turks in Iraq.[3]

The development of the Anglo-Ottoman rivalry and its manipulation by Sheikh Mubarak, who played one side off against another, has been referred to earlier in this book. It was the convergence of the interests of the Sheikh and the British that led to the signature of the January 1899 agreement between them. For the British, the objective of these agreements was to secure its naval control of the Gulf and to have the capacity to exclude other rival European navies from its ports. The rhetoric of Britain's explanations of its policy, however, naturally tended towards such high-minded goals as the achievement of maritime peace in the waters of the Gulf, with the expression of diplomatically acceptable goals such as the struggle against piracy. Kuwait was nevertheless able to remain aloof from British efforts to sign these agreements until the end of the nineteenth century. What made the difference for Sheikh Mubarak, throwing him into the arms of the British, was the Ottoman plan to permit a railway to be built through the region by German companies, and another similar plan put forward by a Russian entrepreneur.

The German project, the southward extension of the so-called Berlin–Baghdad Railway, came about as the result of the Ottoman-German convergence in the last quarter of the nineteenth century. Germany sought to secure economic and commercial interests in Ottoman regions and to open these markets to German goods. Because of this, the Germans, who already planned a modern rail link from Germany to Istanbul, proposed to Sultan Abdul Hamid the idea of a railway line from the Turkish capital to the Gulf. The original plan had been to make Kuwait the terminus of this new rail connection, but after the agreement with the British this was revised to make Basra the end of the line, and an agreement was signed in November 1899. Meanwhile, on 30 December 1898, the Ottoman Government had also granted a concession to a Russian entrepreneur, Count Vladimir Kapnist, to construct a similar project, though this proved to be more of a speculative venture. In the case of the Russian plan, the railway would have been built from the city of Tripoli on the Mediterranean coast of Syria (now in Lebanon), whence it would pass through Homs and Baghdad and on to Kuwait. Had either project reached its intended terminus in Kuwait the result would have been to give the Ottomans the ability to rapidly transport military forces to Kuwait and onward into the Gulf.

Britain's interests in establishing its influence in the Gulf

British interest in Kuwait had first begun in the last quarter of the eighteenth century. When Basra fell briefly into the hands of Persia, British vessels sailing from India to the Gulf turned to Kuwait as an alternative. From Kuwait, their goods would be transported over land to the Arab countries. This continued until the return of Ottoman rule in 1779. A similar situation occurred in December 1821, when the headquarters of the British Resident were temporarily transferred from Basra to Kuwait owing to tension between the British and the Ottoman authorities. Later, in the nineteenth century, Britain also saw its activity in the Gulf as an integral part of its colonial activity in Egypt and Sudan, as well as a means of guaranteeing its influence over the Suez Canal. Meanwhile, the land route from Kuwait and Iraq to the

Mediterranean coast was the best route for land communications. Because of this, Britain made a decision to strengthen Britain's influence and bring Kuwait under its protection. Britain's policy began to be focused on the reinforcement of British power on the coast of Arabia and the control of the northern and southern entrances to the Gulf. However, Britain endeavoured as far as possible to avoid clashing with the various powers in the interior of the Arabian Peninsula.[4]

If the agreement between Britain and Sheikh Mubarak had appeared from the Kuwaiti side as a means for Kuwait to ensure its protection from the results of a German-assisted extension of Ottoman power, from the British point of view an accord with Kuwait analogous to the protection pacts it had already signed with other Gulf sheikhs appeared desirable as an instrument of the consolidation of British naval power in Gulf waters. It was for this reason that the protection agreement was signed with Sheikh Mubarak on 22 January 1899 by Lieutenant Colonel M. J. Meade, the British Political Resident in the Gulf. It stipulated that the Sheikh should not receive the agent or representative of any other country, and that he should not give away, mortgage or lease any part of his land to the government or subjects of any other country without the agreement of the British Government.

This initial agreement was the first of a series of other commitments and agreements that had the effect of giving Britain a prominent role in Kuwait. On 24 May 1900, for instance, an undertaking restricting arms dealing in Kuwait was signed. This contained three separate clauses. The first of these comprised an undertaking from the Sheikh as follows: 'I have agreed to completely prevent the entry and exit of weapons to and from Kuwait and for this ban to take effect, I have issued a public declaration to all those who are concerned with this matter.' The second clause gave British and Iranian ships the right to search boats owned by Kuwaiti subjects and which flew the Sheikh's flag and to confiscate any unlicensed weapons they might find on board. This was signed by the Sheikh and contained the following edict:

Let all those who read this letter know that the ships of imperial Britain and the Iranian imperial state have license to search boats which carry the flags of either of the two above mentioned countries as well as those flying our own flag at sea around Kuwait. And that they can seize, on behalf of the Treasury, all guns and other military weapons on board ... whether such weapons if found are being carried to the cities of India or to foreign countries.

The third section referred to a specific ban on, 'trading in arms with the states of India and with Persia' and also stipulated that, 'the import and export of rifles and ammunition and all other weapons into and out of Kuwait and all areas subject to it is forbidden'. The statement finally states that its purpose is to assist the governments of Britain and Persia to bring an end to the illegal trade in arms.[5]

As has already been indicated, the course of events indicates that Sheikh Mubarak was not necessarily always conscientious in adhering to promises of the variety he made here, which conflicted with his objective of establishing a Kuwaiti military force strong enough to both protect his country and to give him the resources to support those with whom he chose to ally himself in the conflicts in the Arabian Peninsula, foremost amongst whom was Abdul Aziz Al-Saud. Meanwhile, despite the stated intention of British diplomacy to halt the trade in weapons, the truth was that British representatives on the ground did not maintain a sufficient level of vigilance to achieve their objective, whether because it was beyond their means to restrict the activities of the Sheikh sufficiently closely to halt the weapons trade through Kuwait, or because they did not wish in practice to irritate him.[6]

In 1901, two years after the signing of the initial protection agreement with the Sheikh, the British signed a secret agreement with the Ottoman authorities under the terms of which London undertook to preserve the status quo in Arabia and the Gulf and to ensure that Sheikh Mubarak did not attack Ibn Al-Rashid, who was loyal to the Ottomans. In return, Istanbul was to prevent Ibn

Al-Rashid from attacking Kuwait. Sheikh Mubarak was unaware of this agreement. By 1902, however, British power in the Gulf faced grave challenges. The Sultan wished to reassert Ottoman authority in Kuwait, Bahrain and Iraq. At the same time, German influence was strengthening in Iran, while Russia made it clear that it refused to recognize any special status for Britain in Southern Iran or the Gulf. The Russo-French alliance concluded in that year aggravated the anxiety of the British authorities regarding the future of their influence in the Gulf.

In June 1903, the British ambassador in Istanbul, Sir Nicholas O'Conor, suggested that a British agency be established in Kuwait as part of Britain's active policy in the Gulf. Although the British Government of India, which administered the Gulf, supported the suggestion, the Foreign Office in London rejected it on the basis that it was contrary to the commitment made by Britain to the Ottomans in 1901 to respect the status quo. The Foreign Office felt that if it agreed to this suggestion, the move might be construed as British support for the independence of Kuwait. As a compromise, it was agreed that British officials would pay periodic visits to Kuwait to reaffirm the special relationship between the two countries.

On 28 November 1903, in a significant political development, Lord Curzon, the Viceroy of India, visited the Gulf. His tour included a number of Arab emirates, including Kuwait. The aim of the visit was to strengthen the links between Britain and those sheikhs in the area with which it had signed treaties, and to pursue Britain's political and commercial interests in the region.[7] The visit also served as a demonstration of Britain's potential naval power in the Gulf. Curzon arrived in Kuwait at the head of a large naval flotilla, on board the Royal Indian Marine steamship *Hardinge*, accompanied by the first-class Argonaut cruiser *Argonaut*, the second-class cruiser *Hyacinth* and the third-class cruisers *Fox* and *Pomone*, together with a number of smaller vessels. On 28 November, at 10.00 am, the British ships dropped anchor at Bandar Al-Shuwaykh, some 5 kilometres from the city. On their arrival, the guns positioned in front of Sheikh Mubarak's residence fired a 21-gun salute. Anxious to know the purpose of Lord Curzon's visit, Sheikh Mubarak then went aboard the *Hardinge* to welcome his British guest, who was accompanied by the Political Resident in Bushire, Charles Kemball.

At 10.00 am the following day, Lord Curzon himself disembarked in Bandar Al-Shuwaykh, where a carriage had been prepared for him. The Sheikh had provided for the use of his British guest a carriage pulled by four Indian horses.[8] Sheikh Mubarak himself and his sons were waiting at the head of a group of horsemen. The Viceroy rode in the carriage, while his escorts accompanied him on horseback. As the procession set off, a fusillade of rifle shots was fired by the horsemen to express their welcome to the grand guest. In Lorimer's account, we read that Lord Curzon's carriage was surrounded by the group of riders holding up their spears while they fired their rifles in the air, prancing and encircling the carriage. As the cavalcade reached the city, there were more than 200 horsemen, 20 camel riders and about 4,000 people on foot. Lorimer describes the scene as, 'breathtakingly beautiful with the horsemen on their graceful Arabian steeds in bright flapping robes in orange, red and gold that waved in the wind'.[9] A red flag carried before the procession bore the slogan, 'In God we trust'. Flags were also raised over the white walls of the city to enhance the celebratory atmosphere. At the same time, voices were raised in songs of welcome while women ululated and the people cheered.[10] Sheikh Mubarak wanted to impress Lord Curzon and to give him a good impression of Arab and Kuwaiti courtesy.

Once through the gates, Lord Curzon traversed the streets of the city with the people lined up on each side to welcome him. When he came at last to the Sheikh's house, overlooking the sea, a 31-gun salute was fired in his honour. Sheikh Mubarak had organized a grand reception for Lord Curzon, the like of which Kuwait had never seen. Abdul Aziz Al-Rashid, who attended the celebrations, described the reception as 'most beautiful and tasteful'. Sheikh Mubarak spared no expense on the celebrations, intending to enhance the image of Kuwait in British eyes.[11] The formal meeting between the two men was held in the reception room in the Sheikh's house. He had decorated this for the occasion with pictures of the King and Queen of Britain and of the late Queen Victoria. Afterwards, Sheikh Mubarak introduced his sons to the Viceroy. Arabic coffee was served and the two men chatted with each other, before Lord Curzon returned to his ship.

In the afternoon, the Sheikh went to Lord Curzon's ship, accompanied by his son, Jaber, and gifts were exchanged. This was the moment for serious conversation. The Sheikh assured Lord Curzon that he had severed his relations with the Ottomans and that he preferred British protection. He also averred that he had rejected all the inducements that had been made to him by France and Russia to change his position. There was also some conversation about the case of the Sheikh's agent in Basra, who had been detained by the Ottoman authorities and was accused of grand treason. Lord Curzon asked the Sheikh to refrain from interference in the affairs of the Arabian Peninsula. This meeting was attended by the British Minister in Teheran, who was accompanying Lord Curzon, and by the Political Resident in the Gulf, Charles Kemball. Afterwards, he accompanied the Sheikh on a tour of the *Hyacinth*, one of the ships that had accompanied the *Hardinge*. This was the first time the Sheikh had inspected a large military ship and he paid close attention, showing particular interest in the vessel's engines and guns. When the Sheikh disembarked, it fired a five-gun salute in his honour.[12]

After the visit, the British Government agreed to send a political agent to Kuwait. In June 1904, Major Knox was appointed as the first British Agent. When he arrived on 5 August, Sheikh Mubarak personally received him, courteously inviting him to stay temporarily at his palace until he found a suitable residence of his own. Major Knox was soon able to rent a building to serve as the headquarters of the Political Agent. This was in Freij Shamlan, on the coast, on the eastern side of the city. The house now stands opposite the present headquarters of the Kuwaiti Foreign Ministry and is known in Kuwait as the House of Dickson, after Political Agent Dickson who was appointed in 1929.

On 7 September 1904, the duties of the Political Agent in Kuwait were laid down in a letter from the Government of India to the Political Resident in Bushire:

> His main aim is to further and consolidate friendly relations with Sheikh Mubarak and the principal personalities in Kuwait; to ensure British commercial interests in Kuwait and in neighbouring areas; to observe Turkish operations on the borders of Kuwait and to report on any Turkish or other power's intention to interfere or to change the status quo, or on any other development that might indicate the intention of any power to violate the borders of Kuwait.

This letter adds that Major Knox should, 'obtain confidential and precise information about the conflict between the families of Ibn Saud and Ibn Rashid over the control of Najd. The government of India wishes to obtain information about the arms trade in Kuwait and the extent to which weapons are being imported through Kuwait for Ibn Saud.'[13]

Comparison with documents in the Ottoman Archive relating to the appointment of a British Political Agent in Kuwait is illuminating. On 20 October 1904, Fakhri Pasha, the agent of the Governor of Basra, sent a coded telegram to the Sublime Porte saying:

> A British officer called Knox, who used to work in the Indian army, has been sent by the British Government to Kuwait as a political officer, together with eight soldiers from the regular Indian army. He now lives in a house which has been specially allocated to him. He sits in cafes and mixes with people, and interferes in the administrative affairs and business of Kuwait.[14]

The next day, on 21 October 1904, the Ottoman ambassador in London met with the British Foreign Secretary, Lord Landsdowne, to convey this information to him. Landsdowne denied the

Ottoman allegations, responding: 'This is a civilian officer sent by the India government to Kuwait on a temporary basis.' The Foreign Secretary noted the name of the agent and promised to find out more.[15] On 4 November, the ambassador and the Foreign Secretary met once more, and the Ottoman ambassador stressed his government's request that the so-called 'British political officer' be withdrawn immediately. The British Foreign Secretary replied that the Government of India had sent this officer to Kuwait on a temporary basis, to discuss certain specific matters with the Sheikh. The ambassador replied that the situation would be in contravention of international law, whether the officer in question were sent on a temporary or a permanent basis. The Foreign Secretary commented that he had other priorities and interests and that he could not always be concerning himself with Kuwait.[16]

Although the Government of India regarded the appointment of the political agent as permanent, the Foreign Office in London apparently thought of it as temporary. The Ottoman Government was unsatisfied with the situation, since the Sheikh of Kuwait did not have the right to receive diplomatic representatives. In the event, both as a result of the Ottoman protest, and because he was himself indisposed, Major Knox left Kuwait on 19 January 1905 and no one else was appointed in his stead. The management of daily affairs was handled by his assistant, Daoud Al-Rahman, until Knox's return on 25 October 1905. After this, he remained en poste until 1909. He threw himself into his duties. One of his responsibilities was to visit the tribal areas to inspect them and write reports about political and social conditions. In 1904, he went on a tour of the Ottoman borders, visiting Al-Jahra, Sifwan and Umm Qasr. In January 1906, he penetrated as far as the area of Hafar, an area that he was the first European to visit.[17] In March of the same year, he toured the areas south of Kuwait.[18]

There were other agreements between the Sheikh and the British. For example, on 28 February 1904, the Sheikh agreed not to allow any other external government to set up any kind of postal facilities in Kuwait. In a statement, he specified: 'For my part, I agree not to allow any postal office to be established here by any other government. I commit myself and my successors to its undertaking.'[19] On 15 October 1907, the Sheikh agreed to lease an area of land south of Bandar Al-Shuwaykh to the British Government to use as a port for British ships. The lease was signed in exchange for 60,000 rupees a year. This was precisely the same area that Germany had wanted to buy from the Ottoman Empire in 1900, when the Sheikh had obstructed the deal.[20] It is likely that Britain's objective was to prevent any attempt on the part of Germany or the Ottoman authorities to renew the plan to extend the German-built railway project to Kuwait. Abdul Aziz Al-Rashid suggests Sheikh Mubarak's decision was probably also influenced by his apprehension that the Ottomans would occupy that area, as they had already done with the island of Bubyan.[21]

On 23 August 1907, Knox reported to the British Government of India on the details of his talks with Sheikh Mubarak about the lease of the area of land in question. Knox notes that the Sheikh had three reservations. The first of these was his demand that the British Government should endorse the agreement, which should not be made merely at the level of local officials. Second, that the British should not levy any taxes or customs duties within the borders of Kuwait, including the area being leased, reserving to the Sheikh the sole authority to levy and collect taxes. The third was that the Sheikh wished to see the British Government reaffirm its intention not to interfere in Kuwait's internal affairs and its continued wish that the Sheikh should be, 'strong, independent and not responsible to anyone'. The Political Agent advised his superiors to respond swiftly to the Sheikh's stipulations and give him an explicit British mandate to sign the agreement. He added that the ruler of Kuwait and his son, Jaber, had welcomed the agreement, not only for the material profit it would bring them but also, 'as an indicator of the policies that will be followed [by Britain] in the future' and as a guarantee that any railway from Baghdad would be under British control, with its terminus in Bandar Al-Shuwaykh.[22]

A further undertaking given by the Sheikh in response to British pressure was his agreement to halt the slave trade. On 6 September 1910, Percy Cox wrote to the Sheikh to express his regret at having to make an official report of an incident too serious to be ignored. Three Kuwaiti citizens, Salem Tabi' Muhammad ibn Abdullah Al-Hijazi, Muhammad Al-Hawaij and Ahmad bin Muhammad Buzina had transported seven of their servants, including five men and two women, from Kuwait to Dubai to sell them in the slave market. Cox noted that this was contrary to the anti-slavery agreement that the Sheikh had already signed. On 10 September the Sheikh replied, affirming that both he and his subjects abided by all agreements that had been made, 'to prohibit all that is against the law and contrary to the conscience'. He went on to say, however, that the miscreants mentioned in the Political Resident's letter were not from Kuwait and were not his subjects. As he put it: 'We cannot punish those who are not our nationals and who reside in far off countries.' The Sheikh added that he had given orders to officials to be vigilant for any further visit to Kuwait by any of the three named individuals and affirmed that he would inflict punishment upon them were they to be apprehended.[23]

Sheikh Mubarak also granted other concessions to the British. On 29 July 1911 he undertook not to respond to any applications made by other countries to search for pearls or to dive for sponges without consulting the British Political Resident. On 26 July 1912 the Sheikh allowed a wireless telegraph station to be built. On 27 October 1913, at the request of Percy Cox, the British Political Resident, the Sheikh undertook to assign the rights to the exploitation of oil resources in his territories only to those recommended by the British Government. This agreement was part of the so-called 'prohibitive agreements' under which Britain alone had the right to explore and drill for oil. Through this arrangement, Britain sought to prevent other European countries from exploring for oil in Kuwait.[24] At this early stage, Britain had already become aware of the importance of controlling oil. In July

1913 there had been vigorous discussions in the British Parliament relating to the importance of the issue.

After granting oil rights to the British, Sheikh Mubarak agreed to a geological survey to determine where oil might be found. In 1914 Britain sent a delegation of engineers and geologists equipped for the purpose. The Sheikh gave the mission every facility to do its work, delegating his son, Salem, to show the British the existing oil well in the area of Al-Burqan. Salem personally oversaw the necessary arrangements to permit the exploration and excavation to be carried out. The Anglo-Persian Oil Company had already been established in 1909, and it was this company that was granted the subsequent concession to exploit Kuwait's oil resources.[25] Although it was a public company, with private investors, the British Government ensured that it retained a controlling share. The shares owned by the British Government gave it the right to appoint two members on the board of directors. The company's policy was therefore ultimately under the control of the British treasury and the Admiralty Board, the British naval administration.[26]

Knox was succeeded in his post by Captain William Shakespear, who was an accomplished diplomat, an experienced soldier, knowledgeable about education and acquainted with the techniques of geography. He was an expert land surveyor and was able to draw accurate topographical maps. He went on a number of exploratory missions, the most protracted of which took place in 1914, when he traversed the Arabian Peninsula from Kuwait to Riyadh, going on to Jawf, Al-Aqaba and Sinai, and finally reaching Suez in Egypt. He established close relations with Ibn Saud, and was killed in the battle of Jirab against the forces of Ibn Al-Rashid in January 1915.

During all this time, the Ottoman Government was anxiously monitoring the rise of British political influence in Kuwait. Although the Ottoman authorities were unable to exclude Britain's influence or even to contain it, the Ottoman Government nevertheless took care to make its position known, and whenever expedient to register its protests against British activities. One aspect of this was that Istanbul never recognized the Political

Agent, Major Knox, as a diplomatic representative. For example, they refused to extend to him the customs concessions that usually applied to the diplomatic bags of such representatives. Any bag despatched to him was subjected to normal customs inspections on its arrival at the port of Al-Faw, in order to ensure no goods were included on which duty was liable to be paid.[27] They also raised other objections to British activities in Kuwait. For example, at the end of 1904, a memorandum to be found in the Ottoman Archive in Istanbul from the Grand Vizier, Fakhri Pasha, to the Imperial Diwan, presented to the Sultan the memorandum sent by the Ottoman Foreign Minister to the British Government protesting 'the arrival of five British ships in Kuwait and the raising of the British flag in public over the palace of Mubarak Al-Sabah'. It also said: 'If the diplomatic efforts of the Sublime Porte do not have positive results, then international arbitration on this matter will be sought.'[28] Owing to continuing Ottoman objections, which were directed in particular at the presence of a permanent British political agent in Kuwait, negotiations between London and Istanbul resulted in the signing of the Anglo-Ottoman Agreement in 1913. This agreement included the recognition of Anglo-Kuwaiti agreements by the Ottoman authorities as well as the recognition by Britain of Kuwait's legal status as a dependency of the Ottoman Empire. However, owing to the outbreak of World War I on 4 August 1914, the agreement was never ratified.[29]

The onset of war, with the Ottoman Empire and Britain on opposing sides, resulted in a transformation in the political situation in Kuwait. On 18 August 1914, the Political Resident in Bushire officially informed Sheikh Mubarak of the outbreak of war between Britain and Germany. The Sheikh's response came on 21 August. In it, he renewed his support for the British Government, promising that he would deploy his troops to expel the Turkish military from territories and islands belonging to Kuwait, including the islands at the mouth of the Shatt Al-Arab, to which Sheikh Mubarak had a territorial claim. On 3 November 1914 the British Political Resident in Bushire sent a letter to Sheikh Mubarak in which he asked him to co-operate with other Arab sheikhs, particularly with Ibn Saud, the ruler of Najd, and Sheikh Khaz'al, the Sheikh of Al-Muhammara, in order to liberate Basra from Turkish control. The plan was to attack Umm Qasr, Sifwan and Bubyan and to secure British assets in the region protecting British residents in Basra and their property, by preventing Turkish supplies from reaching Basra.[30]

The British proposal included an expression of thanks to the Sheikh of Kuwait for his assistance to Britain, together with a promise not to return Basra back to the Turkish Government and a guarantee that the palm orchards owned by the Sheikh of Kuwait, situated between Al-Faw and Al-Qurna, would remain in the possession of him and his sons and would continue to be exempt from taxes. The British Government also guaranteed to protect the Sheikh of Kuwait from any consequences or effects of any attacks he might undertake against the Ottomans, together with recognition that the 'Sheikdom of Kuwait' would enjoy the status of an independent entity under British protection.[31] Kuwait was included in the area under the control of Force D of the Indian Army campaign in the Gulf. In practice, British and Indian troops occupied Basra on 21 November 1914, after a ten-day campaign. The outcome was total British naval control of the entrance to the Shatt Al-Arab and the headwater of the Gulf. The British imposed their control on the coast of Kuwait in order to tighten their siege of the territory of the Ottoman Empire.

These measures were not undertaken without difficulty for Sheikh Mubarak. He was aware that in throwing in his lot with the British he would meet with resistance from a part of the population of Kuwait. As explained in the previous chapter, Sheikh Khaz'al of Muhammara assisted the British in their operation to occupy Basra, with the result that he had faced a rebellion from some of the tribal people in his territories. When Sheikh Mubarak asked the Kuwaitis to go to Sheikh Khaz'al's aid against those who had rebelled against him, there was resistance in Kuwait to the Sheikh's request. Sheikh Al-Shanqiti and Sheikh

Hafez Wahbah encouraged this reluctance, issuing edicts to the effect that assistance to the Sheikh of Al-Muhammara in these circumstances would be against the teachings of Islam. Sheikh Mubarak reacted with intelligence and diplomacy, declaring that he had not asked them to participate in any fighting, but that they should provide the necessary boats to transport supplies for Sheikh Khaz'al. In response to this explanation, the Kuwaiti people put their boats at Mubarak's disposal.[32]

Sheikh Mubarak took the opportunity of the outbreak of war to reassert his old demands in regard to the borders of Kuwait. His forces besieged the Ottoman garrisons in Sifwan and Umm Qasr, as well as the troops stationed on the southern side of the island of Bubyan. Although the Sheikh's forces were unable to enter Basra, their presence nearby was a factor that helped the British forces that occupied Al-Faw on 6 November 1914 and then marched on to Basra, which was occupied on 22 November. Percy Cox, the British Resident, who accompanied the British expeditionary force on this campaign, informed the Sheikh of this victory so that he could inform the Kuwaiti population. The Sheikh sent a telegram in reply, as follows: 'We are so relieved and are greatly heartened by this joyful news. We have passed on the good tidings to all our subjects, those near and far away, and to all the heads of our loyal tribes. All are utterly pleased and delighted.'[33] The Sheikh sent another telegram on 25 November, expressing the same sentiments and donating 50,000 rupees to a charity for wounded British soldiers.[34] Cox sent a letter to Sheikh Mubarak asking him to specify the date-palm plantations he and his family owned in the neighbourhood of Basra in order to make arrangements to exempt them from tax. Sheikh Mubarak took advantage of this opportunity to resolve the problems raised by previous Ottoman governors of Basra and their refusal to register certain of his properties in the Land Registry in Basra. He wrote to Percy Cox noting the statement made by the Department of Awqaf (religious trusts) in Basra on 13 April 1915 in relation to the issue of land deeds, and asked him to intervene to complete the proper registration of his property.

Once the British were established in Basra, Lord Hardinge, who had become the Viceroy of India in 1901, paid a visit to the Gulf to find out personally what the situation was there and to gain an impression of the views of the various emirs and sheikhs. In January 1915 he visited Bahrain, and took the opportunity to ask the other Gulf rulers to come to Kuwait to meet him. However, owing to the unstable situation that prevailed throughout the Gulf, only Sheikh Hamad bin Issa, the Emir of Bahrain, was able to attend. When Lord Hardinge's naval convoy arrived in Kuwait harbour, Sheikh Jaber boarded his ship to greet him. The next day, Sheikh Mubarak met him and invited him to visit the Kuwait City. Lord Hardinge visited Al-Seif Palace, when Sheikh Mubarak took the opportunity to tell him that the hostility between the sheikhs and the Ottoman authorities was based on pragmatic considerations. As he put it: 'We only became enemies with the Turks, who are Muslims like us, because we fear for our independence.' Then he recited the famous Arab verse: 'He who resorts to Amr in his plight is like he who jumps from the frying pan only to land in the fire.' Mubarak's meaning was that the sheikhs did not simply want to replace one occupier with another. Lord Hardinge, grasping the Sheikh's meaning, replied:

> No, your Highness, the British Government does not covet you or your country. We have only come here to defend you from those who transgress against you. If any representative of the British should behave in a way you do not like, all you have to do is bring the matter to the government's attention and they will give you redress.[35]

French hostility to the British in the Gulf

France did not view the Gulf as a high priority in its foreign policy, nor was it the object of colonial activity. Their efforts were concentrated on the Ottoman provinces in North Africa. Despite this, French diplomatic envoys were active in the Gulf simply in order to curtail British influence. This reflected the competition that existed between the two powers to extend their influence and control. Rivalry between France and Britain continued until the Entente Cordiale was signed in 1904, after which French activity was scaled down. France had first begun to show an interest in the Gulf at the end of the nineteenth century. Their government also established consulates in a number of Gulf emirates, and its navy roamed the ports of the eastern and western shores of the Gulf. In 1898 there was a bitter dispute with Britain over a French attempt to establish a base in the Sultanate of Muscat, and in the same year, the French attempted to negotiate a political co-operation agreement with Sheikh Mubarak.[36]

One of the personalities that played an important role in this was Antonin Goguyer, the French arms dealer, mentioned above. French and British documents reveal that he was not merely a merchant, but enjoyed great influence with the French authorities in the Gulf. He sent them periodic reports about British diplomatic activities and their effects on French interests, with the goal of countering British influence in Kuwait. He published a series of articles in April 1905, in which he indicated that Sheikh Mubarak was always wary of attempts by the British and the Ottomans to interfere in Kuwait's affairs, which the Sheikh sought to obstruct. To counter this, the British sought to drive a wedge between the Sheikh and Goguyer. They accused the latter of being behind an article published by *Al-Ahram* on 16 September 1904, written by its correspondent in Muscat, which included anti-British sentiments. The British Agent in Muscat, Major Grey, accused Goguyer of responsibility for this article, since it contained information on Kuwait that the *Al-Ahram* correspondent in Muscat could not have obtained without having a direct source in Kuwait itself. Major Knox showed the article to the Sheikh, accusing Goguyer of being the source of the information and hoping that this would instill mistrust between the Sheikh and the Frenchman, but he did not succeed.

In November 1904 Goguyer wrote to the Sheikh suggesting that

France and Russia should mediate on his behalf with the Ottoman Sultan in order to resolve the differences between them. However, the Sheikh was not responsive to this suggestion. In his reply, he reminded Goguyer of the hostility of the Ottomans towards him and of their desire to intervene in Kuwait's internal affairs, which in his view was not to be allowed or approved. Goguyer's position, however, was soon to be undermined. On 28 February 1905, Major Knox once more raised with Sheikh Mubarak Goguyer's role in importing weapons into Kuwait. Mubarak denied all knowledge of this, but took the opportunity to inform the British representative that he had issued an order that Goguyer be expelled from Kuwait after writing articles damaging to him.[37]

Germany seeks a foothold

Of the rival European powers, Germany's policy in particular was one of eastward expansion. The main obstacle to this policy was Britain's control over all the routes to India, with the sole exception of that which passed through Turkey and the Arab lands to the Gulf. This led Germany to cultivate closer relations with the Ottoman Empire. The German Emperor declared himself a 'faithful friend' of the Islamic Caliph and sent experts to Istanbul to assist with the reorganization and reform Ottoman administration. In the years leading up to the outbreak of war in 1914, therefore, the Gulf was a theatre for growing economic rivalry between Britain and Germany.[38] In practice, Germany's efforts were concentrated in two principal directions. The first of these was the Berlin–Baghdad Railway project, which was for several years the focus of the Anglo-German conflict. The second was the attempt by German companies to play a greater role in the merchant shipping trade, both from Europe to the Gulf and between the ports of the Gulf itself. Britain believed Germany was seeking to use its shipping lines as an instrument to spread German influence. Lord Curzon remarked that German economic projects would later become the basis of political demands.[39]

In 1899, the same year as the conclusion of the protection agreement between Britain and Kuwait, the Anatolian Railway Company was established, with the support of several German finance companies, to take responsibility for the Berlin–Baghdad Railway project. On 27 November, Sultan Abdul Hamid granted this company the concession to build the extension to the railway that would connect Baghdad with Basra. The German Emperor sent a telegram of thanks to the Ottoman Sultan. Russia's assessment of the Sultan's *firman* was that it was 'a grand victory for German policy'.[40]

In January 1900, a delegation of German surveyors arrived in Baghdad to survey the ground in order to decide what route the railway would take and where its terminus would be located. The delegation was accompanied by the senior German diplomat Paul Graf Wolff Metternich zur Gracht (known to the British as Count Metternich), an adviser to the German Emperor with ambassadorial rank, and by members of the staff of the German embassy in Istanbul including the military attaché. While the delegation was still in Basra, the British Consul, A. C. Wratislaw, met with Metternich and raised with him the question of whether the mission had obtained the agreement of Sheikh Mubarak for the continuation of the railway line to Kuwait. Metternich replied:

> the Anatolian Railway Company would not need the agreement of the Sheikh to extend the Berlin–Baghdad Railway to the region of Kuwait, since German diplomats are able to reach agreement on these matters directly with the Sultan ... the delegation has not yet decided whether it will be necessary to meet with Sheikh Mubarak during its visit to Kuwait, as everything will be decided in Istanbul rather than by him.'[41]

The reality, however, was otherwise, as the German delegation was aware. On 17 January 1900, Metternich was careful to write to Sheikh Mubarak to inform him of the nature of the delegation's work and to express its wish to meet him in the course of its visit to Kuwait.

British documents reveal how interested London was in this mission.[42] On 9 January the British Resident in the Gulf, Colonel Meade, sent a telegram to the Government of India apprising them of the imminent arrival of the German mission in Kuwait. The Government of India replied that they would raise no objection to the German delegation's proposed visit as there were no legal grounds to prevent a German delegation from coming to Kuwait, but added that Colonel Meade should make contact with the Sheikh and emphasize to him that he should refrain from entering into any agreement with the Germans. The following day Meade sent a further telegram to India, to inform the British authorities there that he intended to delegate his assistant, J. C. Gaskin, to travel to Kuwait on HMS *Melpomene* and to deliver a prescribed message to the Sheikh. Together with Captain Denison of the *Melpomene*, Gaskin met the Sheikh on 13 January and warned him against accepting any inducement that might be offered to him by Metternich to persuade him to agree to Kuwait becoming the terminus for the Berlin–Baghdad Railway, stressing to him in addition that he was under an obligation to inform the British authorities of whatever proposal the Germans might make. In response Mubarak said only, 'I will take your recommendations into consideration.' Nevertheless, on 15 January, when the British Resident telegraphed once more to inform the Government of India of the return of the *Melpomene* to Bushire, he was able to report that the Sheikh of Kuwait had undertaken to adhere to the commitments given in the protection agreement.[43]

Gaskin paid several visits to Kuwait in the coming days. First, he returned on 20 January, the day the German delegation left Kuwait, to enquire about what had taken place when the members of the mission had met with the Sheikh. Mubarak wrote a memorandum to the Political Resident detailing what Metternich had requested from him in relation to the proposed railway line, and listed the benefits the Germans had said Kuwait would obtain if the Sheikh gave his agreement. It also transpired that the German had the Sheikh's agreement to the purchase of an area of land to the north of Kuwait known as Kazima. In his note to the Resident, the Sheikh wrote:

> I made no response to his requests. However, I pointed out to him that the project would bring no specific benefit to my people and my tribes, and that I would be unable to agree to something they found unacceptable. He replied that he was aware of my authority over all my subjects, on land and sea, and that, since Kazima lay within my domains, he would undertake to satisfy my wishes and those of my tribe.[44]

On 28 January Gaskin returned once more to gain further information about the German visit. During this visit he spoke to Ali bin Gholoum Rida, a British secret agent in Kuwait, who briefed him thoroughly before he saw Sheikh Mubarak. In the report Gaskin subsequently wrote on 5 February, he recorded the further details Sheikh Mubarak gave him. According to Gaskin's account, the German delegation had sent the Sheikh a letter informing him of their proposed date of arrival and asking for a meeting with him, and had then sent a further letter of confirmation. The delegation had arrived in Kuwait at 1.30 pm on 19 January. During their visit the Sheikh had received its members as his guests. Included in the mission were Count Metternich as the delegation's political leader, Dr Von Kapp (a surveyor for the German state railway system, and effectively the delegation's technical leader), the military attaché Major Morgen and other German members. They were accompanied by Abdul Karim bin Hussein Al-Musharri from Basra. According to Gaskin's account, no Ottoman representative came with them, and they carried no letter of authority from the Sublime Porte or from the governors of Baghdad or Basra. They did have a letter of introduction from the Ottoman military commander in Baghdad, which read as follows: 'The Consul General of the German Empire has come to undertake a survey for the construction of a railway. His visit to you is part of his mission. Treat him with respect, so that he will praise you.'[45]

The report states that the delegation met Sheikh Mubarak immediately after their arrival. The Sheikh received them again the same evening, with several Kuwaiti notables in attendance. It goes on to say that Count Metternich informed the Sheikh that the purpose of the project was to construct a railway line with a terminus in Kuwait, and that if this were to be brought to fruition, Kuwait would experience an era of economic prosperity, trade would flourish and there would be general benefits for the population. The following morning the members of the mission met Sheikh Mubarak alone, wherupon they told him they had been given the concession to build the railway by the Sultan himself, and that he had guaranteed that they would be able to construct it as they intended. They also explained that they had chosen Kazima as the location for the terminus, and requested the Sheikh to sell the railway company the specified area and also to lease to the company an area of land adjacent to it.

The delegation was keen to gain the Sheikh's confidence, informing him that they had been charged with the duty of conveying to him the greetings of the German ambassador, and had been instructed to discuss with him the purchase of the necessary land. They added that they were looking forward to his aid and assistance and that they hoped the Sheikh would lend his good offices in negotiations with the other sheikhs on the banks of the Euphrates on whose land, or on adjacent land, the railway was to be built. In order to offer sufficient inducement to the Sheikh to enlist his co-operation, the members of the mission assured him that a high price would be paid for any land that might be purchased or leased from him, promising him that Kuwait would become a prominent commercial centre. 'Kuwait', they said, could become 'another Bombay' and they indicated that the Sheikh's private income would be enhanced. They also pointed out that the value of land in Kuwait would rise and that there would be widespread opportunities for employment. Maritime trade would prosper, with larger vessels coming to the port of Kuwait to unload their cargo for onward transit by train.

Although the Anglo-Kuwaiti protection agreement was still secret, it had been noticed in diplomatic circles that a special relationship had developed between Sheikh Mubarak and the British. For this reason, the German delegation did not fail to indicate to the Sheikh that if he agreed to their offer they would guarantee German support by land and sea, to him and to his heirs, and that a German gunboat would be sent to protect Kuwait. The Sheikh, however, was keen not to upset either the Ottomans or the British. He therefore showed reluctance to accept the German offer, replying that the delegation had been able to show him a signed letter endorsing their mission from the Sultan, whom, he stressed, was the caliph of all Muslims and the titular head of the Islamic world. The Sheikh sought to underline the spiritual and moral bond that linked all Muslims to him. He explained that his loyalty to the Sultan as caliph was distinct from any political considerations, despite the fact that he did not consider himself an Ottoman subject and did not recognize Ottoman sovereignty over Kuwait.

In addition, the Sheikh pointed out that as an Arab, like others of his kind, he was reluctant to allow foreigners any foothold in Arab lands. He made it clear to the delegation that other Arab sheikhs would also refuse to give up their lands for a foreign railway, and he said they could not guarantee the safety of the line or the lives of those travelling on it. The Arabs of the region were free and independent, and no one could exercise any power over them. His own authority was limited to Kuwait. In conclusion, the delegation said it would return to Istanbul to consider its position and promised to return to Kuwait to make the Sheikh a final offer. Mubarak told Gaskin that the members of the mission had offered him gifts, but that he had refused these with the excuse that he did not accept gifts from guests.[46]

The German documents give a different impression of these events. According to a letter sent by Metternich to Karl Richard, the German consul in Baghdad, for onward transmission by telegraph to Berlin, the reception the German delegation enjoyed in Kuwait was described as 'a real welcome'. He reported that his conversation with Sheikh Mubarak had left him with the impression that the Sheikh had no objection in principle to the idea of building a railway, but that he was not able to discuss the matter of leasing Kuwaiti land. Metternich said that the Sheikh had been critical of the Turks for not appreciating him as they should, because he had done so much to support the Ottoman Empire while receiving only ingratitude in return. Despite this, Metternich reported, the Sheikh was careful in what he said about the Ottoman Sultan. Metternich noted that Sheikh Mubarak, 'spoke of the Sultan with enormous tribute and respect, acknowledging him as his overlord and spiritual master'.[47] He also reported that he felt the Sheikh had been careful not to show any partiality towards Britain.

Russian documents reveal that the Russian consul in Baghdad, Kruglov, visited Kuwait in March 1900, after the German mission. During his visit, Sheikh Mubarak told him that German engineers had selected Kazima as the terminus for the Baghdad–Berlin Railway, but that he had rejected their offer diplomatically by saying to them: 'We are simple Bedouins, we do not plant and cultivate orchards and we have no income; why therefore do we need this railway in the middle of the desert?' Kruglov added that, on the basis of his conversations with other observers, he had come to the conclusion that Mubarak did not welcome the German delegation's visit and that he would not agree to this project.[48]

German anxiety over British activities in Kuwait continued, as did British concern at what was seen as German intrusion. On 3 September 1901, Count Metternich, who had now been promoted to the position of German ambassador in London, wrote to the British Foreign Office to the effect that if the British Government were to prevent the Ottoman Sultan, by threats or by force, from landing troops in Kuwait, this would amount to a refusal to recognize the Sultan's authority. The ambassador pointed out that the British Government, in a memorandum sent by the King to the German Emperor at the time of the Congress of Berlin in 1878, had previously recognized the authority of the Ottoman Sultan and had confirmed that Britain had no wish to interfere in the affairs of the Gulf.[49] Germany endorsed the Ottoman view of Kuwait, viewing it as a province of the Ottoman Empire whose ruler was subject to the orders and instructions of the Ottoman authorities. It therefore refused to recognize the validity of any agreements that might have been signed between Sheikh Mubarak and the British Government on the grounds that the Sheikh had no legal right to sign such agreements. It also regarded the establishment of a British garrison in Kuwait as an unfriendly act that contravened the terms agreed at the Congress of Berlin.

On 9 September the British Foreign Secretary sent a letter to his German counterpart emphasizing Britain's past commitments regarding Kuwait and London's agreement to the maintenance of the status quo:

> His Majesty's government ... did not wish to interfere with the Sultan's current authority as it currently stands. There is no doubt that this authority is very limited, but the Sheikh belongs to a class of tribal leaders and sheikhs who enjoy a great deal of practical independence. His Majesty's government has therefore found that a direct relationship with him is necessary for preserving the calm and protecting British commerce ... Despite London being prepared to preserve the status quo, his Majesty's government cannot accept Turkey's attempts to impose conditions on the Sheikh at a time when he is so far independent from them. The issue has consequently been the subject of a direct and friendly discussion with the Sultan, who considers the matter to be resolved, and Count Metternich has been informed of the guarantees that have been exchanged.[50]

In subsequent correspondence, the German foreign ministry revealed Kuwait's importance to Germany as the designated terminus for the Berlin–Baghdad Railway. The ministry said that it undertook to instruct the railway company to reach an understanding with the British Government at an appropriate time regarding the purchase of the land required for the aforementioned terminus, and to unload the required materials in Kuwait. The British response indicated that Britain would not object to Kuwait being the terminus for the railway, but on condition that this was preceded by discussions between the two governments, owing to the special relationship Britain had with Kuwait. Soon afterwards, Count Metternich confirmed this guarantee to the British Foreign Secretary, Lord Landsdowne, adding that the railway could be built within the coming five years but might be delayed until 50 years in the future, or indefinitely. The important consideration, from Germany's point of view, was that the situation was stable in that part of the Gulf when work began.[51]

Meanwhile, on 11 September 1901, Lord Landsdowne sent a letter to the Ottoman ambassador in London confirming Britain's adherence to the commitments given in the past on preserving the status quo. 'It pleases me to confirm,' he wrote, 'the guarantee given to your excellency by his Majesty's ambassador in Istanbul, on condition that the Turkish government does not send troops to Kuwait and respects the status quo there. In return, his Majesty's government will not occupy the place or establish a British garrison there.' It is noteworthy that he gave these guarantees more than two years after the 1899 protection agreement was signed.

A decade later, in 1913, the Berlin–Baghdad Railway project was the subject of one of the clauses in the Anglo-Ottoman agreement concluded on 29 July in that year. In clause eight of the agreement, Britain agreed to the extension of the railway to the Gulf and for the line to end either in Kuwait or at any other place that might be agreed in the future. Britain also agreed to allow customs offices to be set up, together with any other administrative departments and institutions that might be related to the construction of this line. It seems that the British Government had accepted by this time the economic significance of a railway line and was anxious to ensure that Britain had a role in building it. At the same time as agreement was reached with the Ottomans, the British also entered into talks with Germany, the outcome of which was that Britain agreed that the construction of the line in the area south of Basra would be accomplished under an agreement between the British and German governments. Britain would contribute 40 per cent of the financial cost of the construction, while two British representatives were to be included on the board of the company.

In the first decade of the twentieth century, merchant shipping was a subject of concern to Britain. In 1899, in parallel to German efforts to construct the railway, German ships began to appear in the Gulf. One of the first was a German light cruiser, *Arkona*, which made its appearance in the Gulf in January 1900 in conjunction with the German technical mission to survey likely locations for the Berlin–Baghdad Railway. George Mackenzie, one of the owners of the British-India Steam Navigation Company, wrote a report for the Government of India in which he noted that the German East Africa Steam Company intended to organize voyages to the ports of the Gulf. Mackenzie asked that the routes covered by his own company's ships should be extended to Kuwait to establish their presence in the area before the Germans gained a foothold. He also asked them to obtain the Sheikh's approval.[52] When this was proposed to Sheikh Mubarak he at first agreed, but then withdrew his approval for fear that international quarantine measures would be extended to Kuwait. The Sheikh proposed that the British-India Steam Navigation Company should use the port of Kuwait without the introduction of a quarantine facility. This was, however, not practicable, since without a properly organized quarantine area, ships leaving Kuwait would not be allowed to enter the port of Basra.[53]

The German commercial merchant marine company Wonckhaus was active in shipping in Gulf ports, its main centre being Bahrain, and was one of the companies involved in the construction of the Berlin–Baghdad Railway. Its steam ships competed with those of Messrs Lynch, the British company that had hitherto taken the main part in transporting cargo between the Gulf and Europe. British diplomatic reports contain many indications of the commercial challenges posed by Wonckhaus to British interests.[54] In September 1905 Herr Bahnson, the representative of the company, visited Kuwait to discuss what was described as 'the commercial situation'. According to Lorimer, however, 'the Sheikh did not allow him to stay for long'.[55] Robert Wonckhaus, representing his company, went to Kuwait in 1907 to meet Sheikh Mubarak, proposing to him that he should use the German company for the shipping of goods. The Sheikh replied that his subjects had been accustomed for some time to dealing with the British shipping company.[56]

The Russian search for warm-water ports

Tsarist Russia wanted access to warm-water ports, and by whatever means might be appropriate. In December 1898 the Ottoman Government awarded Count Vladimir Kapnist, a leading Russian business magnate and brother of the Russian ambassador to the Austro-Hungarian Empire, the concession to build a railway connecting Tripoli on the Mediterranean with Kuwait, via Homs and Damascus, with branches reaching Baghdad and Khaniqayn.[57] This followed Russian efforts to gain a foothold in Iran, which resulted in the establishment of a number of economic projects, the exchange of military visits, the opening of Russian consulates and the despatch of medical missions. The British position was clear. London strove to put pressure on Iran to resist the blandishments of the Russians and to warn Teheran against conceding any port on the Gulf to the Russians.

The planned railway concession made British officials anxious, and they followed its construction in every detail. Foremost among British officials expressing concern was Lord Curzon, the Viceroy of India. Even before he was appointed to the post, he had already become aware of the potential danger to British interests from

Russian influence in the Gulf. In his book, *Persia and the Persian Question*, published in 1892, he had already indicated that he considered the littoral of the Gulf region to be a closed British area, where no other power should be allowed to establish a commercial or maritime base. His belief was that if any other power were to obtain a port on the Gulf, this would be a threat to Britain. He added that, in his view, while the establishment of a Russian port on the Gulf 'was be the dream of zealous nationalists from the Volga', the establishment of any such port would be a factor tending to cause turmoil in the Gulf and to disrupt the balance of power that had been established by Britain after much effort.[58]

This view was reflected in Lord Curzon's actions as the Viceroy of India, and in the policies he recommended that Britain should adopt towards Russia's efforts to obtain maritime facilities in the Gulf.[59] An indication of the conviction with which Curzon held this position was his comment that the signature of the protection agreement with Britain by Kuwait was a great achievement and a blow to the Russians. When the Russian railway project was drawn to the attention of Sultan Abdul Hamid II, he referred it to the Ottoman minister for public works, asking that it should be studied and a report be written. At the same time, the Russians also discussed the proposal that a shipping line be opened through the Gulf to be administered by the Black Sea Shipping Company.[60] The Russian Government appointed its own specialists to carry out surveys of the Gulf ports. On 19 January 1900, S. N. Syromyatnikov, a journalist and adventurer with close connections to the Russian royal family, visited Bushire and went on to Baghdad the following month. He arrived in Kuwait on 12 August.

Kuwait was of interest to the Russians because of its potential for use as a storage station for coal. The British concluded that the Russians were planning to use Kuwait as the principal port for Russian ships in the Gulf, particularly as Russia already had a presence on the Persian side of the Gulf coast. This was in part what led the British to accept Sheikh Mubarak's proposal of a protection agreement.

The Russians understood the importance of Kuwait's location, and despatched a series of envoys to compile reports. These purported to be engaged in commerce or to be concerned with public-health issues, but in fact were Russian government agents who were also in touch with the Ottoman authorities in Basra and Istanbul. The purpose of their visits was to befriend the Sheikh of Kuwait and gain his confidence and support, and to inform him of Russia's anxiety over the increased British activity in Kuwait. Their method was to offer help of every description, in the name of the Russian Government, to enable Sheikh Mubarak to preserve his independence, and to reassure him that the Russian Tsar was anxious to assist him. After news of the Anglo-Kuwaiti protection agreement was leaked to the Russians, they feared that it could frustrate their plans, including Count Kapnist's railway project. Russia accused the British Government of violating the status quo policy in the Gulf. Meanwhile, for their part, the British objected to Kapnist's project and considered it a threat to their interests and influence.

In March 1899, the Russian consul in Baghdad, Kruglov, instructed Artine Ovansian, an Armenian resident of Baghdad who had taken Russian nationality, to go to Kuwait on the pretext of purchasing wool. Together with another merchant named Abbas Aliiev, Ovansian visited Kuwait and met Sheikh Mubarak, who expressed great interest in international developments and in the implications of the Russian railway project. From such visits the Russians gained direct knowledge of Kuwaiti affairs.[61] The first years of the twentieth century witnessed Russian diplomatic and military activity on a remarkable level. The archives of the Soviet Navy in Leningrad reveal the entry of Russian ships into the Gulf area and of their visits to several of its cities, including Kuwait.[62]

In March 1900 the coastguard ship *Gilyak*, carrying Kruglov and his deputy Ovseyenko, the Russian representative in Bushire, visited a number of Gulf ports. In preparation for his visit to Kuwait, Kruglov contacted the Naqib of Basra to ensure the ship would be well received in Kuwait. The Naqib informed Kruglov that he had already received a letter from Sheikh Mubarak to let him know that he would give his Russian guests the warmest welcome. On 16 March, when the Russian ship arrived in Kuwait, Sheikh Jaber greeted the Russians at the quayside and in due course Sheikh Mubarak received them at his palace. He told them that he had returned from the desert especially in order to see them, and that the captain of the British ship *Sphinx* had attempted to persuade him to stay where he was and refrain from celebrating their arrival, but that he had not taken this advice. The captain of the *Sphinx* claimed that the Russians intended to occupy Kuwait.[63]

According to Russian diplomatic records, the Sheikh took the opportunity in his meeting with the visiting Russians to criticize Britain and its diplomacy. He revealed to the Russians the pressure to which he was being subjected by the British to approve the inauguration of a regular line between Kuwait and the other Gulf ports and Bombay, to be operated by the British-India Steam Navigation Company. Russian documents also reveal that the Sheikh's men told the delegation that the Sheikh had discovered there were many reasons not to trust the British diplomats.

This contrast provides an illustration of Sheikh Mubarak's diplomatic practice. His objective was to balance skilfully his relations with the British and the Ottomans in order to safeguard his independence. He saw in Russia a potential ally that could be of assistance to him. The Sheikh did not merely meet their delegation; he invited them to his palace and arranged a hunting trip for them, though this did not actually take place because they were obliged to leave immediately and continue their journey. When the Sheikh discovered that the Russian consul's intention was to return to Basra over land, he arranged a caravan and ordered a special guard to accompany him. Upon Kruglov's return to Baghdad, he and Mubarak exchanged letters of thanks and friendship.

In March 1901, Ovseyenko asked the merchant Abbas Aliiev to return to Kuwait and report on the latest developments in the military confrontations between Mubarak's forces and those of Ibn Al-Rashid. Because the Sheikh was absent from the city owing to his involvement in the fighting outside Kuwait, Aliiev left him a letter conveying his regards. On Mubarak's return, he sent an envoy to Basra with a letter asking Aliiev to visit Kuwait as soon as possible for what he described as a 'very important reason'. Aliiev returned to Kuwait and had a further meeting with the Sheikh, who sent him back to Basra with letters for Kruglov and Ovseyenko. These letters included expressions of friendship and affection such as, 'I am your faithful friend to such a great extent as you cannot imagine' and indicated that the Sheikh was ready, 'to undertake with pleasure whatever your country needs'. Aliiev also conveyed a verbal message to Kruglov and Ovseyenko to the effect that Mubarak was asking for Russian protection and was prepared, as he put it, 'to let the Russians take the necessary measures to ensure the security of Kuwait, and if need be to raise the Russian flag over Kuwaiti lands which have belonged to the Al-Sabah since ancient times, independently and untrammelled by any agreements'.

Kruglov and Ovseyenko naturally wished to verify this message, which had been conveyed to them verbally, and to try and secure its contents in writing. On 23 April, therefore, Aliiev returned to Kuwait for a third time. However, Sheikh Mubarak felt unable to do more than to give him a letter for Kruglov to the effect that he could not set down all his ideas in writing as he feared that a written letter could be used against him in the future. Mubarak emphasized the independence of Kuwait, writing that only the obligation to maintain good relations linked him to Turkey. At the close of this letter, he referred to Kruglov's visit.

> When you honoured us by coming to visit last year, and it was what I wished for, I offered you service and favour for the love of your imperial country and its good reputation, and because of the way your country treats anyone who works with them with faithfulness and respect. I have also told your honour by word of mouth that I cannot continue without your attention. Now, with this letter, I hope that your attention will fall on us.

Kruglov believed he understood Mubarak's letter. The Russian consul sent a report to the Russian foreign ministry in which he said: 'The Sheikh of Kuwait is asking for our protection.' On 10 May, Kruglov sent a further report about the situation in Kuwait, and about his meeting with the Sheikh's agent in Baghdad, who had also asked for Russian protection and had offered to raise the Russian flag over Kuwait. Kruglov was anxious to enhance Russia's position in Kuwait. In June 1901 he wrote a report in which he said:

> We are facing fact and a new historical reality. There exists a request, relating to our policy, which requires immediate assessment and a prompt response. This is demanded from us by Sheikh Mubarak, an Emir who is independent and wealthy, and is the Arab owner of the bay of Al-Qurayn, the key to the desert of Arabia as well as to the Tigris and Euphrates Valleys. The Emir has up to now successfully defended his country and freedom from his enemies, be it the British or the Turks, who have long been aware of the importance of Kuwait.

Kruglov went on to urge his government to come off the fence and to cease to limit itself to the role of observer in the Gulf and Kuwait, saying it was necessary to be diplomatically active in order to confront the British, German and Turkish plans to control Kuwait.[64]

There were wide-ranging discussions in the Russian foreign ministry about the Sheikh's approach, how serious it might be and what would be the consequences of accepting it. The ministry officials concluded that the best course was not to interfere in Kuwait in any form, because of the multitude of unknown factors in the situation there. Russia had no wish to enter into a direct clash with Britain in the Gulf. Added to this were Russia's doubts about the seriousness of the Sheikh's request, especially in light of the knowledge they had acquired of the protection agreement signed with Britain. However, Russia did not wish entirely to sever its relations with the Sheikh. The Russian foreign ministry therefore instructed Adamov, the Russian consul in Basra, to inform the Sheikh that the Russians would, 'always use our influence in Istanbul to defend his legitimate interests and any demands he may make to the Turkish government. We will not allow the latter to infringe upon the independence Kuwait enjoys.' Russian diplomats also took this opportunity to give advice to the Sheikh not to ruin his relations with Turkey and warned him to be wary of the British, whose aim they said was to gain control over the whole Gulf coast.[65]

In September 1901 the *Varyag* arrived in the Gulf to tour a number of Gulf ports. *Varyag*, which had been built and launched that same year, was one of the most modern and powerful cruisers in the world. With a tonnage of 6,500 tonnes, it was equipped with 34 rapid-firing guns and six torpedo launchers. Its crew numbered 570. This made it a symbol of the technological advancement and strength of the Russian Navy. Ovseyenko, who accompanied the cruiser on its tour, wrote that it impressed the people of the Gulf with its size and the power of its lights. Another, perhaps surprising factor, was the performance of the ship's orchestra, the likes of which had never been seen before in the region. What the people of the Gulf most enjoyed was that the Russian authorities allowed them to board the cruiser and to see it from the inside, and that the Russian sailors were so welcoming.[66]

According to Russian documents, the aim of sending the *Varyag* was: 'to indicate to the international authorities and to local rulers, by showing the Russian flag in these waters, that we regard these waters to be open to the ships of all nations, in contrast with the ambitions of the British government, which wishes to turn the Arab Gulf into a closed sea, reserved exclusively for its own interests'.[67] The orders of the Admiral in Chief of the Russian Navy to the ship's captain were that he should be cautious and prudent, and that it was imperative that he gain the friendship of local inhabitants, explaining to them that Russia's intentions were not aggressive and that Russia had no wish to steal their land.

The cruiser reached Kuwait on 8 December 1901. According to the captain's report, Sheikh Jaber boarded the cruiser to welcome its crew. He brought a gift of ten sheep and told the Russians that Sheikh Mubarak was once more absent from Kuwait, leading his troops against an attack by Abdul Aziz bin Rashid, who had advanced his own forces to Al-Jahra and had, at the instigation of the Ottomans, stationed men on the borders of Kuwait. The following day, Ovseyenko and his companions travelled on horseback to meet Sheikh Mubarak in Al-Jahra, 'where he welcomed them himself with much warmth and hospitality. He showed them his troops in the army base and put on dances and equestrian military displays in honour of his guests. Moreover, he asked us to convey in his name that he would be very pleased if Russian ships came to visit his possessions as often as possible, and that he would prefer, were hard times to fall on Kuwait, to ask for help from the Russians rather than from any other country.'[68] When the Russian party enquired about the extension of the railway line to Kuwait, the Sheikh said that no work had been carried out on this project and that he was in any case against it.

The author of the report noticed trenches that had been dug by the Sheikh's fighters for protection, noting that they were similar to the trenches used by Russian infantry. The observation reveals the admiration the Russian officers had for Kuwait's use of military techniques similar to those used by European armies, especially as, 'it seemed there were no European advisors'. The report also noted the absence of any evidence of overt British influence in Kuwait, remarking on only two exceptions. In one case, a Persian resident had opened a bakery, with British help, in order to sell goods to the passengers on board British ships visiting Kuwait. The other instance was the presence of a commercial agent for the British-India Steam Navigation Company, who had been appointed in July 1901 to supervise the arrival of the company's ships, which by December of that year came to Kuwait regularly every two weeks.[69]

In Ovseyenko's report of his conversation with the ruler of Kuwait, he indicates that Mubarak, 'asked us, in an emotional manner, to convey to the Russian government his deep gratitude for the honour they had conferred on him by sending a naval cruiser to Kuwait and to confirm that he wanted to see as many Russian visits to Kuwait as possible ... When he bade me farewell, Sheikh Mubarak reminded me yet again of the request he had made, which he had expressed more than once, to see merchant ships with Russian goods and commodities in Kuwait.' Ovseyenko also noted the warm welcome given by the Sheikh and his family to the Russian sailors and the goodwill of the people towards them. He commented that he believed the Sheikh was sincere, and that he really was hoping to strengthen his economic and political ties with Russia.[70]

British documents present a different picture. The British were anxious to know what had taken place in the encounter between Sheikh Mubarak and his foreign visitors. The Sheikh, however, was reluctant to reveal his thinking. As soon as the *Varyag* sailed away, Captain Simmons, the senior British naval commander in the Gulf, called on the Sheikh in order to discover what had passed between him and the Russians. He was unable to obtain a full account, and on 31 December 1901 the Political Resident in the Gulf, Charles Kemball, was sent to Kuwait to find out more.

Mubarak related that the Russian Consul had told him the Russian Government was ready to sign an agreement that would be more advantageous to him than the one between Kuwait and Britain. However, he said he had rejected the offer because Russia had supported Belgian activities in Persia, and had given its support to the installation of Belgian administrators in the Iranian customs service. He particularly objected to the Belgian presence in Al-Muhammara. When Ovseyenko had told him that the Belgian administration in Al-Muhammara was no different to its presence in other Persian cities, Sheikh Mubarak replied that Sheikh Khaz'al, the ruler of Al-Muhammara, was not like any other ruler. The Sheikh also said that Ovseyenko had assured him that the Russian Government regarded him as an independent ruler, and that if he needed help, he should write to him in Bushire.

Nevertheless, the Sheikh confirmed to Kemball that he had told the Russian representative that he preferred British protection. Ovseyenko had suggested that Sheikh Mubarak write a letter of thanks for the Russian visit to the Tsar, but he had declined the suggestion.[71]

The disparity between the Russian and British accounts demands closer examination. None of the reports written by Russians who were present at the meeting with Sheikh Mubarak, including military men and diplomats, refer to the statements allegedly made by the Sheikh in the British documents. The source of the British documents, however, was the Sheikh himself. The disparity, therefore, appears to be explicable as a manifestation of the Sheikh's willingness to exploit the prevailing differences of interest between Britain, Russia and the Ottoman Empire in order to gain advantages for Kuwait and to maintain his independence.

In the spring of 1902 a visit was paid to the Gulf by the Russian zoologist, N. V. Bogoyavlensky, who was a member of the Moscow Society of Naturalists. His itinerary included Al-Muhammara, Kuwait, Bahrain and Muscat. On 23 March, Ovseyenko sent a letter to Mubarak to inform him of the scientist's impending visit and to let him know that he was working on a study of marine animals in the Gulf. Ovseyenko asked the Sheikh to give the visitor whatever assistance he needed in his research and to rent a house for him during his stay in Kuwait, which was expected to last four or five days. On 18 April 1902, Bogoyavlensky arrived in Kuwait to carry out his research. Sheikh Mubarak was in the desert at the time, but the visitor was, as was becoming customary, received by Sheikh Jaber 'with the warmest welcome' and housed in the Sheikh's palace. On being informed of Bogoyavlensky's arrival by Sheikh Jaber, Sheikh Mubarak came back to Kuwait to greet him, and he also returned four days later to bid him farewell.

According to Bogoyavlensky's own report to Ovseyenko, sent on 14 June, Sheikh Mubarak spoke to him as follows: 'I consider the Russians to be my brothers. I am very pleased to receive their visits and I am always prepared to offer them as much assistance as I am able. Please convey to Mr. Ovseyenko, the Russian general consul in Bushire, who I consider to be my brother, my greetings and tell him of my wish to correspond with him.' In his second meeting with Sheikh Mubarak, the Russian scientist thanked the Sheikh for the hospitality he had received and asked how he could return the favour. The Sheikh replied: 'Only one thing: inform His Majesty the Emperor that I am a friend to the Russians and that I consider them to be my brothers.'[72] It is noteworthy, however, that on the day after Bogoyavlensky's arrival in Kuwait the Sheikh sent the British Political Agent a brief note of such information as he had gleaned about the Russian visitor together with a copy of Ovseyenko's letter of recommendation.

Although the Russians had not succeeded in gaining Sheikh Mubarak's support for the Berlin–Baghdad Railway project, this did not discourage them from contacting him again. The Russian consuls in Bushire, Basra and Baghdad visited Kuwait and regularly met with the Sheikh. These visits were assiduously monitored by the British authorities, and British ships tracked the movements of Russian naval vessels in the Gulf. Reports by the captains of Russian ships that visited Kuwait confirm that as they arrived they would find either that a British ship was already anchored in the port, or that the Royal Navy was aware of their movements. Bogoyavlensky's visit to Kuwait and his activities were monitored like the rest. A report to Lord Curzon noted that Bogoyavlensky was seen taking photographs in Kuwait.

Visits by Russian naval ships to Kuwait continued, including that of the cruiser *Askold*, which arrived on 28 November 1902 with the Russian consul in Basra, A. Adamov. He was greeted by a representative of Mubarak, who informed him that the Sheikh had decided to travel to Al-Jahra but had changed his mind when he heard of the arrival of the cruiser. Sheikh Jaber and his son, Ahmad, then arrived at the quayside to welcome the crew of the cruiser and were invited to inspect the Russian vessel's guns and other weaponry. Sheikh Mubarak sent a gift of three calves and ten sheep. The Russians reciprocated by giving the Sheikh and his son a handgun and a hunting rifle. The *Askold's* crew, Adamov reported, were appreciative of the warm welcome given to them by the Sheikh, and he expressed his joy to see the Russian cruiser in the port of Kuwait. The Sheikh appeared to echo his earlier statements with an assurance that in future he would also offer his warmest hospitality to all Russian ships, 'be they military vessels or merchant ships'. The Sheikh also reportedly expressed his regret that Russian merchant ships did not come regularly to Kuwait as they already did to several other Gulf ports. A report noted optimistically that the Sheikh knew very well that, 'the value of Kuwait city lay in its being the closest port to the Baghdad railway, which is under development'.[73]

Adamov added that Mubarak showed great interest in the Berlin–Baghdad Railway and asked about the latest news published on it in European newspapers. Adamov went on to say that in his opinion, the Sheikh, 'would not hesitate to take advantage of this situation when it comes to the final resolution of the issue'. Adamov told Mubarak that the newspapers had published news of the British Government's intention to concede to the Germans the port of Kazima so that it can be used as a terminus for the railway. Reportedly, this infuriated Mubarak, who said that he alone would take decisions on Kuwait's affairs, and took the opportunity to reaffirm his interest in developing his relations with Russia on all issues. A few days later the Sheikh met the captain of a British destroyer that had been despatched to Kuwait to report on the visit of the Russian cruiser and on the contacts between the Russians and the Sheikh. When Mubarak did not refer at all to the Russian visit, the British expressed surprise.[74] The Sheikh's silence was deliberate, intended to give an air of mystery to what had passed between Mubarak and his Russian visitors. The Sheikh used this occasion to influence the British. He sent a letter to the Assistant Political Resident in January 1903 complaining about the lack of urgency the British were showing towards giving Kuwait the necessary military assistance in its conflict with Ibn Al-Rashid and the Ottomans.

Oddly, Wratislaw, the British consul in Basra, reported on the basis of what he had gleaned from his secret sources in Kuwait that Sheikh Mubarak had refused the invitation of the captain of the *Askold* to board the ship and inspect it. In contrast, Russian documents indicate that the captain had not extended such an invitation to the Sheikh in order not to embarrass him, as he knew the Sheikh did not wish to be seen to be on too close terms with his Russian visitors.

Although the discussions between the Sheikh and the Russians during the *Askold* visit did not cover any specific political topics, Mubarak and his entourage started a rumour that the negotiations had touched on some significant proposals. This reached the ears of the British, who sought to verify the information through their agents in Kuwait. Their efforts failed, however, due to the silence of the Sheikh and his son Jaber. On 18 January 1903, therefore, Kemball hastened to Kuwait to discover what he could for himself.

On 5 March 1903 the Russian cruiser *Boyarin* visited Kuwait, accompanied by the French vessel *Infernet*. The presence of the French vessel was a reflection of the level of co-operation between Russia and France in the region at the time. Sheikh Sabah bin Mubarak went on board the cruiser, accompanied by Sheikh Ahmad bin Jaber, to welcome the Russians in Sheikh Mubarak's name and to agree on a time for the consul and the ship's officers to visit him. The Sheikh received them at his palace in the city. When the subject of the Berlin–Baghdad Railway arose, the Sheikh made very clear his objection to the line reaching as far as Kuwait. Asked about his view of the British plan to build a road from Port Said to Kuwait, he answered diplomatically that, 'if this road were to be built by Britain and France then he would most likely not object to it'. A member of the delegation who had met the Sheikh before noticed that he had not changed much in the past three years, recording that, 'he gives the impression that he is a man who knows his own value and status very well'.[75]

Of course, British officials were far from happy about these exchanges. Their anxiety was further aggravated when the Russians also contacted Emir Abdul Aziz Al-Rashid and Emir Abdul Aziz bin Saud after the latter captured Riyadh.[76] This was part of the so-called 'game of nations' experienced by Kuwait and the other Gulf states at the end of the nineteenth and the beginning of the twentieth centuries. It was a time of alliances, conflicts and rivalries between the great European powers on the one hand, whose goal was to spread their influence, and the Ottoman Empire on the other, which remained the nominal sovereign power. Sheikh Mubarak's concern was to manipulate the relationships between Kuwait and all these conflicting factions in such a way as to best protect the independence of Kuwait and maintain its borders.

Conclusion

———◆◆◆———

S heikh Mubarak combined a warrior's bold instincts with the sagacity of a politician. He possessed the attributes of a man of war, such as strength of will, determination and decisiveness, together with the statesmanlike qualities of intelligence, flexibility, vision and prudence. He was ambitious, and could be ruthless, but he hitched his ambitions to a vision for the development of Kuwait as an independent political entity and the enhancement of its economic and commercial standing.

This book has attempted to show that Sheikh Mubarak's management of Kuwait's international relations was conducted in such a way as to safeguard the country's independence. Although he entered into an agreement with the British Government, the British were not able to impose their policies upon him. He was careful to maintain his connection with the Ottoman Empire and to establish relations with other European powers. Prudence brought him closer to the British, since Britain was the power with political hegemony over the Gulf. But when British policies conflicted with the interests of Kuwait and the Sheikh's independence as Kuwait's ruler, he kept his distance from them.

The British diplomatic correspondence on Kuwait reveals a number of instances in which the Sheikh did not respond positively to British demands, or where he concealed news of his movements and communications from them or even circulated false information in order to influence British policy. One such example was his resistance to British pressure between 1899 and 1900 to obtain the concession for a direct shipping line between Kuwait and India, though he had to change his position on this after the battle of Al-Sarif in 1901.[1] In September 1901 he objected to the British demand that he should fly a specifically Kuwaiti flag over his palace instead of the Ottoman flag. Another instance was his rejection of Major Knox's request to be allowed to raise the British flag over the shipping agency headquarters, a request to which he finally acceded to only in 1907 after a great deal of insistence.[2]

In March 1908, the Sheikh rejected a request to set up a British quarantine agency in Kuwait.[3] In the same year, he refused Knox's demand that passengers of a ship belonging to a British commercial shipping company be allowed to bypass quarantine. When Knox threatened that the company would halt its regular trips to Kuwait, the Sheikh simply replied that he had never asked for the establishment of a shipping line to his country. In 1911, the Sheikh removed the quarantine facility established by Political Agent Shakespear.[4]

After the battle of Al-Sarif in 1901, the Sheikh withheld details of the battle from the assistant to Political Resident Kemball, who visited Kuwait on 31 March, going as far as to give the impression that his forces had defeated Ibn Al-Rashid.[5] The Sheikh proceeded in a similar manner in 1901 during the crisis with the Ottoman authorities. According to Lorimer, 'the Sheikh contacted the Russian representative in Baghdad on a matter that remains unknown'.[6] In 1902 Mubarak followed the same tactic when he concealed from the British what had taken place during his meeting with the Russians who had arrived on the cruiser *Askold*, despite their enquiries about his encounter with the Russian visitors. A rumour was spread to the effect that the talks between the Russians and the Sheikh included important political recommendations, which was not actually true.

Similarly, Mubarak gave false information to the British in order to conceal the despatch of troops to support Ibn Saud against the threat posed by Ibn Al-Rashid. The Sheikh knew that sending his forces to assist Ibn Saud was contrary to British policy and ran counter to the advice repeatedly given to him by British diplomats, who had stressed the folly of getting involved in the wars in Arabia. For this reason, Mubarak hastened to write to the Political Resident on 14 April 1903 to explain that the situation that had developed was simply a confrontation between Ibn Saud and Ibn Al-Rashid and that Kuwait had nothing to do with it. He stressed this in the conclusion to his letter, where he wrote, 'This information is true.'[7]

Between 1899 and 1904, Ali bin Gholoum Rida was Britain's agent and informer in the Gulf. Sheikh Mubarak sought to influence the content of his reports and to use him to transmit whatever information he wished to convey to the British authorities, in Kuwait's interests. 'This was revealed by Ali Gholoum's reports, which often included, to the point of exaggeration, Sheikh Mubarak's praise for Britain, his partiality towards the British, and his rejection of the Ottoman Empire. The style of these letters reveals that Sheikh Mubarak Al-Sabah had in fact taken control of Hajj Ali bin Gholoum, turning him into little more than the Sheikh's scribe.'[8] A noteworthy example of this was the report sent by Bin Gholoum on the visit by Kruglov, the Russian consul in Baghdad, on board the Russian vessel *Gilyak*. These say nothing about the ship and do not go into the topics discussed in the meetings between the Sheikh and the Russian diplomat, which indicates that Mubarak was deliberately concealing information on this matter.[9]

In 1907, in a further instance, Mubarak deliberately failed to inform Knox that he was mounting a military campaign to assist Sheikh Khaz'al, the Emir of Al-Muhammara, in quelling a tribal rebellion. This was a sensitive matter because Iran regarded Al-Muhammara as its territory and Iranian policy was particularly anti-British. For this reason, Knox did not hesitate to recommend to his superiors that a strong warning should be given to the Sheikh, and that if he failed to heed it the British Political Agent should be withdrawn from his position.[10] Mubarak told Knox in December 1908 that the Ottoman Sultan was keen to improve his relations with him and had offered him the governorships of Al-Qatif and Al-Hasa, but that he had rejected the offer. Although the British were not in a position to confirm or deny this, they did convey it to the Foreign Office in London.[11] On 15 June 1910, Shakespear reported that he had received independent information that Abdul Aziz bin Salem Al-Badr, the Sheikh's agent in Basra, was attempting to improve relations between Kuwait and the Ottoman Empire, and had become aware that the Sheikh was failing to inform the Political Agent of his actions.[12]

It also became habitual for the Sheikh to evade questions from the British and to disregard their warnings, while he constantly found excuses for not disclosing the activities of Kuwait's armed forces. The British Political Agent in Kuwait continued to warn the Sheikh about the dangers of such a course. One such admonition can be seen in the report written by Shakespear to the Political Resident in Bushire on 12 July 1910, which relates to his discussion with the Sheikh on the subject of the campaign his troops carried out in the Al-Zubayr area in an action that had aroused the ire of the Ottoman authorities.[13]

Sheikh Mubarak never hesitated to express his feelings of dissatisfaction towards Britain, and this was frequently noted by British diplomats. For example, in a report of what was said to have been a long and detailed meeting held between the Sheikh and Political Resident Kemball in January 1903, Kemball says that the Sheikh's letters to him had revealed, 'that he feels that the British government was failing him', though Kemball had tried to convince him otherwise.

On 7 August 1904, in another example of the Sheikh's dissatisfaction, this time in a report by Percy Cox, as Political Resident in Bushire, on the appointment of Captain Knox as a political agent in Kuwait, the Sheikh took the opportunity to highlight the problems he believed he was facing because of his relationship with Britain. According to him, 'Until now I have not had the justice I deserve from your government for the losses inflicted on me by the Turkish government for no reason other than the friendship that links me to you.' After welcoming the appointment of Knox, he was careful to add, 'I wish to see him establish peace and security and for this to include my interests. If this is not forthcoming, then there is no point in him residing in my province.'[14] This constituted a clear statement, made by the Sheikh before the arrival of the first political agent to Kuwait, confirming his conception of mutual interests. The Sheikh realized that Britain was pursuing very substantial strategic, political and economic interests in Kuwait, and he wished to take advantage of Britain's concern, obtaining in return British assistance in safeguarding the borders of Kuwait and its independence.

In January 1905, Sheikh Mubarak told Knox that he must improve his relations with the Ottoman Empire because, as he put it, 'the British government is far from this Emirate, which makes it difficult for Britain to look after our interests'. In a mocking tone, he mused: 'We do not know what the real aims of Britain's policies are.' Mubarak also expressed surprise at Britain's apparent reluctance to take the necessary measures to prevent the Ottoman authorities from mobilizing fresh troops in Arabia. Knox explained to the Sheikh that Lord Curzon had suggested such a course of action to the Foreign Office in London, but that agreement had not been forthcoming. Mubarak's scathing comment was that the Lord Viceroy should therefore have resigned from his position.[15]

Despite his eagerness for British support, the Sheikh was concerned about his country's independence, anxious that Britain should not interfere in its internal affairs. This was noticed by the Ottoman authorities, who sought to make use of it. Pertev Pasha, the highest-ranking officer in the Sixth Turkish Army, who met Sheikh Mubarak in June 1907, noted in his report that 'there is no doubt that Sheikh Mubarak is very irritated by Britain's interference in his internal affairs and therefore it is the right time for the Turks to do something'.[16] A report sent by Knox to Percy Cox in July 1908 described the tension in his relationship with the Sheikh: 'I cannot ignore the reality of there being hundreds of different means Mubarak can employ to convince me that I cannot go above him in this city.'[17] Knox's statement was apparently based on events. It seems that he had interfered in some internal matters in a manner that had infuriated the Sheikh. In a report dated 30 October 1904, the agent of the Governor of Basra reported to the Sublime Porte that Knox was, 'trying to force the market to accept Indian currency and to prevent it from expanding its activities, and is closing shops, as well as interfering in other ways. Mubarak Al-Sabah is angry and full of regret because of this behaviour and interference.'[18]

It must be concluded, therefore, that the image of Sheikh Mubarak that has emerged from research based solely on British documents is incorrect, particularly in the light of the Sheikh's discussions and correspondence with the Russians and French. Antonin Goguyer's account tells a story that contrasts with what the British documents appear to reveal, bringing to the fore the Sheikh's determination to safeguard his independence and his apprehension of British influence. Sheikh Mubarak was determined to have his own sources of information, gathered by his own secret agents. He also developed a close relationship with the director of the telegraph office in Faw, who kept him informed about the content of the most important telegrams sent and received. The Sheikh had agents whom he entrusted to deliver his letters and messages to the Political Resident in Bushire, whose names appear in various British documents, including among others Abdullah Al-Latif Al-Harun and Abdullah bin Ibrahim Al-Samaka. He was also always keen to meet foreigners who came to Kuwait, including diplomats, merchants and travellers, and to hear their assessments of what was happening in the region and the world. Antonin Goguyer spoke truthfully when he described Sheikh Mubarak as a politician who sought to create a balance between the British and the Ottomans.[19] Goguyer's assessment was that Sheikh Mubarak, 'only pays the British what is necessary for the services they provide, and his desire to maintain independence lies behind his constant readiness to stand up against the treacherous conspiracies which surround him'.[20]

Sheikh Mubarak always kept his eye on all the factors that might affect his independence and Kuwait's security, and was willing to talk to any party that might bring him advantage. Lorimer notes, for example, that in October 1899 the Sheikh, acting through Sheikh Khaz'al as his intermediary, asked the Shah of Iran to accord him Iranian protection. The Sheikh's objective, about which he was quite open in a letter he wrote to Muhammad Rahim Sifr, the acting British Political Agent in Bahrain, was apparently to test the strength of the British Government's interest in Kuwait. Lorimer comments that the Sheikh, 'was not inclined to trust in the efficacy of Britain's support in the light of the hostility shown to him by the Turks. Acting through the Sheikh of Al-Muhammara, he has asked for the Shah's protection.'[21] When the British consul in Basra was first informed of this, he found it hard to believe. When he was convinced it was true, he sent a report on 2 October 1899 to Sir Nicholas O'Conor, the British ambassador in Istanbul, stating that the acting British Political Agent in Bahrain had confirmed the veracity of this news to the captain of the British naval vessel HMS *Lapwing*, averring that he had received a letter from Sheikh Mubarak to that effect.[22]

In 1907, there occurred another event significant for British-Kuwaiti relations when the Sheikh placed the Ottoman emblem on his palace. The British Political Agent objected, so the Sheikh also put up the emblem of the Shah of Iran. The Sheikh informed the British Agent that his intention in putting up the emblem was not to express any political position, but simply to decorate his palace, which, as he said, 'looks impressive, decorated with the emblems of the two great Islamic states'.[23] The Russian writer Grigori Bondarevsky comments that Sheikh Mubarak's objective was, from the first day he took the reins of power to play a double game, and sometimes even on three sides at the same time. This confused the foreign diplomats and spies, as well as the Turkish authorities, leaving them all floundering. Therefore it can be said that up to this day the multilateral diplomacy of Mubarak has not been comprehensively assessed.[24]

My hope is that this book has brought into view new material relevant to the attempt to understand this multilateral diplomacy, and has offered an analysis of an important period in the history of Kuwait. The years of Sheikh Mubarak's rule saw the country break through into modernity, with education and health services being provided and the foundations laid for the economic and commercial activities that characterized Kuwait's subsequent history. All these changes began with the Sheikh vision and his strategy for the establishment of a modern state, the definition of its frontiers and the protection of its independence.

Notes

Introduction

1   Yaqub Youssef Al-Hajji, *Al-Sheikh Abdul Aziz Al-Rashid, Sirat Hayatihi* [Al-Sheikh Abdul Aziz Al-Rashid: A Biography] (Kuwait, 1993).

Chapter 1 – Making a State

1   Lewis R. Scudder III, *The Arabian Mission's Story* (Grand Rapids, MI, 1998), p. 98.

2   Brian Cooper Busch, *Britain and the Persian Gulf 1894–1914* (Berkeley, CA, 1967), p. 95.

3   Abdullah Salem Abdullah Muhammad Al-Mizyan, *Ta'rikh wa Amjad* [History and Glory] (Kuwait, n.d.), pp. 96–98.

4   Hafez Wahbah, *Jazirat Al-Arab fi Al-Qarn Al-Ishrin* [The Arabian Peninsula in the Twentieth Century] (Cairo, 1967), p. 81.

5   Hussein Khalaf Al-Sheikh Khaz'al, *Tarikh Al-Kuwait Al-Siyasi* [Political History of Kuwait] (Beirut, 1962), part 2, p. 12.

6   Abd Al-Massih Antaki, *Al-Riyad Al-Muzhira Bayn al-Kuwait wa Al-Muhammara* [Flowery Gardens between Kuwait and Muhammara] (Cairo, 1907), p. 678. Abd Al-Massih Antaki was a young Syrian who travelled to Egypt and worked there as a journalist. He published *Al-Imran* magazine and visited Kuwait in 1907. For his biography, see Khaled Al-Bassam, *Marfa' Al-*

Dhikrayat: Rihlat lIa Al-Kuwait Al-Qadima [The Port of Memories: Voyages to Old Kuwait] (Kuwait, 1995), pp. 49–61.

7 Jamal Zakariyya Qassem, *Al-Khalij Al-Arabi, Dirasa li Tarikh Al-Imarat Al-Arabiyya 1840–1914* [The Arab Gulf: A Study of the History of the Arab Emirates 1840–1914] (Cairo, 1966), pp. 374–375.

8 Abdullah Yusuf Al-Ghoneim, ed., *Akhbar Al-Kuwait: Rasail Ali Bin Gholoum Reda Al-Wakil Al-Ikhbari li Britaniya fi Al-Kuwait* [News from Kuwait: The Letters of Ali Bin Gholoum Reda, the British Agent for Information in Kuwait] (Kuwait, 2007), pp. 45–46.

9 Walid Hamdi Al-Azami, *Al-Kuwait fi Al-Wathaiq Al-Inglisiyya 1752–1960* [Kuwait in British Documents 1752–1960] (London, 1991), p. 74.

10 Qassem, *Al-Khalij Al-Arabi*, pp. 262–263.

11 Abdullah Al-Nuri, *Khalidun fi Tarikh Al-Kuwait* [Legends in the History of Kuwait] (Kuwait, 1988), p. 15.

12 Letter from the Viceroy Governor of India to Political Resident Kemball, 28 February 1901.

13 One *kara* was approximately one and a half tonnes.

14 J. G. Lorimer, *Gazetteer of the Persian Gulf, Oman and Central Arabia* (reprinted edition, Cambridge University Press Archive Editions, 1986). For details of the first year of Sheikh Mubarak's rule and his relations with the Ottoman authorities see Sultan Muhammad Al-Qassimi, *Bayan Al-Kuwait: Sirat Hayat Al-Sheikh Mubarak Al-Sabah* [A Biography of Sheikh Mubarak Al-Sabah] (Sharja, 2004), pp. 21–74.

15 A *sanjak* was an Ottoman administrative division.

16 Al-Azami, *Al-Kuwait fi Al-Wathaiq*, pp. 27–28.

17 Grigori Bondarevsky, *Al-Kuwayt wa-ʿalāqatuhā al-duwalīyah khilāla al-qarn al-tāsiʿ ʿashara wa-awāʾil al-qarn al-ʿishrīn* [Kuwait and its International Relations during the Nineteenth and Beginning of the Twentieth Century], trans. from the Russian by Maher Salama (Kuwait, 1994), p. 198.

18 Al-Azami, *Al-Kuwait fi Al-Wathaiq*, pp. 27–28.

19 'The leader of the descendants of the Prophet': this was an official Ottoman position.

20 Ottoman Archive in Istanbul, 14 Shaban AH 1317, no. 2–4/69.

21 Ottoman Archive in Istanbul, 7 Ramadan, AH 1317, no. 2–4/69.

22 The word 'mirmirat' means 'Emir of Emirs'.

23 Ottoman Archive in Istanbul, 12 Shawwal, AH 1317, no. 2–5/69.

24 Ottoman Archive in Istanbul, 7 Muharram AH 1318, no. 2–5/69.

25 Ottoman Archive in Istanbul, 1 Rabi Al-Thani AH 1319, no. 2–8/69.

26 A rank equivalent to brigadier general.

27 Ottoman Archive in Istanbul, 5 Rabi Al-Thani AH 1319, no. 4, part 36/1319.

28 Ottoman Archive in Istanbul, 9 Rabi Al-Akhir, AH 1319, no. 4, part 36/1319.

29 Ottoman Archive in Istanbul, 15 Rabi Al-Akhir, AH 1319, no. 4, part 36/1319.

30 Ottoman Archive in Istanbul, 12 Jamadi Al-Awwal AH 1319, no. 2–19/ 69.

31 Ottoman Archive in Istanbul, 14 Jamadi Al-Awwal, AH 1319, no. 2–9/ 69.

32 Ottoman Archive in Istanbul, 21 Jamadi Al-Awwal, AH 1319, no. 81/419.

33 Ottoman Archive in Istanbul, 5 September 1901, no. 81/419.

34 Ottoman Archive in Istanbul, 5 September 1901, no. 68/422.

35 Bondarevsky, *Al-Kuwayt*, p. 241.

36 Ottoman Archive in Istanbul, 6 September 1901, no. 81/419.

37 Ottoman Archive in Istanbul, 13 September 1901, no. 68/422.

38 'Miralay': an Ottoman rank equivalent to colonel.

39 See Captain Simmons, the captain of HMS *Pomone*, to the British Naval Authorities on 14 December 1901, in Captain Simmons, Kuwait to Rear-Admiral Bosanquet, 14 December 1901 in *Records of Kuwait 1899–1961* (Cambridge, 1989), pp. 200–202.

40 Ottoman Archive in Istanbul, 11 December 1901, no. 8/443.

41 Ottoman Archive in Istanbul, 15 December 1901, no. 8/433.

42 Ottoman Archive in Istanbul, 18 December 1901, no. 18/432.

43 Ottoman Archive in Istanbul, 30 December 1901, no. 29/423.

44 Ottoman Archive in Istanbul, 31 December 1901, no. 29/423; 3 January 1902, no. 2–16/69. For an analysis and documentation of

this important military and diplomatic confrontation see Sultan bin Muhammad Al-Qassimi, *Bayan Al-Kuwait*, pp. 177–202.

45   H. R. P. Dickson, *Kuwait and Its Neighbours*, trans. Fattuh Abdul Muhsin Al-Khatrash (Kuwait, 1995), p. 102.

46   Maymouna Al-Khalifa Al-Sabah, *Al-Kuwait fi Dhil Al-Himaya Al-Britaniyya* [Kuwait under British Protection] (Kuwait, 1988), pp. 240–241. Bondarevsky, *Al-Kuwayt*, p. 423.

47   Khaz'al, *Tarikh Al-Kuwait Al-Siyasi*, pp. 122–127.

48   *Al-Manar* magazine, vol. 16, p. 398, in Khaz'al, *Tarikh Al-Kuwait Al-Siyasi*, pp. 69–70.

49   *Al-Imran*, 254, ninth year, quoted in Khaz'al, *Tarikh Al-Kuwait Al-Siyasi*, pp. 70–73.

50   Abd Al-Massih Antaki, *Al-Ayaat al-Subah fi Tarikh Mawlana Sahib Al-Summuw Emir Al-Kuwait Al-Sheikh Mubarak Pasha Bin Al-Sabah* [The Highlights of the History of Our Master His Majesty the Emir of Kuwait, Sheikh Mubarak Pasha Al-Sabah] (Cairo, A H 1326). On the other side, there were newspapers that expressed the Ottoman position and supported the right of the Ottomans to extend their influence and exercise their sovereignty over Kuwait. For example, see the Egyptian newspaper *Al-Liwa*, 4 November 1902, 26 April 1904, 14 June 1904, 20 June 1904, 25 June 1904, 10 July 1904. See also the weekly magazine *Al-Aalam Al-Islami* [Islamic World], 28 April 1905.

51   Memorandum by Marquess of Landsdowne, Foreign Office, 21 March 1902, in *Records of Kuwait 1899–1961*, pp. 224–225.

52   *Kuwait Political Agency, Arabic Documents 1899–1949* (London, 1994), vol. 1, pp. 129–130.

53   Ibid., p. 131.

54   William Shakespear, Political Agent in Kuwait to Political Resident, Bushire, 10 November 1913. I.O,R/15/1/73/1, no. c, 22.

55   *Al-Ahram*, 16 September 1904.

56   Ahmad Mustafa Abu Hakima, *Tarikh Al-Kuwait Al-Hadith 1750–1965* [Modern History of Kuwait 1750–1965] (Kuwait, 1984), pp. 320–321.

57   For example, see *Al-Manar* magazine, 'The Fitna of Kuwait', vol. 20, 1 December 1901, p. 799. *Fitna* means 'internal strife or dissension within the Muslim community'.

58 Al-Sabah, *Al-Kuwait* pp. 228–229. Also see Fattuh Abdul Muhsin Al-Khatrash, *History of British-Kuwaiti Political Relations 1890–1921* (Kuwait, 1974).

59 Meade to India Office, Bushire, 25 September 1897. F.O.406/14, inc. 4 no. 23.

60 Salah Al-Aqqad, *Al-Tayyarat Al-Siyasiyya fi Al-Khalij Al-Arabi* [Political Currents in the Arab Gulf] (Cairo, 1965), pp. 193–195. Also Abdul Aziz Hussein, *Muhadarat An Al-Mujtama Al-Arabi bi Al-Kuwait* [Lectures on Arab Society in Kuwait] (Cairo, 1960), pp. 28–29.

61 Al-Ghoneim, *Akhbar Al-Kuwait*, pp. 5–10, 19.

62 Ibid., p. 24.

63 Bondarevsky, *Al-Kuwayt*, pp. 135–136.

64 Ibid., pp. 121–125, 135.

65 Ottoman Archive in Istanbul, 6 Jamadi Al-Akher 1318, no. 2–6/69.

66 Lorimer, *Gazetteer of the Persian Gulf*, vol. 3, p. 1560. Khaz'al, *Tarikh Al-Kuwait Al-Siyasi*, pp. 77–78.

67 Yaqub Youssef Al-Hajji, *Al-Sheikh Abdul Aziz Al-Rashid, Sirat Hayatihi* [Al-Sheikh Abdul Aziz Al-Rashid: A Biography] (Kuwait, 1993), p. 200.

68 *Kuwait Political Agency, Arabic Documents*, p. 132.

69 Khaz'al, *Tarikh Al-Kuwait Al-Siyasi*, pp. 93–94.

70 Ottoman Archive in Istanbul, 19 Muharram A H 1331, no. 62/25.

71 Ottoman Archive in Istanbul, 3 Safar A H 1331, no. 64/25.

Chapter 2 – The Building of a Nation

1 Najat Abdul Qadir Al-Jasim, *Al-Tatawwur Al-Siyasi wa Al-Iqtisadi lil Kuwait bayn Al-Harbayn 1912–1939* [Political and Economic Progress in Kuwait between the Two Wars 1912–1939] (Kuwait, 1997), p. 23.

2 B. J. Slot, *Mubarak Al-Sabah, Founder of Modern Kuwait 1896–1915* (London, 2005), p. 276.

3 See ibid., pp. 278–279, for a discussion of Goguyer's background and his earlier career in Tunisia, where he practised law before going to Muscat and Kuwait.

4   Abdullah Yusuf Al-Ghoneim, ed., *Akhbar Al-Kuwait: Rasail Ali Bin Gholoum Reda Al-Wakil Al-Ikhbari li Britaniya fi Al-Kuwait* [News from Kuwait: The Letters of Ali bin Gholoum Reda, the British Agent for Information in Kuwait] (Kuwait, 2007), pp. 32–35.

5   J. G. Lorimer, *Gazetteer of the Persian Gulf, Oman and Central Arabia* (reprinted edition, Cambridge University Press Archive Editions, 1986), vol. 6, pp. 3734–3736.

6   Jamal Zakariyya Qassem, *Al-Khalij Al-Arabi, Dirasa li Tarikh Al-Imarat Al-Arabiyya 1840–1914* [The Arab Gulf: A Study of the History of the Arab Emirates 1840–1914] (Cairo, 1966), p. 285.

7   Ottoman Archive in Istanbul, 1 Rabi Al-Awwal, AH 1322, no. 3/473.

8   *Al-Ahram*, 16 September 1904.

9   Al-Jasim, *Al-Tatawwur*, p. 72.

10   *Kuwait Political Agency, Arabic Documents 1899–1949* (London, 1994), vol. 3, pp. 172–180.

11   Ibid., pp. 181–183.

12   Ibid., pp. 184–186.

13   Ibid., pp. 188–193.

14   Ibid., pp. 194–195.

15   Ibid., pp. 218–220.

16   Ibid., pp. 224–226.

17   Ibid., pp. 228–229.

18   Ibid., pp. 231–235.

19   Ibid., pp. 236–238.

20   Ibid., pp. 240–243.

21   Ibid., pp. 244–247.

22   From Sheikh Mubarak to Political Resident Cox, 18 May 1913, ibid., pp. 20–21. Sir Percy Cox came to be regarded as one of the most authoritative British diplomats in regard to Gulf affairs. On his life and activities see Philip Graves, *The Life of Sir Percy Cox* (London, 1941).

23   From British Political Agent Shakespear to Sheikh Mubarak, 7 May 1910. The Sheikh replied on 8 May. See *Kuwait Political Agency, Arabic Documents 1899–1949*, vol. 1, pp. 718–721.

24 From Shakespear to Sheikh Mubarak, 30 February 1913, and from Sheikh Mubarak to Shakespear, 31 February 1913, ibid., pp. 729–730.

25 From Sheikh Mubarak to Percy Cox, 16 May 1912, ibid., pp. 733–734.

26 Shafa Al-Muhdaris Al-Matiri (introduction and comment by Muhammad bin Ibrahim Al-Shaybani), *Alam Al-Kuwait Mundh Al-Nash'a Hatta Al-Istiqlal 1746–1961* [The Kuwaiti Flag: From the Beginning to Independence 1746–1961] (Kuwait, 1996), pp. 61–69. Hussein Khalaf Al-Sheikh Khaz'al, *Tarikh Al-Kuwait Al-Siyasi* [Political History of Kuwait] (Beirut, 1962), p. 99. Also see Hamad Muhammad Al-Saidan, *Tarikh Al-Alam Al-Kuwaiti* [The History of the Flag of Kuwait] (Kuwait, 1985), pp. 3–52.

27 From Political Resident Cox, Bushire, to Foreign Office, No. 337, 1 July, 1905.

28 See British correspondence on the flag of Kuwait in *Records of Kuwait 1899–1961* (Cambridge, 1989), vol. 1, pp. 525–540.

29 Abdullah Khaled Al-Hatem, *Min Huna Bada'at Al-Kuwait* [This is How Kuwait Began] (Kuwait, 1980), p. 16.

30 Khaz'al, *Tarikh Al-Kuwait Al-Siyasi*, pp. 99–100.

31 The issue of the borders of Kuwait is one that has been of particular interest to historians and international lawyers, especially after the Iraqi invasion of Kuwait in August 1990. See, for example, Maymouna Al-Khalifa Al-Sabah, *Mushkilat Al-Hudud Al-Kuwaitiyya Bayn Al-Dawlatayn Al-Uthmaniyya wa Al-Baritaniyya 1899–1913* [Problems of Kuwaiti Border between the Ottoman and British Empires 1899–1913], Thesis 82, Journal of Faculty of Arts, Kuwait University (Journal 13 1413/1993). See also *Tarsim Al-Hudud Al-Kuwaitiyya Al-Iraqiyya. Al-Haq Al-Tariki wa Al-Irada Al-Duwaliyya* [Drawing the Kuwaiti-Iraqi Borders. The Historical Rights and International Will] (Kuwait, 1992).

32 Lorimer, *Gazetteer of the Persian Gulf*, vol. 3, pp. 1546–1548. For these developments see Ahmad Zakariyya Al-Shalaq, 'Al-Wad' Al-Duwali Lil Kuwait Mundhu Itifaq Al-Himaya Hatta Al-Itifaq Al-Baritani-Al-Uthmani 1913' [The International Position of Kuwait From the Protection Agreement to the Anglo-Ottoman

Agreement in 1913], in Ahmad Al-Rushed, ed., *Al-Kuwait Min Al-Imara lIa Al-Dawla* [Kuwait: From Emirate to State] (Cairo, 1993), pp. 141–213.

33 Ottoman Archive in Istanbul, 30 Shawwal A H 1319, no. 7/45.

34 Ottoman Archive in Istanbul, 14 Dhu l-Hujja A H 1319, no. 53/426.

35 Ottoman Archive in Istanbul, 18 Dhu l-Hujja A H 1319, no. 89/426.

36 See British diplomatic correspondence on this issue in *Records of Kuwait 1899–1961*, vol. 1, pp. 41–105.

37 Al-Shalaq, 'Al-Wad' Al-Duwali', pp. 191–192.

38 From Sheikh Mubarak to Political Resident Cox, Bushire, FO 371/154, 13 July 1905. F.O 371/154.

39 Memorandum Respecting Kuwait, FO 371/149, 11 December 1905. See British correspondence on Umm Qasr, Warba and Bubyan 1902–1910 in *Records of Kuwait 1899–1961*, vol. 1, pp. 49–92.

40 Qassem, *Al-Khalij Al-Arabi*, p. 284.

41 For details of how Britain's position developed with regard to Kuwait in the Anglo-Ottoman negotiations, see *Records of Kuwait 1899–1961*, vol. 1, pp. 357–423.

42 From Political Agent in Kuwait Shakespear to Political Resident in Bushire Percy Cox, 28 May 1913.

43 For the development of maps of Kuwait see Mounira Abdul Qadir Al-Jassem, *Tatawwur Al-Khara'it Al-Kuwaitiyya* [The Development of Kuwaiti Maps] (Kuwait, 1993). Also Muhammad Rashid Al-Fil, *Al-Jughrafiya Al-Tarikhiyya lil Kuwait* [The Geographical History of Kuwait] (Kuwait, 1985), p. 311. See also Abdullah Yusuf Al-Ghoneim, *Al-Kuwait: Qiraa'a Fi Al-Khara'it Al-Tarikhiyya* [Kuwait: A Reading of Historical Maps] (Kuwait, 1992).

44 See the map provided facing p. 334 in Brian Cooper Busch, *Britain and the Persian Gulf 1894–1914* (Berkeley, CA, 1967).

45 From Political Agent Shakespear to Political Resident, 28 May 1913. *Records of Kuwait, 1899–1961*, vol. 1, pp. 394–397.

46 From Political Resident Cox to Sheikh Mubarak, 7 July 1913. I.O, R/15/5/65.

Chapter 3 – Social Development and the Outside World

1 Hussein Khalaf Al-Sheikh Khaz'al, *Tarikh Al-Kuwait Al-Siyasi* [Political History of Kuwait] (Beirut, 1962), p. 294.

2 Stanley Mylrea, 'Memoirs', trans. by Muhammad Ghanem Al-Rumayhi and Bassem Sarhan as *Al-Kuwait Qabl Al-Naft* [Kuwait before Oil] (Kuwait, 1997), p. 36. A copy of a privately printed edition of the English text *Kuwait before Oil: Memoirs of Dr C. Stanley G. Mylrea, Pioneer Medical Missionary of the Arabian Mission, Reformed Church in America*, OCLC number 190774041, is held by the Library of Columbia University in New York. Quotations in this book are from the Arabic translation of this text cited above, re-translated into English. There are also typescript copies of two versions of Dr Mylrea's memoirs in the Middle East Centre Archive at St Antony's College, Oxford, MECA GB 165–0214.

3 Mylrea, *Al-Kuwait Qabl Al-Naft*, pp. 37–38.

4 Barclay Raunkiær, *Abr Al-Jazira Al-Arabiyya al Dhahr Jamal* [Through Wahhabiland on a Camel], translated from English to Arabic by Mansour Muhammad Al-Khariji (Riyadh, 1999), p. 62. Also Muhammad bin Ibrahim Al-Shaybani, ed., *Al-Kuwait Kama Ra'aha Al-Siyasi Al-Denmarki Barclay Raunkiær 1330/1912* [Kuwait as Seen by the Danish Politician Barclay Raunkiær in 1330/1912] (Kuwait, Center for Manuscripts, Heritage and Documents, 2004), p. 15. Also see analysis of Raunkiær's trip in Peter Brent, *Far Arabia, Explorers of the Myth* (London, 1979), pp. 180–193.

5 Mylrea, *Al-Kuwait Qabl Al-Naft*, p. 36.

6 Raunkiær, *Abr Al-Jazira*, p. 63.

7 H. V. F. Winstone, *Captain Shakespear: A Portrait* (London, 1976), p. 112.

8 Raunkiær, *Abr Al-Jazira*, pp. 60–61.

9 Abd Al-Massih Antaki, *Al-ayat Al Sabbah fi Tarikh Mawlana Saheb El Somow Amir Al Kuwait Al Sheikh Mubarak Pasha Ibn Al Sabbah* [The Shining Glimpses of the History of His Excellency the Amir of Kuwait Sheikh Mubarak Pasha Ibn Al Sabbah] (Cairo, Al Arab Printing Shop, AH 1326), pp. 644–646. It is worth mentioning that in 1917, Sheikh Salem renovated the old building in the

palace and added a new wing. He wrote on the northern gate: 'Had it been enough for others, it would not have come to you.' Sheikh Abdullah Al-Salem also renovated the palace in 1961.

10 Abdullah Zakariyya Al-Ansari, *Fahd Al-Askar, Hayatahu wa Shi'rihi* [Fahd Al-Askar: His Life and Poetry] (Kuwait, 1967), p. 39.

11 Ibid., pp. 39–40.

12 J. G. Lorimer, *Gazetteer of the Persian Gulf, Oman and Central Arabia* (reprinted edition, Cambridge University Press Archive Editions, 1986), p. 1567.

13 Abd Al-Massih Antaki, *Al-Riyad Al-Muzhira Bayn al-Kuwait wa Al-Muhammara* [Flowery Gardens Between Kuwait and Muhammara] (Cairo, 1907), pp. 674–675.

14 Yaqub Youssef Al-Hajji, *Al-Sheikh Abdul Aziz Al-Rashid, Sirat Hayatihi* [Al-Sheikh Abdul Aziz Al-Rashid: A Biography] (Kuwait, 1993), p. 220.

15 Abdullah Khaled Al-Hatem, *Min Huna Bada'at Al-Kuwait* [This is How Kuwait Began] (Kuwait, 1980), pp. 179–180.

16 See Dr Mylrea's description of this incident in Zubayda Ali Ashkenani, trans. and ed., *Min Nafidhat 'Al-Americani': Taqarir Al-Aamilin fi Mustashfa al-Irsaliyya Al-Americiyya An al-Kuwait Qabl Al-Naft* [From the Window of the 'American' Hospital: The Reports of Those Who Worked at the American Mission Hospital about Kuwait before the Oil] (Kuwait, 1995), pp. 33–40.

17 Ibid., p. 135.

18 Al-Hajji, *Al-Sheikh Abdul Aziz Al-Rashidi*, p. 373.

19 Khalil Muhammad Audah Abu Milal, *Ulama Al-Kuwait Du'aat Al-Islah* [Kuwait's Ulema Call for Reform] (Kuwait, 1987), pp. 92–94. Al-Hajji, *Al-Sheikh Abdul Aziz Al-Rashidi*, pp. 372–374.

20 Mubarak Al-Khater, *Al-Mu'asasat Al-Thaqafiyya Al-Ula fi l-Kuwait* [The First Cultural Foundations in Kuwait] (Kuwait, 1997), pp. 33–56. Also Milal, *Ulama Al-Kuwait Du'aat Al-Islah*, pp. 44–45.

21 Najat Abdul Qadir Al-Jassem, *Sheikh Youssef Bin Issa Al-Qinai, Dawarahu fi Al-Hayat Al-Iztima'iyya wal Siyasiyya fi Al-Kuwait* [Sheikh Youssef bin Issa Al-Qinai, His Role in the Social and Political Life of Kuwait] (Kuwait, n.d.), pp. 33–34.

22 Youssef Al-Shihab, *Rijal fi Tarikh Al-Kuwait* [Men in the History of Kuwait] (Kuwait 1993), vol. 1, p. 422.

23 'Madrasa Ilmiyya fi Al-Kuwait' [A Scientific School in Kuwait], *Al-Manar*, 15(2) (1912), pp. 327–328.

24 Sheikh Hafez Wahbah was an Egyptian who lived in Kuwait and then moved to Najd, later becoming the Saudi ambassador in London. For a biography see Khaled Al-Bassam, *Rijal fi Jazair Al-Lu'lu'* [Men in the Pearl Islands] (Manama, 1991), pp. 33–44.

25 Al-Hatem, *Min Huna Bada'at Al-Kuwait*, pp. 77–79. Also Al-Hajji, *Al-Sheikh Abdul Aziz Al-Rashidi*, pp. 367–369.

26 Al-Jassem, *Sheikh Youssef Bin Issa Al-Qinai*, p. 24.

27 Abdullah Al Nouri, *Qissat Al-Ta'lim fi Al-Kuwait fi Nisf Qarn* [The Story of Education in Kuwait in Half a Century] (Kuwait, n.d.), p. 45.

28 For the text of the interview see Khaled Al-Bassam, trans. and ed., *Sadmat Al-Ihtikak: Hikayat Al-Irasaliyya Al-Amerikiyya fi Al-Khalij wa Al-Jazira Al-Arabiyya, 1892–1925* [The Shock of Contact: The Story of the American Mission in the Gulf and Arabia] (Beirut, 1998), pp. 159–161.

29 For a biography of Sheikh Abdul Aziz Al-Rashid, see Al-Hajji, *Al-Sheikh Abdul Aziz Al-Rashid, Sirat Hayatihi*.

30 May Muhammad Al-Khalifa, *Ma Sheikh Al-Udaba fi al-Bahrain: Ibrahim Bin Muhammad Al-Khalifa 1850–1933* [With Bahrain's Leading Writer: Ibrahim bin Muhammad Al-Khalifa 1850–1933] (Bahrain, 1993), p. 34.

31 Mubarak Al-Khater, *Min A'lam Al-Khalij Al-Arabi: Nabighat Al-Bahrain Abdullah Al-Zayed Hayatihi wa A'malihi 1894–1945* [Notables of the Arab Gulf: The Genius of Bahrain Abdullah al-Zayed: His Life and Works 1894–1945] (Beirut, 1972), p. 146.

32 *Al-Manar*, 16 (1913), pp. 396–399, from Al-Hajji, *Al-Sheikh Abdul Aziz Al-Rashid, Sirat Hayatihi*, p. 228. Also Youssef Ibish, *Rihlat Al-Imam Muhammad Rashid Rida* [Imam Muhammad Rashid Rida's Journey] (Beirut, 2000), pp. 71–72.

33 Ibid., p. 353.

34 Al-Hajji, *Al-Sheikh Abdul Aziz Al-Rashid, Sirat Hayatihi*, pp. 345–347.

35 Khaz'al, *Tarikh Al-Kuwait Al-Siyasi*, p. 260.

36   Al-Hajji, *Al-Sheikh Abdul Aziz Al-Rashid*, pp. 206–207.

37   Dr Muhammad Hassan Abdullah, *Al-Shi'r we Al-Shu'ara fi Al-Kuwait* [Poetry and Poets in Kuwait] (Kuwait, 1987), pp. 11–12.

38   Abdullah Abdul Aziz Al-Duwaysh, *Diwan Hammud Al-Nasser Al-Badr* [The Poetry of Hammud Al-Nasser Al-Badr] (Kuwait, 1981), pp. 8–9. Also see Khaled Saud Al-Zayd, *Udaba' Al-Kuwait fi Qarnayn* [Kuwaiti Writers in Two Centuries] (Kuwait, 1976), vol. 1, pp. 36–40.

39   Al-Hajji, *Al-Sheikh Abdul Aziz Al-Rashid, Sirat Hayatihi*, p. 352.

40   Abdullah Yusuf Al-Ghoneim, ed., *Akhbar Al-Kuwait: Rasail Ali Bin Gholoum Reda Al-Wakil Al-Ikhbari li Britaniya fi Al-Kuwait* [News from Kuwait: The Letters of Ali bin Gholoum Reda, the British Agent for Information in Kuwait] (Kuwait, 2007), p. 26.

41   *Kuwait Political Agency, Arabic Documents 1899–1949* (London, 1994), vol. 1, pp. 283–288.

42   Khaled Fahd Jarallah, *Tarikh Al-Khadamat Al-Sihiyya fi Al-Kuwait Min Al-Nasha Hatta Al-Istiqlal* [The History of Healthcare in Kuwait from the Beginning to Independence] (Kuwait, 1996), p. 58.

43   *Kuwait Political Agency, Arabic Documents 1899–1949*, vol. 1, p. 289.

44   From Political Resident Cox to Sheikh Mubarak, 7 June 1908.

45   Al-Jarallah, *Tarikh Al-Khadamat*, p. 157.

46   Ibid., pp. 73–76.

47   See Zwemer's report of his visit to Kuwait in 1903 in Al-Bassam, *Sadmat Al-Ihtikak*, pp. 171–174.

48   Mylrea, *Al-Kuwait Qabl Al-Naft*, pp. 40–42. Also Jarallah, *Tarikh Al-Khadamat*, pp. 107–108.

49   Zubayda Ali Ashkenani, trans. and ed., *'Al-Americani': Taqarir Al-Aamilin fi Mustashfa al-Irsaliyya Al-Americiyya An al-Kuwait Qabl Al-Naft* [From the Window of the 'American' Hospital: The Reports of Those Who Worked at the American Mission Hospital about Kuwait before the Oil] (Kuwait, 1995), p. 5.

50   Al-Jarallah, *Tarikh Al-Khadamat*, pp. 110–111. Also Al-Hatem, *Min Huna Bada'at Al-Kuwait*, pp. 90–93, 103.

51   Eleanor Calverley, *Kuntu Awal Tabiba fi Al-Kuwait* [I was the First Female Doctor in Kuwait], trans. Abdullah Al-Hatem (Kuwait, 1968), pp. 39–40.

52   Ibid., p. 44.

53   Ibid., p. 52.

54   Ibid., p. 55.

55   Al-Bassam, *Sadmat Al-Ihtikak*, p. 86. It should be noted that the date of the visit was wrongly reported as 27 January 1916. This would have been impossible as Sheikh Mubarak died in November 1915.

56   Ayyub Hussein, *Ma Dhikrayatina Al-Kuwaitiyya* [Our Kuwaiti Memories] (Kuwait, 1984), p. 55.

57   From Mubarak to Political Agent in Kuwait Knox, 10 June 1907, *Kuwait Political Agency, Arabic Documents 1899–1949*, pp. 410–411.

58   Ibid., p. 416.

59   Shakespear was also an accomplished artist and it was he who painted the celebrated portrait of Sheikh Mubarak that is still the best-known image of the Sheikh.

60   See the British Diplomatic Correspondence on the postal and telegraphic service to Kuwait in *Records of Kuwait 1899–1961* (Cambridge, 1989), vol. 4, pp. 3–21.

61   Ibid., p. 118.

62   Ibid., pp. 296–297.

63   *Kuwait Political Agency, Arabic Documents 1899–1949*, vol. 1, pp. 696–704.

64   Calverley, *Kuntu Awal Tabiba fi Al-Kuwait*, pp. 105–107, 113, 116, 140–141, 160.

65   Khaz'al, *Tarikh Al-Kuwait Al-Siyasi*, p. 138.

66   This stamp was designed in 1904 when the first Political Agent was appointed in Kuwait, but it was left unused for 11 years.

67   In 1923, the spelling was changed to the one used today – 'Kuwait'.

68   Muhammad Abdul Hadi Jamal, *Ta'rikh Al-Khadamat Al-Baridiyya fi Al-Kuwait* [History of the Postal Services in Kuwait] (Kuwait, 1994), pp. 133–136. See also Adel Muhammad Al-Abd Al-Maghni, *Lamahat Min Tawabi Al-Barid Fi Al-Kuwait* [Glimpses of

the Postage Stamps of Kuwait] (Kuwait, 1994), pp. 11–13. Also see Neil Donaldson, *The Postal Agencies in Eastern Arabia and the Gulf* (London, 1975), pp. 94–103.

69 Antaki, *Al-Riyad*, p. 624.

70 Ibid., p. 651.

71 Khaled Al-Bassam, ed. and trans., *Al-Qawafil: Rihlat Al-Irsaliyya Al-Amerikiyya fi Mudun Al-Khalij wa Al-Jazira Al-Arabia 1901–1926* [The Caravans: The Journeys of the American Mission in the Cities of the Gulf and Arabia 1901–1926] (Bahrain, 1993), pp. 74, 85.

72 Ibid., p. 93.

73 Al-Hajji, *Al-Sheikh Abdul Aziz Al-Rashid*, pp. 41–46.

74 Khaz'al, *Tarikh Al-Kuwait Al-Siyasi*, vol. 3, p. 181.

75 See Zwemer's report on his visit to Kuwait in 1903 in Al-Bassam, *Al-Qawafil*, pp. 171–174.

76 For the history of the *diwaniyyas* and the development of their social and political role see Yaqub Youssef Al-Kundari, *Al-Diwaniyya Al-Kuwaitiyya* [The Kuwaiti Diwaniyya] (Kuwait, 2002).

77 Al-Hajji, *Al-Sheikh Abdul Aziz Al-Rashid*, p. 335.

78 Mylrea, *Al-Kuwait Qabl Al-Naft*, pp. 36, 46.

79 Al-Bassam, *Al-Qawafil*, pp. 108–110.

80 Anastace Al-Karmali, 'Al-Kuwait', *Al-Mashriq*, 7(10) (1904), p. 455.

81 Hussein, *Ma Dhikrayatina Al-Kuwaitiyya*, p. 135.

82 For details of the importation and distribution of water, see ibid., pp. 130–143. Also see Yaqoub Youssef Al-Hajji, ed., *Al-Kuwait Al-Qadima: Siwar wa Dhikrayat* [Old Kuwait: Photographs and Memories], (Al Kuwait, Center for Kuwaiti Research and Studies, 1997), pp. 92–100.

83 Hussein, *Ma Dhikrayatina Al-Kuwaitiyya*, p. 137.

84 Calverley, *Kuntu Awal Tabiba fi Al-Kuwait*, p. 156.

85 Ibid., p. 157.

86 'Safahat wa Watha'iq Min Qissat Al-Ma' fi Al-Kuwai' [Pages and Documents from the Story of Water in Kuwait], *Risalat Al-Kuwait*, 3(10) (2005), p. 10.

87   Adnan bin Salem bin Muhammad Al-Rumi, *Tarikh Masajid Al-Kuwait Al-Qadima* [The History of the Old Mosques in Kuwait] (Kuwait, 2002), p. 130.

88   Calverley, *Kuntu Awal Tabiba fi Al-Kuwait*, p. 112.

89   Ibid., p. 110.

90   Violet Dickson (Um Saud), intro. Sayf Marzouq Al-Shamlan Al Sayf, *Arba'un Aam fi Al-Kuwait* [Forty Years in Kuwait] (Kuwait, 1994), p. 11.

91   Grigori Bondarevsky, *Al-Kuwayt wa-'alāqatuhā al-duwalīyah khilāla al-qarn al-tāsi' 'ashara wa-awā'il al-qarn al-'ishrīn* [Kuwait and its International Relations during the Nineteenth and Beginning of the Twentieth Century], trans. from the Russian by Maher Salama (Kuwait, 1994), p. 202.

92   Raunkiær, *Abr Al-Jazira*, p. 71.

93   Muhammad bin Ibrahim Al-Sahybani, ed., *Risala Fiha Hawadith wa Wafiyyat Al-A'yan min Tadwinat Khan Bahader, Abdullah Al-Qinai,* [An Account of the Lives and Deaths of the Notables, According to Khan Bahader and Abdullah al-Qinai] (Kuwait, 2006), p. 113. Also see Khaz'al, *Tarikh Al-Kuwait Al-Siyasi*, pp. 288–299.

Chapter 4 – Economic Development

1   Youssef bin Issa Al-Qinai, *Safahat Min Tarikh Al-Kuwait* [Pages from the History of Kuwait] (Cairo, 1946), pp. 22–23.

2   Salim Touma, ed. and trans., *Sufun Russiyya fi Al-Khalij Al-Arabi 1899–1903, Mawad Min Arsheef Al-Dawla Al-Markazi lil Ustuul Al-Bahri Al-Harbi* [Russian Ships in the Arab Gulf 1899–1903, Material from the Central Government Archives of the Navy] (Moscow, 1990), p. 92.

3   Muhammad Rashid Al-Fil, *Al-Jughrafiya Al-Tarikhiyya lil Kuwait* [The Geographical History of Kuwait] (Kuwait, 1985), p. 110.

4   Abdullah Al-Saleh Al-Uthaymni, *Al-Alaqat Bayn Al-Dawla Al-Saudiyya Al-Ula wa Al-Kuwait* [Relations between the First Saudi State and Kuwait] (Riyadh, 1990), p. 85.

5   Barclay Raunkiær, *Abr Al-Jazira Al-Arabiyya al Dhahr Jamal* [Through Wahhabiland on a Camel], trans. Mansour Muhammad Al-Khariji (Riyadh, 1999), p. 75. Also Muhammad bin Ibrahim

Al-Shaybani, ed., *Al-Kuwait Kama Ra'aha Al-Siyasi Al-Denmarki Barclay Raunkiær 1330/1912* [Kuwait as Seen by the Danish Politician Barclay Raunkiær in 1330/1912] (Kuwait, n.d.), p. 23.

6 Abd Al-Massih Antaki, *Al-Riyad Al-Muzhira Bayn al-Kuwait wa Al-Muhammara* [Flowery Gardens between Kuwait and Muhammara] (Cairo, 1907), p. 651.

7 Political Resident, Turkish Arabia to Political Resident, Bushire, 25 June 1900, in *Records of Kuwait 1899–1961* (Cambridge, 1989), vol. 6, p. 4.

8 Hafez Wahbah, *Jazirat Al-Arab fi Al-Qarn Al-Ishrin* [The Arabian Peninsula in the Twentieth Century] (Cairo, 1967), p. 74. The Political Agent reported periodically on the traffic in the port of Kuwait, recording the number of boats arriving and the goods they carried. See 'Notes on Kuwait Harbour' prepared by the Political Agent, Kuwait, 1907, in *Records of Kuwait 1899–1961*, vol. 4, pp. 731–753.

9 Hussein Khalaf Al-Sheikh Khaz'al, *Tarikh Al-Kuwait Al-Siyasi* [Political History of Kuwait] (Beirut, 1962), p. 289.

10 Raunkiær, *Abr Al-Jazira*, pp. 76–77; Al-Shaybani, *Al-Kuwait Kama Ra'aha*, pp. 24–25.

11 Yaqoub Youssef Al-Hajji, *Al-Nashatat Al-Bahriyya Al-Qadima fi Al-Kuwait* [Maritime Activities of Yesteryear in Kuwait] (Kuwait, 2007), pp. 182–183.

12 Antaki, *Al-Riyad Al-Muzhira Bayn al-Kuwait wa Al-Muhammara*, p. 653.

13 *Kuwait Political Agency, Arabic Documents 1899–1949* (London, 1994), pp. 529–532, 543–548.

14 Khaz'al, *Tarikh Al-Kuwait Al-Siyasi*, pp. 157–158.

15 From Sheikh Mubarak to Al-Sayyid Faisal bin Turki, 29 March 1910, in *Kuwait Political Agency, Arabic Documents 1899–1949*, vol. 1, p. 716.

16 From Sheikh Mubarak to Political Agent Shakespear, 4 November 1912, and Shakespear's reply, in ibid., pp. 117–119.

17 Muhammad bin Ibrahim Al-Shaybani, ed., *Risala fiha Hawadith wa Wafiyyat Al-Ayan min Tadwinat Khan Bahader, Abdullah Al-Qinai* [An Account of the Lives and Deaths of the Notables, According to Khan Bahader and Abdullah Al-Qinai] (Kuwait, Center for

Manuscripts and Documents, 2006), p. 27. See also Khaz'al, *Tarikh Al-Kuwait Al-Siyasi*, p. 291.

18 From Sheikh Mubarak to Political Resident Cox, 16 May 1913, in *Kuwait Political Agency, Arabic Documents 1899–1949*, pp. 733–734.

19 For a copy of the certificate, see ibid., p. 114.

20 For a copy of the certificate, see ibid., p. 115.

21 For a copy of the certificate, see ibid., pp. 3–8.

22 Hasanayn Tawfiq Ibrahim, 'Imarat Al-Kuwait min Al-Nash'a hatter Al-Himaya Al-Baritaniyya aam 1899 – Al-Alaqat Al-Khalijiyya' [The Emirate of Kuwait from the Beginning to the British Protectorate in 1899 – Relations with the Gulf], in Ahmad Al-Rashidi, ed., *Al Kuwait min Al Imara Ila Al Dawla* [Kuwait from Emirate to State], (Cairo, Center for Political Studies and Research, Cairo University, 1993), p. 193.

23 Al-Hajji, *Al-Nashatat Al-Bahriyya Al-Qadima fi Al-Kuwait*, pp. 84, 89–90.

24 Sayf Marzouq Al-Shamlan, *Ta'rikh Al-Ghaws ala L-Lulu' fi Al-Kuwait wa Al-Khalij Al-Arabi* [The History of Pearl Diving in Kuwait and the Arab Gulf] (Kuwait, 1986), p. 275.

25 Yaqoub Youssef Al-Hajji, *Sina'at Al-Sufun Al-Shira'iyya fi Al-Kuwait* [The Sailing Boat Industry in Kuwait] (Qatar, 1988), pp. 253–254.

26 Issa Al-Qitami, *Dalil Al-Muhtar fi Ilm Al-Biha* [The Guide to the Sea for the Bewildered] (Kuwait, 1964), pp. 193–196.

27 Yaqoub Youssef Al-Hajji, ed., *Al-Kuwait Al-Qadima: Siwar wa Dhukrayat* [Old Kuwait: Photographs and Memories], (Al Kuwait, Center for Kuwaiti Research and Studies, 1997), p. 37.

28 See Ahmad Abdul Aziz Al-Mazini, *Al-Kuwait wa Tarikhuha Al-Bahri Aw Rihlat Al-Shiraa'* [Kuwait and its Maritime History: Stories of Sail] (Kuwait, 1986).

29 Al-Hajji, ed., *Al-Kuwait Al-Qadima: Siwar wa Dhukrayat*, pp. 164–165.

30 Ibid.

31 Touma, *Sufun Russiyya fi Al-Khalij Al-Arabi 1899–1903*, p. 132.

32 Abdul Malik Khalaf Al-Tamimi, *Abhath fi Tarikh Al-Kuwait* [Studies in the History of Kuwait] (Kuwait, 1999), p. 93. See also

Ali Hassan Al-Hamadani, *Al-Hiraf Al-Yadawiyya bayn Al-Tarikh wa Al-Qanun fi Al-Mujtama Al-Kuwaiti Al-Qadim, min fatrat 1896–1950* [Handcrafts between History and Law in Old Kuwaiti Society 1896–1950] (London, 1994).

33 H. V. F. Winstone, *Captain Shakespear: A Portrait* (London, 1976), p. 119.

34 Ibid., pp. 94–95.

35 Yaqub Youssef Al-Hajji, *Al-Sheikh Abdul Aziz Al-Rashid, Sirat Hayatihi* [Al-Sheikh Abdul Aziz Al-Rashid: A Biography] (Kuwait, 1993), pp. 47–48.

36 See Ibrahim Al-Shakli, *Al-Badawa fi Al-Kuwait, Dirasa Maydaniyya* [Bedouin Life in Kuwait: A Field Study] (Kuwait, 1987). See also Muhammad Al-Haddad et al., *Turath Al-Badiya Muqaddima li Dirasat Al-Badiya fi Al-Kuwait* [The Culture of the Desert: An Introduction to the Study of the Desert in Kuwait] (Kuwait, 1987). Also see H. R. P. Dickson, *The Arab of the Desert: A Glimpse into Badawin Life in Kuwait and Saudi Arabia* (London, 1949).

37 See British diplomats' view of these developments in *Records of Kuwait 1899–1961*, vol. 4, pp. 615–629.

38 Stanley Mylrea, 'Memoirs', trans. by Muhammad Ghanem Al-Rumayhi and Bassem Sarhan as *Al-Kuwait Qabl Al-Naft* [Kuwait before Oil] (Kuwait, 1997), p. 37.

39 Abdullah Khaled Al-Hatem, *Min Huna Bada'at Al-Kuwait* [This is How Kuwait Began] (Kuwait, 1980), p. 271.

40 Antaki, *Al-Riyad Al-Muzhira Bayn al-Kuwait wa Al-Muhammara*, pp. 561–562.

41 Raunkiær, *Abr Al-Jazira*, pp. 77–78. Also Al-Shaybani, ed., *Risala fiha Hawadith wa Wafiyyat Al-Ayan min Tadwinat Khan Bahader*, pp. 25–26.

42 Khaled Al-Bassam, *Rijal fi Jazair Al-Lu'lu'* [Men in the Pearl Islands] (Manama, 1991), pp. 74–75.

43 Adel Muhammad Al-Abd Al-Mughni, *Dalil Ma'rad Al-Imlah Al-Kuwaitiyya abr Al-Tarikh* [The Guide to the Exhibition of Kuwaiti Currency through the Ages] (Kuwait, 1996), pp. 11–17.

44 Khaz'al, *Tarikh Al-Kuwait Al-Siyasi*, p. 163.

45 Youssef Al-Shihab, *Rijal fi Tarikh Al-Kuwait* [Men in the History of Kuwait] (Kuwait 1993), vol. 1, p. 422.

46 Al-Hajji, *Al-Sheikh Abdul Aziz Al-Rashid*, p. 189.

47 Abdullah Yusuf Al-Ghoneim, ed., *Akhbar Al-Kuwait: Rasail Ali Bin Gholoum Reda Al-Wakil Al-Ikhbari li Britaniya fi Al-Kuwait* [News from Kuwait: The Letters of Ali bin Gholoum Reda, the British Agent for Information in Kuwait] (Kuwait, 2007), p. 49.

48 J. G. Lorimer, *Gazetteer of the Persian Gulf, Oman and Central Arabia* (reprinted edition, Cambridge University Press Archive Editions, 1986), vol. 3, pp. 1566–1567.

49 Antaki, *Al-Riyad Al-Muzhira Bayn al-Kuwait wa Al-Muhammara*, p. 640.

50 Lorimer, *Gazetteer of the Persian Gulf*, pp. 1548–1549, 1560.

51 Khaz'al, *Tarikh Al-Kuwait Al-Siyasi*, pp. 79–80.

52 Jamal Zakariyya Qassem, *Al-Khalij Al-Arabi, Dirasa li Tarikh Al-Imarat Al-Arabiyya 1840–1914* [The Arab Gulf: A Study of the History of the Arab Emirates 1840–1914] (Cairo, 1966), p. 289.

53 Ashraf Muhammad Abdul Rahman, *Tarikh Al-Iraq Al-Siyasi min Nihayat Hukm Midhat Pasha ila Qiyam Hukm Al-Itihadiyyeen 1872–1908* [The Poltical History of Iraq from the End of Midhat Pasha's Rule to the Beginning of the Unionists' Rule, 1872–1908] (Cairo, 1993), pp. 326–330.

54 *Kuwait Political Agency, Arabic Documents 1899–1949*, pp. 101–108.

55 Ibid., pp. 120–122.

56 Ibid., pp. 123–127.

57 Ibid., p. 128.

58 Khaz'al, *Tarikh Al-Kuwait Al-Siyasi*, p. 89.

59 Ibid., pp. 95–97.

60 Lorimer, *Gazetteer of the Persian Gulf*, p. 1566.

Chapter 5 – Regional Relations and the Employment of Political Resources

1 Stanley Mylrea, 'Memoirs' trans. by Muhammad Ghanem Al-Rumayhi and Bassem Sarhan as *Al-Kuwait Qabl Al-Naft* [Kuwait before Oil] (Kuwait, 1997), p. 28.

2   Khair Al-Din Al-Zarakli, *Al-Wajiz Sirat Al-Malik Abdul Aziz* [The Concise History of King Abdul Aziz] (Beirut, Dar Al Elm Lil Malaveen, 1970), p. 21.

3   Jibran Shamiyya, *Al Saud: Madihum wa Mustaqbalihim* [The Saud Family: Their Past and Future] (London, Dar Riyad Al Rayess, n.d.), p. 91.

4   Banwa Mishan, *Abdul Aziz Al Saud: Sirat Batal wa Mawlid Mamlaka* [Abdul Aziz Al Saud: the Story of a Hero and the Birth of a Kingdom], trans. into Arabic by Abdul Fattah Yaseen (Beirut, Dar Al Kateb Al Arabi, n.d.), p. 61.

5   H. R. P. Dickson, *Kuwait and Her Neighbours* (London, 1956), p. 136.

6   Jamal Zakariyya Qassem, *Al-Khalij Al-Arabi, Dirasa li Tarikh Al-Imarat Al-Arabiyya 1840–1914* [The Arab Gulf: A Study of the History of the Arab Emirates 1840–1914] (Cairo, 1966), pp. 268–269.

7   Abdullah Salem Abdullah Muhammad Al-Mizyan, *Ta'rikh wa Amjad* [History and Glory] (Kuwait, n.d.), pp. 98–99. Also Khaz'al, *Tarikh Al-Kuwait Al-Siyasi* [Political History of Kuwait] (Beirut, 1962), vol. 2, pp. 35–36.

8   The text of the letter from Sheikh Mubarak is to be found in Khaz'al, *Tarikh Al-Kuwait Al-Siyasi*, p. 33.

9   Al-Sarif is the site of a water well close to the town of Al-Tanuma, between Ha'il and Al-Qasim.

10   Qadri Qalaji, *Adwa' ala Tarikh Al-Kuwait* [Spotlight on the History of Kuwait] (Beirut, 1962), pp. 78–79.

11   Grigori Bondarevsky, *Al-Kuwayt wa-'alāqatuhā al-duwalīyah khilāla al-qarn al-tāsi' 'ashara wa-awā'il al-qarn al-'ishrīn* [Kuwait and Its international Relations during the Nineteenth and Beginning of the Twentieth Century], trans. from the Russian by Maher Salama (Kuwait, 1994), p. 185.

12   Political Resident Col Kemball, Bushire, to the Viceroy and Governor of India, 18 April 1901.

13   Ottoman Archive in Istanbul, 31 December 1901, no. 29/423.

14   Ottoman Archive in Istanbul, 1 January 1902, no. 60/423.

15   Qassem, *Al-Khalij Al-Arabi*, p. 279.

16 *Kuwait Political Agency, Arabic Documents 1899–1949* (London, 1994), p. 580. On 5 September 1904, Political Agent Knox replied to Abdul Rahman Al-Faisal Al-Saud's letter informing him that he had forwarded his letter to Political Resident Cox to be conveyed to the British Government.

17 Sultan bin Muhammad Al-Qassimi, *Bayan Al-Kuwait: Sirat Hayat Al-Sheikh Mubarak Al-Sabah* [A Biography of Sheikh Mubarak Al-Sabah] (Sharja, 2004), p. 126

18 Ibid., p. 228.

19 Bondarevsky, *Al-Kuwayt*, p. 231.

20 Al-Hajji, *Al-Sheikh Abdul Aziz Al-Rashid*, p. 175.

21 Khaled Hammoud Al-Sa'dun, *Al-Alaqat bayn Najd wa Al-Kuwait 1319–1341 AH/ 1902–1922 A D* [Relations Between Najd and Kuwait 1319–1341/ 1902–1922] (Kuwait, 1990), p. 100. All historians agree on the role Sheikh Mubarak played in preparing and equipping Emir Abdul Aziz. See, for example, Abdullah Al-Saleh Al-Uthaymini, *Tarikh Al-Mamlaka Al-Arabiyya Al-Saudiyya* [The History of the Kingdom Of Saudi Arabia] (Riyadh, 1999), vol. 2, p. 50. See also Salah Al-Din Al-Mukhtar, *Tarikh Al-Mamlaka Al-Arabiyya Al-Saudiyya Madiha wa Hadiruha* [The History of the Kingdom of Saudi Arabia: its Past and Present] (Beirut, n.d.), p. 33.

22 Zubayda Ali Ashkenani (trans. and ed.), *Min Nafidhat 'Al-Americani': Taqarir Al-Aamilin fi Mustashfa al-Irsaliyya Al-Americiyya An al-Kuwait Qabl Al-Naft* [From the Window of the 'American' Hospital: The Reports of Those Who Worked at the American Mission Hospital about Kuwait before the Oil] (Kuwait, 1995), p. 11.

23 Al-Mizyan, *Ta'rikh wa Amjad*, pp. 120–121.

24 Al-Sa'dun, *Al-Alaqat bayn Najd wa Al-Kuwait*, p. 165.

25 Al-Hajji, *Al-Sheikh Abdul Aziz Al-Rashid*, pp. 211–217.

26 Munira Abdullah Al-Araynan, *Alaqat Najd bil Qiwa Al-Muhita 1319–1323 A.H./ 1902–1914 A D* [Najd's Relations with Surrounding Powers] (Kuwait, 1990), pp. 195–197.

27 Al-Sa'dun, *Al-Alaqat bayn Najd wa Al-Kuwait*, p., 118.

28   Moudi bint Mansour bint Abdul Aziz, *Al-Malik Abdul Aziz wa Mu'tamar Al-Kuwait 1923–1924* [King Abdul Aziz and the Kuwait Conference, 1923–1924] (Beirut, 1992), p. 82.

29   For the close relationship between Sheikh Mubarak and Sheikh Khaz'al see Abdul Aziz Muhammad Al-Mansour, *Al-Kuwait wa Alaqatiha bi Arabistan wa Al-Basra 1896–1915* [Kuwait and Its Relations with Arabistan and Basra 1896–1915] (Kuwait, 1980). Also see Khaz'al, *Tarikh Al-Kuwait Al-Siyasi*, pp. 246–260. Also see *Al-Sheikh Khaz'al Emir Al-Muhammara* [Sheikh Khaz'al, the Emir of Al-Muhammara] (Beirut, 1989), pp. 52–56.

30   *Kuwait Political Agency, Arabic Documents 1899–1949*, vol. 1, p. 112.

31   Al-Mansour, *Al-Kuwait wa Alaqatiha bi Arabistan wa Al-Basra 1896–1915*, pp. 68–73.

32   Ali Nima Al-Hilw, *Al-Ahwaz (Arabistan) Imarat Ka'b Al-Arabiyya fi Al-Muhammara* [Al-Ahwaz (Arabistan) The Arab Emirate of Ka'b in Al-Muhammara] (Baghdad, 1969), vol. 3, p. 131.

33   Ibid.

34   Mahmoud Ali Al-Dawid, *Ahadith an Al-Khalij Al-Arabi* [Stories about the Arab Gulf] (Baghdad, 1960), pp. 15–18.

35   Ali Nima Al-Hilo, pp. 125–143. Also Al-Hajji, *Al-Sheikh Abdul Aziz Al-Rashid*, p. 34.

36   For these developments see William Theodore Strunk, 'The Reign of Sheikh Khazal ibn Jabir and the Suppression of the Principality of Arabistan: A Study in British Imperialism in Southwestern Iran, 1897–1925' (Unpublished PhD thesis, University of Indiana, August 1977), trans. Abdul Jabbar Naji as *Hukm Al-Sheikh Khaz'al Bin Jaber wa Ihtilal Imarat Arabistan* [The Rule of Sheikh Khaz'al bin Jaber and the Occupation of the Emirate of Arabistan] (Basra, 1983).

37   Abdul Aziz Al-Mansour, *Al-Tatawwur Al-Siyasi li Qatar fi Fatrat ma bayn 1868–1916* [The Political Development of Qatar 1868–1916] (Kuwait, 1980), p. 151. For details of this period, see also Mahmoud Hilmi Mustafa et al., *Tatawwur Qatar Al-Siyasi wa Al-Ijtimai fi Ahd Al-Sheikh Qassem Bin Muhammad Al Thani* [Qatar's Political and Social Development in the Reign of Al-Sheikh Qassem bin Muhammad Al Thani] (Doha, 1980).

38 Ottoman Archive in Istanbul, 2 Rajab AH 1315, no. 4/170.

39 Ottoman Archive in Istanbul, 2 Rajab AH 1315, no. 48/170.

40 Ottoman Archive in Istanbul, 9 Rajab AH 1315, no. 25/90.

41 Ottoman Archive in Istanbul, 9 Shawwal AH 1315, no. 29/91.

42 Ottoman Archive in Istanbul, 22 Rajab AH 1315, no. 56/90.

43 Ottoman Archive in Istanbul, 24 Rajab AH 1315, no. 56/90.

44 Ottoman Archive in Istanbul, 27 January 1898, no. 29/91.

45 Nouriyya Muhammad Nasser Al-Saleh, *Alaqat Al-Kuwait Al-Siyasiyya bi Sharq Al-Jazira Al-Arabiyya wa Al-Iraq Al-Uthmani 1866–1902* [Kuwait's Political Relations with Eastern Arabia and Ottoman Iraq] (Kuwait, 1977), pp. 57–58.

46 Al-Mansour, *Al-Tatawwur Al-Siyasi li Qatar fi Fatrat ma bayn 1868–1916*, pp. 162–165.

47 B. J. Slot, *Mubarak Al-Sabah, Founder of Modern Kuwait 1896–1915* (London, 2005), p. 279, p. 383.

48 Abd Al-Massih Antaki, *Al-Riyad Al-Muzhira Bayn al-Kuwait wa Al-Muhammara* [Flowery Gardens between Kuwait and Muhammara] (Cairo, 1907), pp. 682–683.

49 *Al-Manar*, vol. 16 (1913), pp. 396–399. Youssef Ibish, *Rihlat Al-Imam Muhammad Rashid Rida* [Imam Muhammad Rashid Rida's Journey] (Beirut, 2000), p. 72.

50 Ibrahim Hilmi, 'Madi Al-Jazira wa Mustaqbaliha' [The Past and Future of Arabia] (Beirut, April 1914).

51 Khaz'al, *Tarikh Al-Kuwait Al-Siyasi*, pp. 80–81, 228.

52 Ibid., pp. 170–171.

53 Ibid., pp. 275–276.

Chapter 6 – The International Struggle for Kuwait

1 Grigori Bondarevsky, *Al-Kuwayt wa-'alāqatuhā al-duwalīyah khilāla al-qarn al-tāsi' 'ashara wa-awā'il al-qarn al-'ishrīn* [Kuwait and its International Relations during the Nineteenth and Beginning of the Twentieth Century], trans. from the Russian by Maher Salama (Kuwait, 1994).

2 Barclay Raunkiær, *Abr Al-Jazira Al-Arabiyya al Dhahr Jamal* [Through Wahhabiland on a Camel], trans. from English to Arabic by Mansour Muhammad Al-Khariji (Riyadh, 1999), p. 73. Also Muhammad bin Ibrahim Al-Shaybani, ed., *Risala fiha*

Hawadith wa Wafiyyat Al-Ayan min Tadwinat Khan Bahader, Abdullah Al-Qinai [An Account of the Lives and Deaths of the Notables, According to Khan Bahader and Abdullah al-Qinai] (Kuwait, Center for Manuscripts and Documents, 2006), p. 22.

3   See Philip Perceval Graves, *The Life of Sir Percy* Cox (London, 1941). See also Ghanem Sultan, *Jawanib Min Shakhsiyyat Al-Kuwait* [Perspectives on Kuwaiti Personalities] (Kuwait, 1990), p. 120. For these developments also see Lieutenant Colonel Sir Arnold T. Wilson, *The Persian Gulf: A Historical* Sketch, trans. Muhammad Amin Abdullah as *Tarikh Al-Khalij* [The History of the Gulf] (Muscat, 1981), pp. 179–203. For European policy towards the Gulf, particularly Kuwait, see Badr Al-Din Abbas Al-Khususi, *Dirasat fi Tarikh Al-Khalij Al-Arabi Al-Hadith wa Al-Mu'asir* [Studies in the Modern and Contemporary History of the Arab Gulf] (Kuwait, 1988).

4   Abdul Aziz Abdul Ghani Ibrahim, *Al-Salam Al-Baritani fi Al-Khalij Al-Arabi 1899–1947, Dirasa Wathaiqiyya* [British Peace in the Arab Gulf, 1899–1947: A Documentary Study] (Riyadh, 1981); Abdul Aziz Abdul Ghani Ibrahim, *Umara wa Guzat, Qadiyyat Al-Hudud wa Al-Siyada Al-Iqlimiyya fi Al-Khalij, Dirasa Wathaiqiyya* [Emirs and Conquerers: The Question of Borders and Regional Sovereignty in the Gulf: A Documentary Study] (Beirut, 1995). See also Brian Cooper Busch, *Britain and The Persian Gulf 1894–1914* (Berkeley, CA, 1967), pp. 95–132, 187–234, 304–347; Frederick F. Anscombe, *The Ottoman Gulf, The Creation of Kuwait, Saudi Arabia and Qatar* (New York, 1997), pp. 91–112.

5   *Kuwait Political Agency, Arabic Documents 1899–1949* (London, 1994), vol. 1, pp. 726–728.

6   B. J. Slot, *Mubarak Al-Sabah, Founder of Modern Kuwait 1896–1915* (London, 2005), p. 276.

7   J. G. Lorimer, *Gazetteer of the Persian Gulf, Oman and Central Arabia* (repr., Cambridge University Press Archive Editions, 1986), vol. 7, pp. 3833–3834.

8   Abdullah Khaled Al-Hatem, *Min Huna Bada'at Al-Kuwait* [This is How Kuwait Began] (Kuwait, 1980), pp. 42–43.

9 Lorimer, *Gazetteer of the Persian Gulf, Oman and Central Arabia*, vol. 7, pp. 3874–3875.

10 Hussein Khalaf Al-Sheikh Khaz'al, *Tarikh Al-Kuwait Al-Siyasi* [Political History of Kuwait] (Beirut, 1962), p. 138.

11 Al-Hatem, *Min Huna Bada'at Al-Kuwait*, pp. 42–43.

12 Lorimer, *Gazetteer of the Persian Gulf, Oman and Central Arabia*, pp. 3,876–3,877.

13 Penelope Touzon, *Sijillat Al-Mu'tamad Al-Baritani wa Al-Wikalat Al-Tabi'a lahu fi Al-Khalij* [Records of the British Agent and the Agencies Dependent on Him in The Gulf] (Kuwait, 1993), pp. 13–14.

14 Ottoman Archive in Istanbul, 20 October 1904, no. 113/480.

15 Ottoman Archive in Istanbul, 21 October 1904, no. 113/480.

16 Ottoman Archive in Istanbul, 5 November 1904, no. 113/480.

17 For a text of the report of this trip written by Knox in February 1906, which includes a list of the names of the areas he visited, see Report on Tour of Political Agent at Kuwait to Hafar Al-Batin in February 1906, with glossary of vernacular words used in report, January 1906, in *Records of Kuwait 1899–1961* (Cambridge, 1989), vol. 1, pp. 6–28.

18 See report of Political Agent Knox to Political Resident Cox in Political Agent, Kuwait, to Political Resident, Bushire enclosing notes of Agent's tour in March 1906 of southern Kuwait, 28 March 1906 in ibid., pp. 29–31.

19 Khaz'al, *Tarikh Al-Kuwait Al-Siyasi*, p. 138.

20 This lease was terminated in 1922.

21 Yaqub Youssef Al-Hajji, *Al-Sheikh Abdul Aziz Al-Rashid, Sirat Hayatihi* [Al-Sheikh Abdul Aziz Al-Rashid: A Biography] (Kuwait, 1993), pp. 198–199.

22 Knox to J. H. Bill, 23 August 1907 in *Kuwait Political Agency, Arabic Documents 1899–1949* (London, 1994), pp. 396–397.

23 Political Resident Cox to Sheikh Mubarak, 6 September 1910; the Sheikh's reply, 10 September, *Kuwait Political Agency, Arabic Documents 1899–1949* (London, 1994), pp. 58–62. See also British diplomatic correspondence on slavery in Kuwait and the Gulf area in *Records of Kuwait 1899–1961*, vol. 4, pp. 227–284.

24 See British diplomatic correspondence on drilling for oil in Kuwait in *Records of Kuwait 1899–1961*, vol. 5, pp. 3–14.

25 In 1935 its name changed to the Anglo-Iranian Oil Company.

26 Najat Abdul Qader Jassem, *Al-Uthmaniyun wa Shamal Shibh Jazirat Al-Arab, 1840–1909* [The Ottomans and North Arabia 1840–1909] (Cairo, 1976), pp. 197–198. For details see, Archibald H. T. Chisholm, *The First Kuwait Oil Concession Agreement: A Record of Negotiations 1911–1934* (London, 1975).

27 Jassem, *Al-Uthmaniyun wa Shamal Shibh Jazirat Al-Arab, 1840–1909*, p. 212.

28 Ottoman Archive in Istanbul, 22 Shawwal AH 1322, no. 129/482.

29 Walid Hamdi Al-Azami, *Al-Kuwait fi Al-Wathaiq Al-Inglisiyya 1752–1960* [Kuwait in British Documents 1752–1960] (London, 1991), pp. 14–15.

30 Jamal Zakariyya Qassem, 'Baritaniyya wa Al-Khalij Al-Arabi fi Al-Harb Al-Alamiyya Al-Ula' [Britain and the Gulf in the First World War], in *Majallat Dirasat Al-Khalij wa Al-Jazira Al-Arabiyya*, 3 (1975), pp. 88–95.

31 Sayyed Nawfal, *Al Khalig Al Arabi Awe Al Houdoud Al Sharkia Lil Watan Al Arabi* [The Arab Gulf or the Eastern Frontiers of the Arab Nation] (Beirut, 1969), pp. 185–186.

32 Al-Hajji, *Al-Sheikh Abdul Aziz Al-Rashid*, pp. 203–205.

33 Khaz'al, *Tarikh Al-Kuwait Al-Siyasi*, pp. 155–160.

34 Ibid., p. 161.

35 Al-Hajji, *Al-Sheikh Abdul Aziz Al-Rashid*, p. 203.

36 Bondarevsky, *Al-Kuwayt*, pp. 126–127.

37 Slot, *Mubarak Al-Sabah, Founder of Modern Kuwait 1896–1915*, pp. 280, 284–285.

38 Maymouna Al-Khalifa Al-Sabah, *Al-Kuwait fi Zil Al-Himaya Al-Baritaniyya* [Kuwait Under British Protection] (Kuwait, 1988), pp. 29–32.

39 Qassem, 'Baritaniyya wa Al-Khalij Al-Arabi fi Al-Harb Al-Alamiyya Al-Ula', p. 424. For details of European rivalry over this project see, Merle, Edward, *Turkey, the Great Powers and the Baghdad Railway, A Study in Imperialism* (New York, 1923).

40 Bondarevsky, *Al-Kuwayt*, pp. 143–144.

41 Ibid., pp. 146–147.

42   Sultan bin Muhammad Al-Qassimi, *Bayan Al-Kuwait: Sirat Hayat Al-Sheikh Mubarak Al-Sabah* [A Biography of Sheikh Mubarak Al-Sabah] (Sharja, 2004), p. 107.

43   See British Diplomatic Correspondence on the Berlin–Baghdad Railway and the development of their position in *Records of Kuwait 1899–1961*, vol. 1, pp. 427–482. From Sheikh Mubarak to Political Resident Meade, Bushire, 13 January 1900. See also Bondarevsky, *Al-Kuwayt*, p. 147.

44   Al-Qassemi, *Bayan Al-Kuwait*, p. 108.

45   From Political Resident Meade, Bushire, to Viceroy of India, 23 January 1900.

46   From Gaskin, Memo of an interview with Sheikh Mubarak, Bushire, 5 February 1900.

47   Al-Qassemi, *Bayan Al-Kuwait*, p. 114.

48   Bondarevsky, *Al-Kuwayt*, pp. 148–149.

49   Al-Azami, *Al-Kuwait fi Al-Wathaiq Al-Inglisiyya 1752–1960*, pp. 28–30.

50   Ibid., pp. 31–32.

51   Ibid., p. 33.

52   See British diplomatic correspondence on the British-India Steam Navigation Company and Britain's commercial interests in Kuwait in *Records of Kuwait 1899–1961*, vol. 4, pp. 161–180.

53   From Mubarak to Lyle, 4 Rabi Thani, A H 1318.

54   See the report sent by Political Agent Knox to the Political Resident in Bushire on 3 September 1907, on the activity of this company in Major S. G. Knox, Political Agent, Kuwait to Political Resident, Bushire, 3 September 1907, *Records of Kuwait 1899–1961*, vol. 4, pp. 699–700. For correspondence on the same topic see also pp. 701–704.

55   Lorimer, *Gazetteer of the Persian Gulf, Oman and Central Arabia*, vol. 3, p. 1,565.

56   Jassem, *Al-Uthmaniyun wa Shamal Shibh Jazirat Al-Arab, 1840–1909*, p. 26.

57   For the development of Russian interest in the Gulf see A. Lutsky, *Modern History of the Arab Countries* (Moscow, 1969).

58   Lord Curzon, *Persia and the Persian Question* (London, 1892), p. 465. Also see Al-Sayyed Rajab Haraz, *Al-Dawla Al-Uthmaniyya*

wa Shibh Al-Jazira Al-Arabiyya 1840–1909 [The Ottoman Empire And the Arabian Peninsula 1840–1909] (Cairo, 1970), pp. 172–173.

59   Government of India to Lord Hamilton, 14 February 1899.

60   Badr Al-Din Al-Khususi, 'Al-Nashat Al-Russi fi Al-Khalij Al-Arabi 1887–1907' [Russian Activity in the Arab Gulf 1887–1907] in *Majallat Dirasat Al-Khalij wa Al-Jazira Al-Arabiyya*, 5/18 (1979), p. 118.

61   Bondarevsky, *Al-Kuwayt*, p. 193.

62   Efim Rezvan, *Russian Ships in the Gulf 1899–1903* (London, 1993), p. 11.

63   Ibid., pp. 54–55. Also Bondarevsky, *Al-Kuwayt*, pp. 214–218.

64   Bondarevsky, *Al-Kuwayt*, pp. 267–268. See the text of the secret telegram sent by Kruglov on 13 April 1901 and Ovseyenko's report dated 20 April, ibid., pp. 460–462.

65   Ibid., pp. 219–223.

66   Ibid., pp. 276–277.

67   Rezvan, *Russian Ships in the Gulf 1899–1903*, p. 11.

68   Ibid., p. 91.

69   Ibid., pp. 92–93.

70   Bondarevsky, *Al-Kuwayt*, p. 279.

71   Al-Khususi, 'Al-Nashat Al-Russi fi Al-Khalij Al-Arabi 1887–1907', pp. 119–122. Bondarevsky, *Al-Kuwayt*, pp. 287–288.

72   Rezvan, *Russian Ships in the Gulf 1899–1903*.

73   Ibid., p. 133.

74   Bondarevsky, *Al-Kuwayt*, p. 367.

75   Ibid., p. 158.

76   Al-Khususi, 'Al-Nashat Al-Russi fi Al-Khalij Al-Arabi 1887–1907', pp. 119–122.

Conclusion

1   J. J. Saldanha, ed., *Al-Tarikh Al-Siyasi lil Kuwait fi Ahd Mubarak, Dirasa Watha'iqiyya Muqarina bi Al-Mu'arrikhin Al-Mahalliyyin* [The Poltical History of Kuwait Under Mubarak, a Comparative Study Between Local Historians], trans. Fattouh Al-Khatrash (Kuwait: 1990), pp. 105–106.

2   Sultan bin Muhammad Al-Qassimi, *Bayan Al-Kuwait: Sirat Hayat Al-Sheikh Mubarak Al-Sabah* [A Biography of Sheikh Mubarak Al-Sabah]. Sharja, 2004, p. 164 and p. 312.

3   From Political Agent Knox, Kuwait, to Political Resident Cox, Bushire, 22 April 1908.

4   Sultan bin Muhammad Al-Qassimi, *Bayan Al-Kuwait*, p. 319.

5   Saldanha, ed., *Al-Tarikh Al-Siyasi lil Kuwait fi Ahd Mubarak*, p. 118.

6   J. G. Lorimer, *Gazetteer of the Persian Gulf, Oman and Central Arabia* (reprinted edition, Cambridge University Press Archive Editions, 1986), vol. 1, p. 575.

7   Khaled Hammoud Al-Sa'dun, *Al-Alaqat bayn Najd wa Al-Kuwait 1319–1341 A H/1902–1922 A D* [Relations between Najd and Kuwait 1319–1341/1902–1922] (Kuwait, Zat Al Salassel, 1990), pp. 92–93.

8   Abdullah Yusuf Al-Ghoneim, ed., *Akhbar Al-Kuwait: Rasail Ali Bin Gholoum Reda Al-Wakil Al-Ikhbari li Britaniya fi Al-Kuwait* [News from Kuwait: The Letters of Ali bin Gholoum Reda, the British Agent for information in Kuwait] (Kuwait, 2007), p. 13.

9   Ibid., p. 86.

10   Grigori Bondarevsky, *Al-Kuwayt wa-'alāqatuhā al-duwalīyah khilāla al-qarn al-tāsi' 'ashara wa-awā'il al-qarn al-'ishrīn* [Kuwait and its international Relations during the Nineteenth and the Beginning of the Twentieth Century], translated from the Russian by Maher Salama (Kuwait, 1994), p. 439.

11   From Political Resident Cox, Bushire, to Monto, Foreign Office, London, 9 December 1908.

12   W. H. Shakespear, Political Agent, Kuwait, to Political Resident, Bushire, 15 June 1910, in *Records of Kuwait 1899–1961* (Cambridge, 1989), vol. 1, pp. 329–330.

13   W. H. Shakespear, Political Agent, Kuwait, to Political Resident, Bushire, 12 July 1910, in *Records of Kuwait 1899–1961* (Cambridge, 1989), vol. 1, pp. 332–333.

14   Sultan bin Muhammad Al-Qassimi, *Bayan Al-Kuwait*, p. 258, pp. 281–282 and p. 293.

15   Bondarevsky, *Al-Kuwayt*, p. 422.

16   Ibid., p. 312.

17   From Political Agent Knox, Kuwait, to Political Resident Cox, Bushire, 8 July 1908.

18   Sultan bin Muhammad Al-Qassimi, *Bayan Al-Kuwait*, p. 287.

19   B. J. Slot, *Mubarak Al-Sabah, Founder of Modern Kuwait 1896–1915* (London, 2005), pp. 280–281.

20   Al-Ghoneim, ed., *Akhbar Al-Kuwait*, p. 35.

21   Lorimer, *Gazetteer of the Persian Gulf, Oman and Central Arabia*, p. 1536. Saldanha, ed., *Al-Tarikh Al-Siyasi lil Kuwait fi Ahd Mubarak*, p. 93.

22   Consul Wratislaw, Basra, to Sir N. O'Conor, British Ambassador, Constantinople, 2 October 1899 in *Records of Kuwait 1899–1961* (Cambridge, 1989), vol. 6, p. 673.

23   Sultan bin Muhammad Al-Qassimi, *Bayan Al-Kuwait*, p. 312.

24   Bondarevsky, *Al-Kuwayt*, p. 103.

Bibliography

Manuscript sources

Archives of the Ottoman Empire, Istanbul
British National Archives, London

Published archive collections

ENGLISH DOCUMENTS

The Affairs of Kuwait 1896–1905, ed. Robin Bidwell. London, 1971.

Arabian Boundaries: Primary Documents 1853–1957, ed. Richard Schofield. Cambridge, 1988.

Arabian Gulf Oil Concessions 1911–1953. Cambridge, 1989.

British Documents on Foreign Affairs: Reports and Papers from the Foreign Office Confidential Print, ed. Kenneth Bourne and D. Cameron Watt, Series B, parts I and II.

Kuwait Political Agency, Arabic Documents 1899–1949. London, 1994.

Persian Gulf Administration Reports 1873–1957. Cambridge, 1986.

Persian Gulf Trade Reports 1905–1940. Cambridge, 1987.

Political Diaries of the Persian Gulf 1904–1958. Cambridge, 1990.

Records of Kuwait 1899-1961, ed. A. de L. Rush. Cambridge, 1989.

Records of the Persian Gulf Pearl Fisheries, ed. Anita L. P. Burdett. Cambridge, 1989.

Royal Families of Arabia, ed. A. de L. Rush. Cambridge, 1991.

OTTOMAN DOCUMENTS
*Watha'iq al-Archif Al-Othmani Mutarjama ila al-Lugha Al-'Arabiyya
wa Mahfuza lada Markaz al-Buhuth wa al-Dirasat al-Kuwaitiyya*
[Documents from the Ottoman Archives translated into Arabic and
held at the Centre for Kuwaiti Research and Studies].

ARABIC DOCUMENTS
Kuwait Political Agency: Arabic Documents 1899–1949. Cambridge,
1994.

English published sources

Anscombe, Frederick F., *The Ottoman Gulf: The Creation of Kuwait, Saudi Arabia and Qatar.* New York, 1997.

Brent, Peter, *Far Arabia, Explorers of the Myth.* London, 1979.

Busch, Brian Cooper, *Britain and the Persian Gulf 1894–1914.* Berkeley, 1967.

Chisholm, Archibald H. T., *The First Kuwait Oil Concession Agreement: A Record of Negotiations 1911–1934.* London, 1975.

Curzon, Lord George, *Persia and the Persian Question.* London, 1892.

Dickson, H. R. P., *The Arab of the Desert: A Glimpse into Badawin Life in Kuwait and Saudi Arabia.* London, 1949.

———, *Kuwait and Her Neighbours.* London, 1968.

Donaldson, Neil, *The Postal Agencies in Eastern Arabia and the Gulf.* London, repr. 1994.

Graves, Philip Perceval, *The Life of Sir Percy Cox.* London, 1941.

Lorimer, J. G., *Gazetteer of the Persian Gulf, Oman and Central Arabia.* Cambridge, repr. 1986.

Lutsky, A., *Modern History of the Arab Countries.* Moscow, 1969.

Merle, Edward, *Turkey, the Great Powers and the Baghdad Railway, A Study in Imperialism.* New York, 1923.

Mylrea, Stanley, *Kuwait before Oil: Memoirs of Dr C. Stanley G. Mylrea, Pioneer Medical Missionary of the Arabian Mission, Reformed Church in America.* Privately printed. Copy held by the Library of Columbia University in New York. (Typescript copies of two versions of Dr Mylrea's memoirs are also held by the Middle East Centre Archive at St Antony's College, Oxford MECA GB 165-0214.)

Rezvan, Efim, *Russian Ships in the Gulf*. London, 1993.

Scudder, Lewis R., *The Arabian Mission's Story*. Grand Rapids, MI, 1998.

Slot, B. J., *Mubarak Al-Sabah, Founder of Modern Kuwait 1896–1915*. London, 2005.

Winstone, H. V. F., *Captain Shakespear: A Portrait*. London, 1976.

Arabic published sources in translation from European languages

Abdul Rahman, Ashraf Muhammad, 'Tarikh Al-Iraq Al-Siyasi min Nihayat Hukm Midhat Pasha ila Qiyam Hukm Al-Itihadiyyeen 1872–1908' [The Political History of Iraq from the End of Midhat Pasha's Rule to the Beginning of the Unionists Rule, 1872–1908], MA thesis, Faculty of Arts, Ayn Shams University, 1993.

Anon., 'Safahat wa Watha'iq Min Qissat Al-Ma' fi Al-Kuwait' [Pages and Documents from the Story of Water in Kuwait], *Risalat Al-Kuwait*, 3/10, 2005.

Bondarevsky, Grigori, *Al-Kuwayt wa-'alaqatuha al-duwaliyah khilala al-qarn al-tasi' 'ashara wa-awa'il al-qarn al-'ishrīn* [Kuwait and its International Relations during the Nineteenth and Beginning of the Twentieth Century], trans. from the Russian by Maher Salama. Kuwait, 1994.

Calverley, Eleanor, *My Arabian Days and Nights: A Medical Missionary in Old Kuwait*. New York, 1958; trans. Abdullah Al-Hatem as *Kuntu Awal Tabiba fi Al-Kuwait* [I was the First Female Doctor in Kuwait]. Kuwait, 1968.

Dickson, H. R. P., *Kuwait and Her Neighbours*, trans. Fattuh Abdul Muhsin Al-Khatrash. Kuwait, 1995.

Dickson, Violet (Um Saud), *Arba'un Aam fi Al-Kuwait* [Forty Years in Kuwait], with introduction by Sayf Marzouq Al-Shamlan Al Sayf. Kuwait, 1994.

Mylrea, Stanley, 'Memoirs', trans. Muhammad Ghanem Al-Rumayhi and Bassem Sarhan as *Al-Kuwait Qabl Al-Naft* [Kuwait before Oil]. Kuwait, 1997.

Raunkiær, Barclay, *Abr Al-Jazira Al-Arabiyya al Dhahr Jamal* [Through Wahhabiland on a Camel], trans. Mansour Muhammad Al-Khariji. Riyadh, 1999.

Saldanha, J. J., *Al-Tarikh Al-Siyasi lil Kuwait fi Ahd Mubarak, Dirasa Watha'iqiyya Muqarina bi Al-Mu'arrikhin Al-Mahalliyyin* [The Political History of Kuwait under Mubarak, a Comparative Study between Local Historians], trans. and ed. Fattouh Al-Khatrash. Kuwait, 1990.

Strunk, William Theodore, 'The Reign of Sheikh Khazal ibn Jabir and the Suppression of the Principality of Arabistan: A Study in British Imperialism in Southwestern Iran, 1897–1925', PhD thesis, University of Indiana, 1977; trans. Abdul Jabbar Naji as *Hukm Al-Sheikh Khaz'al Bin Jaber wa Ihtilal Imarat Arabistan* [The Rule of Sheikh Khaz'al bin Jaber and the Occupation of the Emirate of Arabistan]. Basra, 1983.

Touma, Salim (ed. and trans.), *Sufun Russiyya fi Al-Khalij Al-Arabi 1899–1903, Mawad Min Arsheef Al-Dawla Al-Markazi lil Ustuul Al-Bahri Al-Harbi* [Russian Ships in the Arab Gulf 1899–1903, Material from the Central Government Archives of the Navy]. Moscow, 1990.

Touzon, Penelope, *Sijillat Al-Mu'tamad Al-Baritani wa Al-Wikalat Al-Tabi'a lahu fi Al-Khalij* [Records of the British Agent and the Agencies Dependent on Him in the Gulf]. Kuwait, 1993.

Wilson, Arnold T., *The Persian Gulf: A Historical* Sketch; trans. Muhammad Amin Abdullah as *Tarikh Al-Khalij* [The History of the Gulf]. Muscat, 1981.

Arabic published sources

Abdullah, Muhammad Hassan, *Al-Shi'r we Al-Shu'ara fi Al-Kuwait* [Poetry and Poets in Kuwait]. Kuwait, 1987.

Abu Hakima, Ahmad Mustafa, *Ta'rikh Al-Kuwait Al-Hadith 1750–1965* [Modern History of Kuwait 1750–1965]. Kuwait, 1984.

Abu Milal, Khalil Muhammad Audah, *Ulama Al-Kuwait Du'aat Al-Islah* [Kuwait's Ulema Call for Reform]. Kuwait, 1987.

Ansari, Abdullah Zakariyya Al-, *Fahd Al-Askar, Hayatahu wa Shi'rihi* [Fahd Al-Askar: His Life and Poetry]. Kuwait, 1967.

Antaki, Abd Al-Massih, *Al-Riyad Al-Muzhira Bayn al-Kuwait wa Al-Muhammara* [The Flowered Gardens between Kuwait and Muhammara]. Cairo, 1907.

———, *Al-Ayaat al-Subah fi Ta'rikh Mawlana Sahib Al-Summuw Emir Al-Kuwait Al-Sheikh Mubarak Pasha Bin Al-Sabah* [The Highlights of the History of Our Master His Majesty the Emir of Kuwait, Sheikh Mubarak Pasha Al-Sabah]. Cairo, AH 1326.

Aqqad, Salah Al-, *Al-Tayyarat Al-Siyasiyya fi Al-Khalij Al-Arabi* [Political Currents in the Arab Gulf]. Cairo, 1965.

Araynan, Munira Abdullah Al-, *Alaqat Najd bil Qiwa Al-Muhita 1319– 1323 AH/1902–1914 AD* [Najd's Relations with Surrounding Powers]. Kuwait, 1990.

Ashkenani, Zubayda Ali (trans. and ed.), *Min Nafidhat 'Al-Americani': Taqarir Al-Aamilin fi Mustashfa al-Irsaliyya Al-Americiyya An al-Kuwait Qabl Al-Naft* [From the Window of the 'American' Hospital: The Reports of Those Who Worked at the American Mission Hospital about Kuwait before the Oil]. Kuwait, 1995.

Azami, Walid Hamdi Al-, *Al-Kuwait fi Al-Wathaiq Al-Inglisiyya 1752– 1960* [Kuwait in British Documents 1752–1960]. London, 1991.

Bassam, Khaled Al-, *Rijal fi Jaza'ir Al-Lu'lu'* [Men in the Pearl Islands]. Manama, 1991.

———, *Marfa' Al-Dhikrayat: Rihlat lIa Al-Kuwait Al-Qadima* [The Port of Memories: Voyages to Old Kuwait]. Kuwait, 1995.

——— (ed. and trans.), *Al-Qawafil: Rihlat Al-Irsaliyya Al-Amerikiyya fi Mudun Al-Khalij wa Al-Jazira Al-Arabia 1901–1926* [The Caravans: The Journeys of the American Mission in the Cities of the Gulf and Arabia 1901–1926]. Bahrain, 1993.

——— (ed. and trans.), *Sadmat Al-Ihtikak. Hikayat Al-Irasaliyya Al-Amerikiyya fi Al-Khalij wa Al-Jazira Al-Arabiyya, 1892–1925* [The Shock of Contact: The Story of the American Mission in the Gulf and Arabia]. Beirut, 1998.

Bint Mansour bint Abdul Aziz, Moudi, *Al-Malik Abdul Aziz wa Mu'tamar Al-Kuwait 1923–1924* [King Abdul Aziz and the Kuwait Conference, 1923–1924]. Beirut, 1992.

Center for Kuwaiti Research and Studies, *Tarsim Al-Hudud Al-Kuwaitiyya Al-Iraqiyya: Al-Haq Al-Tarikhi wa Al-Irada Al-Duwaliyya* [Drawing the Kuwaiti-Iraqi Borders: Historical Rights and International Decrees]. Kuwait, 1992.

Dawid, Mahmoud Ali Al-, *Ahadith an Al-Khalij Al-Arabi* [Stories about the Arab Gulf]. Baghdad, 1960.

Duwaysh, Abdullah Abdul Aziz Al-, *Diwan Hammud Al-Nasser Al-Badr* [The Poetry of Hammud Al-Nasser Al-Badr]. Kuwait, 1981.

Fil, Muhammad Rashid Al-, *Al-Jughrafiya Al-Ta'rikhiyya lil Kuwait* [The Historical Geography of Kuwait]. Kuwait, 1985.

Ghoneim, Abdullah Yusuf Al-, *Al-Kuwait: Qiraa'a Fi Al-Khara'it Al-Ta'rikhiyya* [Kuwait: A Reading of Historical Maps]. Kuwait, 1992.

——— (ed.), *Akhbar Al-Kuwait: Rasail Ali Bin Gholoum Reda Al-Wakil Al-Ikhbari li Britaniya fi Al-Kuwait* [News from Kuwait: The Letters of Ali bin Gholoum Reda, the British Agent for Information in Kuwait]. Kuwait, 2007.

Haddad, Muhammad Al-, et al., *Turath Al-Badiya Muqaddima li Dirasat Al-Badiya fi Al-Kuwait* [The Culture of the Desert, an Introduction to the Study of the Desert in Kuwait]. Kuwait, 1987.

Hajji, Yaqoub Youssef Al-, *Al-Nashatat Al-Bahriyya Al-Qadima fi Al-Kuwait* [Maritime Activities of Yesteryear in Kuwait]. Kuwait, 2007.

———, *Al-Sheikh Abdul Aziz Al-Rashid, Sirat Hayatihi* [Al-Sheikh Abdul Aziz Al-Rashid: A Biography]. Kuwait, 1993.

———, *Sina'at Al-Sufun Al-Shira'iyya fi Al-Kuwait* [The Sailboat Industry in Kuwait]. Qatar, 1988.

——— (ed.), *Al-Kuwait Al-Qadima: Siwar wa Dhikrayat* [Old Kuwait: Photographs and Memories].

Hamadani, Ali Hassan Al-, *Al-Hiraf Al-Yadawiyya bayn Al-Tarikh wa Al-Qanun fi Al-Mujtama Al-Kuwaiti Al-Qadim, min fatrat 1896–1950* [Hand Crafts between History and Law in Old Kuwaiti Society 1896–1950]. London, 1994.

Haraz, Al-Sayyid Rajab, *Al-Dawla Al-Uthmaniyya wa Shibh Al-Jazira Al-Arabiyya 1840–1909* [The Ottoman Empire and the Arabian Peninsula 1840–1909]. Cairo, 1970.

Hatem, Abdullah Khaled Al-, *Min Huna Bada'at Al-Kuwait* [This is How Kuwait Began]. Kuwait, 1980.

Hilmi, Ibrahim, 'Madi Al-Jazira wa Mustaqbaliha' [The Past and Future of Arabia], *Fata Al-Arab*, Beirut, April 1914.

Hilw, Ali Nima Al-, *Al-Ahwaz (Arabistan) Imarat Ka'b Al-Arabiyya fi Al-Muhammara* [Al-Ahwaz (Arabistan) the Arab Emirate of Ka'b in Al-Muhammara]. Baghdad, 1969.

Hussein, Abdul Aziz, *Muhadarat An Al-Mujtama Al-Arabi bi Al-Kuwait* [Lectures on Arab Society in Kuwait]. Cairo, 1960.

Hussein, Ayyub, *Ma'a Dhikrayatina Al-Kuwaitiyya* [With our Kuwaiti Memories]. Kuwait, 1984.

Ibish, Youssef, *Rihlat Al-Imam Muhammad Rashid Rida* [Imam Muhammad Rashid Rida's Journey]. Beirut, 2000.

Ibrahim, Abdul Aziz Abdul Ghani, *Al-Salam Al-Baritani fi Al-Khalij Al-Arabi 1899–1947, Dirasa Wathaiqiyya* [British Peace in the Arab Gulf, 1899–1947: A Documentary Study]. Riyadh, 1981.

———, *Umara wa Guzat, Qadiyyat Al-Hudud wa Al-Siyada Al-Iqlimiyya fi Al-Khalij, Dirasa Wathaiqiyya* [Emirs and Conquerors: The Question of Borders and Regional Sovereignty in the Gulf. A Documentary Study]. Beirut, 1995.

Jamal, Muhammad Abdul Hadi, *Ta'rikh Al-Khadamat Al-Baridiyya fi Al-Kuwait* [History of the Postal Services in Kuwait]. Kuwait, 1994.

Jarallah, Khaled Fahd, *Ta'rikh Al-Khadamat Al-Sihiyya fi Al-Kuwait Min Al-Nasha Hatta Al-Istiqlal* [The History of Healthcare in Kuwait from the Beginning to Independence]. Kuwait, 1996.

Jasim, Mounira Abdul Qadir Al-, 'Al-Uthmaniyun wa Shamal Shibh Jazirat Al-Arab, 1840–1909' [The Ottomans and North Arabia 1840–1909], PhD thesis, Ayn Shams University, Cairo, 1976.

———, *Tatawwur Al-Khara'it Al-Kuwaitiyya* [The Development of Kuwaiti Maps]. Kuwait, 1993.

———, *Al-Tatawwur Al-Siyasi wa Al-Iqtisadi lil Kuwait bayn Al-Harbayn 1912–1939* [Political and Economic Progress in Kuwait between the Two Wars 1912–1939]. Kuwait, 1997.

———, *Sheikh Youssef Bin Issa Al-Qinai, Dawarahu fi Al-Hayat Al-Iztima'iyya wal Siyasiyya fi Al-Kuwait* [Sheikh Youssef bin Issa Al-Qinai, His Role in the Social and Political Life of Kuwait]. Kuwait, n.d.

Karmali, Anastace Al-, 'Al-Kuwait', *Al-Mashriq*, 7/10, 1904, pp. 450–458.

Khalifa, May Muhammad Al-, *Ma'a Sheikh Al-Udaba fi al-Bahrain: Ibrahim Bin Muhammad Al-Khalifa 1850–1933* [With Bahrain's Leading Writer: Ibrahim bin Muhammad Al-Khalifa 1850–1933]. Bahrain, 1993.

Khater, Mubarak Al-, *Min A'lam Al-Khalij Al-Arabi: Nabighat Al-Bahrain Abdullah Al-Zayed Hayatihi wa A'malihi 1894–1945* [Notables of the Arab Gulf: The Genius of Bahrain Abdullah al-Zayed: His Life and Works 1894–1945]. Beirut, 1972.

———, *Al-Mu'asasat Al-Thaqafiyya Al-Ula fi l-Kuwait* [The First Cultural Foundations in Kuwait]. Kuwait, 1997.

Khatrash, Fattouh Abdul Muhsin Al-, *History of British–Kuwaiti Political Relations 1890–1921*. Kuwait, 1974.

Khazal, Hussein Khalaf Al-Sheikh, *Ta'rikh Al-Kuwait Al-Siyasi* [Political History of Kuwait]. Beirut, 1962.

Khususi, 'Al-Nashat Al-Russi fi Al-Khalij Al-Arabi 1887–1907' [Russian Activity in the Arab Gulf 1887–1907], *Majallat Dirasat Al-Khalij wa Al-Jazira Al-Arabiyya*, 5/18, 1979.

―――, Badr Al-Din Al-, *Dirasat fi Tarikh Al-Khalij Al-Arabi Al-Hadith wa Al-Mu'asir* [Studies in the Modern and Contemporary History of the Arab Gulf]. Kuwait, 1988, pp. 113–134.

Kundari, Yaqub Youssef Al-, *Al-Diwaniyya Al-Kuwaitiyya* [The Kuwaiti Diwaniyya]. Kuwait, 2002.

Maghni, Adel Muhammad Al-, *Lamahat Min Tawabi Al-Barid Fi Al-Kuwait* [Glimpses of the Postage Stamps of Kuwait]. Kuwait, 1994.

Mansour, Abdul Aziz Al-, *Al-Kuwait wa Alaqatiha bi Arabistan wa Al-Basra 1896–1915* [Kuwait and its Relations with Arabistan and Basra 1896–1915]. Kuwait, 1980.

―――, *Al-Tatawwur Al-Siyasi li Qatar fi Fatrat ma bayn 1868–1916* [The Political Development of Qatar 1868–1916]. Kuwait, 1980.

Matiri, Shafa Al-Muhdaris Al-, *Alam Al-Kuwait Mundh Al-Nash'a Hatta Al-Istiqlal 1746–1961* [The Kuwaiti Flag: From the Beginning to Independence 1746–1961], with introduction and comment by Muhammad bin Ibrahim Al-Shaybani. Kuwait, 1996.

Mazini, Ahmad Abdul Aziz Al-, *Al-Kuwait wa Tarikhuha Al-Bahri Aw Rihlat Al-Shiraa'* [Kuwait and its Maritime History: Stories of Sail]. Kuwait, 1986.

Mizyan, Abdullah Salem Abdullah Muhammad Al-, *Ta'rikh wa Amjad* [History and Glory]. Kuwait, n.d.

Mughni, Adel Muhammad Al-Abd Al-, *Dalil Ma'rad Al-Imlah Al-Kuwaitiyya abr Al-Tarikh* [The Guide to the Exhibition of Kuwaiti Currency through the Ages]. Kuwait, 1996.

Mukhtar, Salah Al-Din Al-, *Tarikh Al-Mamlaka Al-Arabiyya Al-Saudiyya Madiha wa Hadiruha* [The History of the Kingdom of Saudi Arabia: Its Past and Present]. Beirut, n.d.

Mustafa, Mahmoud Hilmi, et al., *Tatawwur Qatar Al-Siyasi wa Al-Ijtimai fi Ahd Al-Sheikh Qassem Bin Muhammad Al Thani* [Qatar's Political and Social Development in the Reign of Al-Sheikh Qassem bin Muhammad Al Thani]. Doha, 1980.

Nishan, Banwa, *Abdul Aziz Al Saud: Sirat Batal wa Mawlid Mamlaka* [Abdul Aziz Al Saud: The Story of a Hero and the Birth of a Kingdom], trans. into Arabic by Abdul Fattah Yaseen. Beirut, n.d.

Nuri, Abdullah Al-, *Khalidun fi Ta'rikh Al-Kuwait* [Legends in the History of Kuwait]. Kuwait, 1988.

———, *Qissat Al-Ta'lim fi Al-Kuwait fi Nisf Qarn* [The Story of Education in Kuwait in Half a Century]. Kuwait, n.d.

Qalaji, Qadri, *Adwa' ala Tarikh Al-Kuwait* [Spotlight on the History of Kuwait]. Beirut, 1962.

Qassem, Jamal Zakariyya, *Al-Khalij Al-Arabi, Dirasa li Ta'rikh Al-Imarat Al-Arabiyya 1840–1914* [The Arab Gulf: A Study of the History of the Arab Emirates 1840–1914]. Cairo, 1966.

———, 'Baritaniyya wa Al-Khalij Al-Arabi fi Al-Harb Al-Alamiyya Al-Ula' [Britain and the Gulf in the First World War], *Majallat Dirasat Al-Khalij wa Al-Jazira Al-Arabiyya*, 3, 1975, pp. 88–95.

Qassimi, Sultan Muhammad Al-, *Bayan Al-Kuwait: Sirat Hayat Al-Sheikh Mubarak Al-Sabah* [A Biography of Sheikh Mubarak Al-Sabah]. Sharja, 2004.

Qinai, Youssef bin Issa Al-, *Safahat Min Tarikh Al-Kuwait* [Pages from the History of Kuwait]. Cairo, 1946.

Qitami, Issa Al-, *Dalil Al-Muhtar fi Ilm Al-Biha* [The Guide to the Sea for the Bewildered]. Kuwait, 1964.

Rida, Muhammad Rashid, 'Madrasa Ilmiyya fi Al-Kuwait' [A Scientific School in Kuwait], *Al-Manar*, 15/2, 1912, pp. 237–239.

Rumi, Adnan bin Salem bin Muhammad Al-, *Tarikh Masajid Al-Kuwait Al-Qadima* [The History of the Old Mosques in Kuwait]. Kuwait, 2002.

Rushd, Ahmad Al- (ed.), *Al-Kuwait Min Al-Imara lIa Al-Dawla* [Kuwait: From Emirate to State]. Cairo, 1993.

Sabah, Maymouna Al-Khalifa Al-, *Al-Kuwait fi Dhil Al-Himaya Al-Britaniyya* [Kuwait under British Protection]. Kuwait, 1988.

———, 'Mushkilat Al-Hudud Al-Kuwaitiyya Bayn Al-Dawlatayn Al-Uthmaniyya wa Al-Baritaniyya 1899–1913' [Problems of Kuwaiti Border between the Ottoman and British Empires (1899–1913]),

Thesis 82, *Journal of Faculty of Arts, Kuwait University,* 13, AH 1413/ 1993.

Sa'dun, Khaled Hammoud Al-, *Al-Alaqat bayn Najd wa Al-Kuwait 1319–1341 AH/1902–1922 AD* [Relations between Najd and Kuwait 1319–1341/1902–1922]. Kuwait, 1990.

Saidan, Hamad Muhammad Al-, *Ta'rikh Al-Alam Al-Kuwaiti* [The History of the Flag of Kuwait]. Kuwait, 1985.

Saleh, Nouriyya Muhammad Nasser Al-, *Alaqat Al-Kuwait Al-Siyasiyya bi Sharq Al-Jazira Al-Arabiyya wa Al-Iraq Al-Uthmani 1866–1902* [Kuwait's Political Relations with Eastern Arabia and Ottoman Iraq]. Kuwait, 1977.

Shakli, Ibrahim Al-, *Al-Badawa fi Al-Kuwait, Dirasa Maydaniyya* [Bedouin Life in Kuwait, A Field Study]. Kuwait, 1987.

Shalaq, Ahmad Zakariyya Al-, 'Al-Wad' Al-Duwali Lil Kuwait Mundhu Itifaq Al-Himaya Hatta Al-Itifaq Al-Baritani-Al-Uthmani 1913' [The International Position of Kuwait from the Protection Agreement to the Anglo-Ottoman Agreement in 1913], in Ahmad Al-Rushd (ed.), *Al-Kuwait Min Al-Imara lIa Al-Dawla* [Kuwait: From Emirate to State]. Cairo, 1993.

Shamiyya, Jibran, *Al Saud: Madihum wa Mustaqbalihim* [The Saud Family: Their Past and Future]. London, n.d.

Shamlan, Sayf Marzouq Al-, *Ta'rikh Al-Ghaws ala L-Lulu' fi Al-Kuwait wa Al-Khalij Al-Arabi* [The History of Pearl Diving in Kuwait and the Arab Gulf]. Kuwait, 1986.

Shaybani, Muhammad bin Ibrahim Al- (ed.), *Risala Fiha Hawadith wa Wafiyyat Al-A'yan min Tadwinat Khan Bahader, Abdullah Al-Qinai* [An Account of the Lives and Deaths of the Notables, According to Khan Bahader and Abdullah al-Qinai]. Kuwait, 2006.

—— (ed.), *Al-Kuwait Kama Ra'aha Al-Siyasi Al-Denmarki Barclay Raunkiær 1330/1912* [Kuwait as Seen by the Danish Politician Barclay Raunkiær in 1330/1912]. Kuwait, n.d.

Al-Sheikh Khaz'al Emir Al-Muhammara [Sheikh Khaz'al, the Emir of Al-Muhammara]. Beirut, 1989.

Shihab, Youssef Al-, *Rijal fi Tarikh Al-Kuwait* [Men in the History of Kuwait], vol. 1. Kuwait, 1993.

Sultan, Ghanem, *Jawanib Min Shakhsiyyat Al-Kuwait* [Perspectives on Kuwaiti Personalities]. Kuwait, 1990.

Tamimi, Abdul Malik Khalaf Al-, *Abhath fi Tarikh Al-Kuwait* [Studies in the History of Kuwait]. Kuwait, 1999.

Uthaymni, Abdullah Al-Saleh Al-, *Al-Alaqat Bayn Al-Dawla Al-Saudiyya Al-Ula wa Al-Kuwait* [Relations between the First Saudi State and Kuwait]. Riyadh, 1990.

———, *Tarikh Al-Mamlaka Al-Arabiyya Al-Saudiyya* [The History of the Kingdom of Saudi Arabia]. Riyadh, 1999.

Wahbah, Hafez, *Jazirat Al-Arab fi Al-Qarn Al-Ishrin* [The Arabian Peninsula in the Twentieth Century]. Cairo, 1967.

Zarakli, Khair Al-Din Al-, *Al-Wajiz Sirat Al-Malik Abdul Aziz* [The Concise History of King Abdul Aziz]. Beirut, n.d.

Zayd, Khaled Saud Al-, *Udaba' Al-Kuwait fi Qarnayn* [Kuwaiti Writers in Two Centuries], vol. 1. Kuwait, 1976.

Index

O'Conor, Sir Nicholas 22, 54, 55, 56,
  177, 221
officialdom 70–1
oil 119, 183–4
Oman 113, 118, 151, 153
Ottoman Empire xiii, xiv–xv, xvi–xvii,
  163–4, 167, 171–2
  and Arab Gulf 2–3, 35, 166,
    168–70
  and Arabistan 152, 157
  and arms trade 40, 41
  and borders 53–6, 57, 58–60, 61
  and customs 128
  and date farms 129–34
  and flag 51, 52–3
  and Germany 64
  and Great Britain 16–18, 19–20,
    28, 180–1, 184–5, 219–20
  and Al-Hasa campaign 4
  and Ibn Saud 150
  and intellectuals 80
  and Kuwait 6, 7, 10–16, 27, 29,
    31–2, 62–4, 141, 144–5
  and Mubarak 20–1, 22–4, 25–6,
    36–8
  and Qatar 139, 159, 160–1, 162,
    163
  and Riyadh 147
  and trade 109, 110
Ovansian, Artine 202
Ovseyenko 202, 203, 204, 206, 207–8,
  209–10

pearl diving 45, 47, 49, 71, 105,
  107–8, 116–19
  and taxes 126–7
Pears, Captain 15
Persia 40, 152, 153, 154, 174, 208; see
  also Iran
Persian Gulf see Gulf, the
Pertev Pasha 219–20
pharmacies 86
photography 94

piracy 30–1, 45, 49, 109–10, 153–4,
  156, 173
poetry 82
Pomone, HMS 19, 20
postal system 96–7, 181–2
press reports 23–4, 26, 36
punishment 71, 72

Qarruh island 60
Al-Qasaba 156, 157
Al-Qasim 150
Qassim bin Muhammad Al-Ibrahim
  76, 94
Qasim Pasha 11
Qatar 10, 32, 50, 118, 151, 158–63
  and Mubarak 2, 4
  and Najd 138, 139
Al-Qatif 4, 22, 152, 218
Al-Qattami, Issa 118
Al-Qinai, Youssef bin Issa xvi, 75, 76,
  78, 107, 117
  and reforms 107
Al-Qira 60
quarantine 85–6, 216
Al-Qurin 60
Al-Qurna tribe 168
Qut Al-Zain island 129

Rafih, Ismail bin Muhammad 44
Al-Rahman, Daoud 84, 181
Rahmatullah, Dr Nur Muhammad
  84
railways 28, 31, 35, 36, 54, 172,
  200–1; see also Berlin–Baghdad
  Railway
Rajab Al-Naqib Efendi 8, 19, 161
Ramadan 74, 100, 117
Ras Al-Ajuza 21
Al-Rashaydeh tribe 5
Al-Rashid, Abdul Aziz xiii–xiv, xvi, 7,
  81, 182, 213
  and intellectuals 78, 79, 82
  and Islam 71–2, 101

Plate 1. Sheikh Mubarak in 1901.

Plate 2. Sheikh Mubarak with officers of the Russian naval ship *Varyag*, 1901. The *Varyag*, commissioned into the Russian Navy in 1901, arrived on a goodwill mission in early December. The ship and her crew later became iconic in Russia: in 1902 they engaged heroically in an unequal battle with a Japanese squadron and, when defeated, scuttled their ship.

Plate 3. Sheikh Mubarak, mounted, receiving Lord Curzon, 1903. One of his soldiers hoists Kuwait's first flag, which bears the country's name.

Plate 4. Sheikh Mubarak and his friend Sheikh Khaz'al of Muhammurah, 1907.

Plate 5. Sheikh Mubarak standing on a bridge that connected the old and new sections of Al-Seif Palace.

Plate 6. The Summer Palace, 1907.

Plate 7. Sheikh Mubarak in his outdoor council.

Plate 8. Sheikh Mubarak with Emir 'Abd al-'Aziz Al S'aud on his right hand, among a group of the two families, 1910.

Plate 9. Sheikh Mubarak, 1912.

Plate 10. Sheikh Mubarak in his last years. Standing at the back to his left is his son, Sheikh Jaber.

Plate 11. Sheikh Mubarak with the commander of Basra forces, most likely before the battle of Basra, 1914.

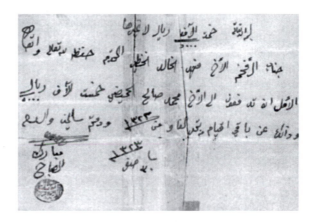

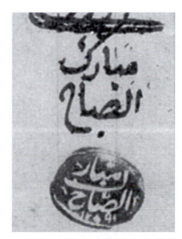

Plate 12. Mubarak's seal and signature, in the archives of the Kuwaiti Research and Studies Center, 1908.

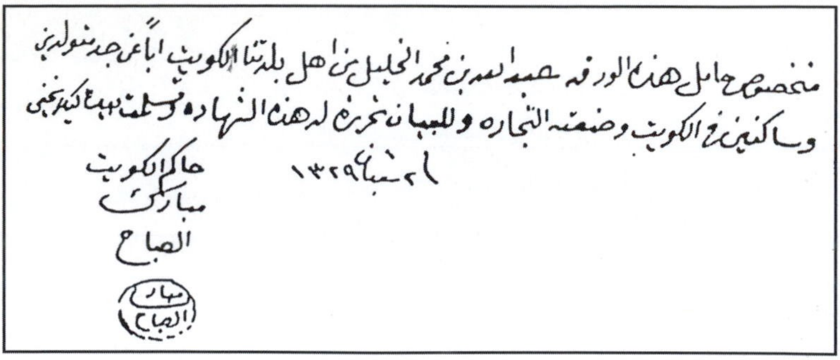

مخصوص حامل هذه الورقة عبد الله بن محمد الخليل من اهل بلدتنا الكويت ابا عن جد متولدين وساكنين في الكويت وصنعته التجاره وللبيان تحرر له هذه الشهاده وسلمت بيده كيلا يخفى

١٢ شعبان ١٣٢٩

حاكم الكويت
مبارك
الصباح

مبارك الصباح

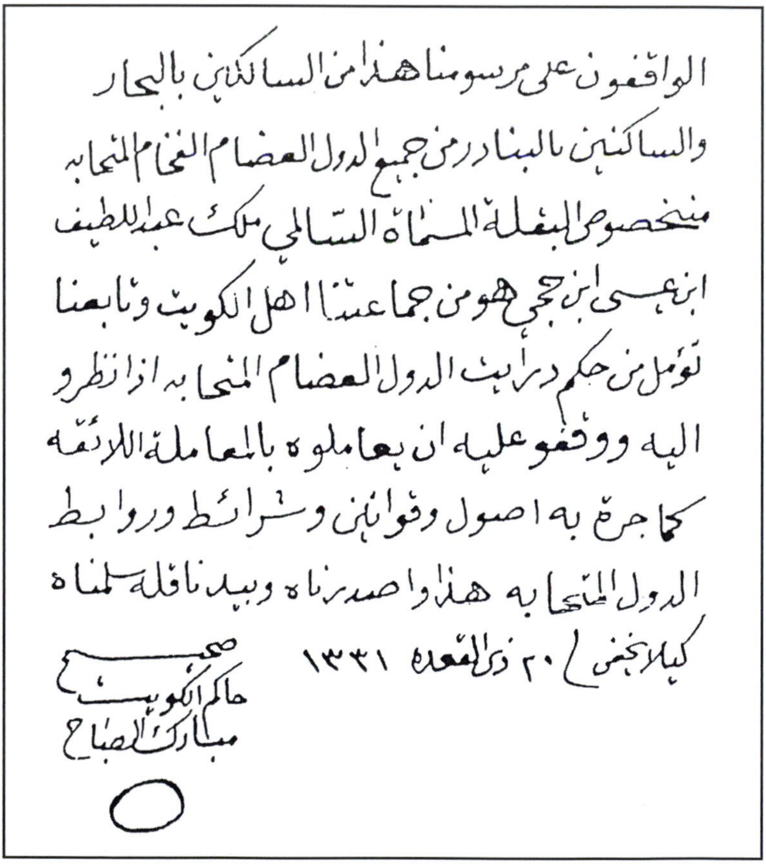

الواقفون على مرسومنا هذا من السالكين بالبحار
والساكنين بالبنادر من جميع الدول العظام الفخام المتحابه
مخصوص البغلة المسماة السالمي ملك عبد اللطيف
ابن عيسى ابن حجي هو من جماعتنا اهل الكويت وتابعنا
نؤمل من حكم درايت الدول العظام المتحابه اذا نظرو
اليه ووقفو عليه ان يعاملوه بالمعاملة اللائقه
كما جرى به اصول وقوانين وشرائط وروابط
الدول المتحابه بهذا واصدرناه وبيد ناقلة سلمناه
كيلا يخفى ٢٠ ذي القعده ١٣٣١

صح
حاكم الكويت
مبارك الصباح

Plate 13. A certificate issued by the Sheikh attesting to the identity of Kuwaiti merchants and, below, a certificate issued by Sheikh Mubarak for Kuwaiti ships, 1908.

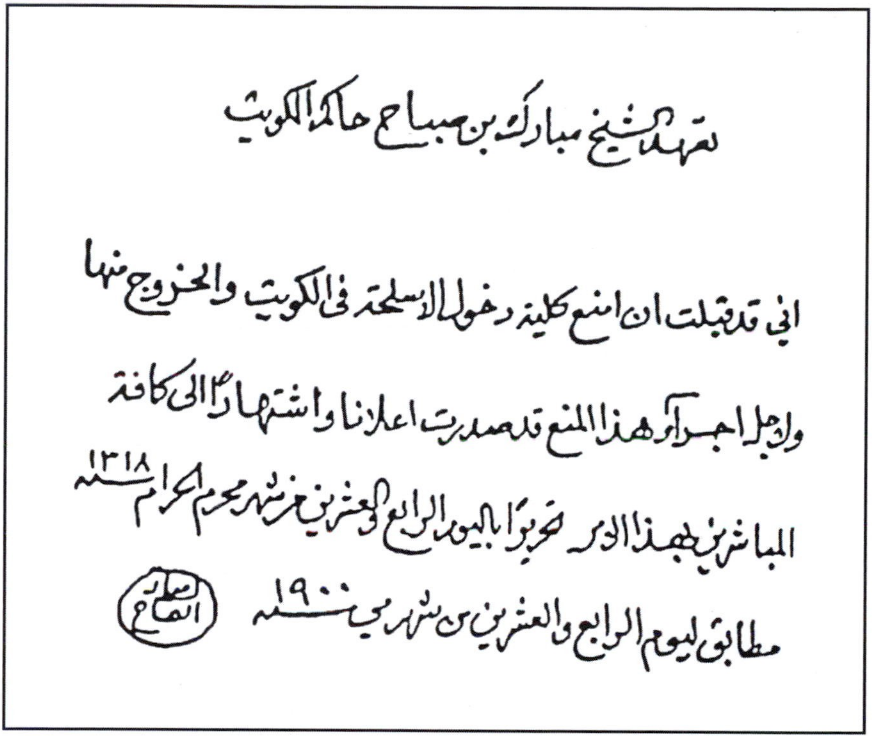

نتعهد نحن شيخ مبارك بن صباح حاكم الكويت

اني قد قبلت ان امنع كلية دخول الاسلحة في الكويت والخروج منها
ولاجل اجراء هذا المنع قد صدرت اعلاننا واشتهارا الى كافة
المباشرين بهذا الامر تحريرا باليوم الرابع والعشرين من شهر محرم الحرام سنة ١٣١٨
مطابق ليوم الرابع والعشرين من شهر يونيه سنة ١٩٠٠ ه (الختم)

Plate 14. A document prepared by the Sheikh to prevent the
dealing of arms in Kuwait, 1900.

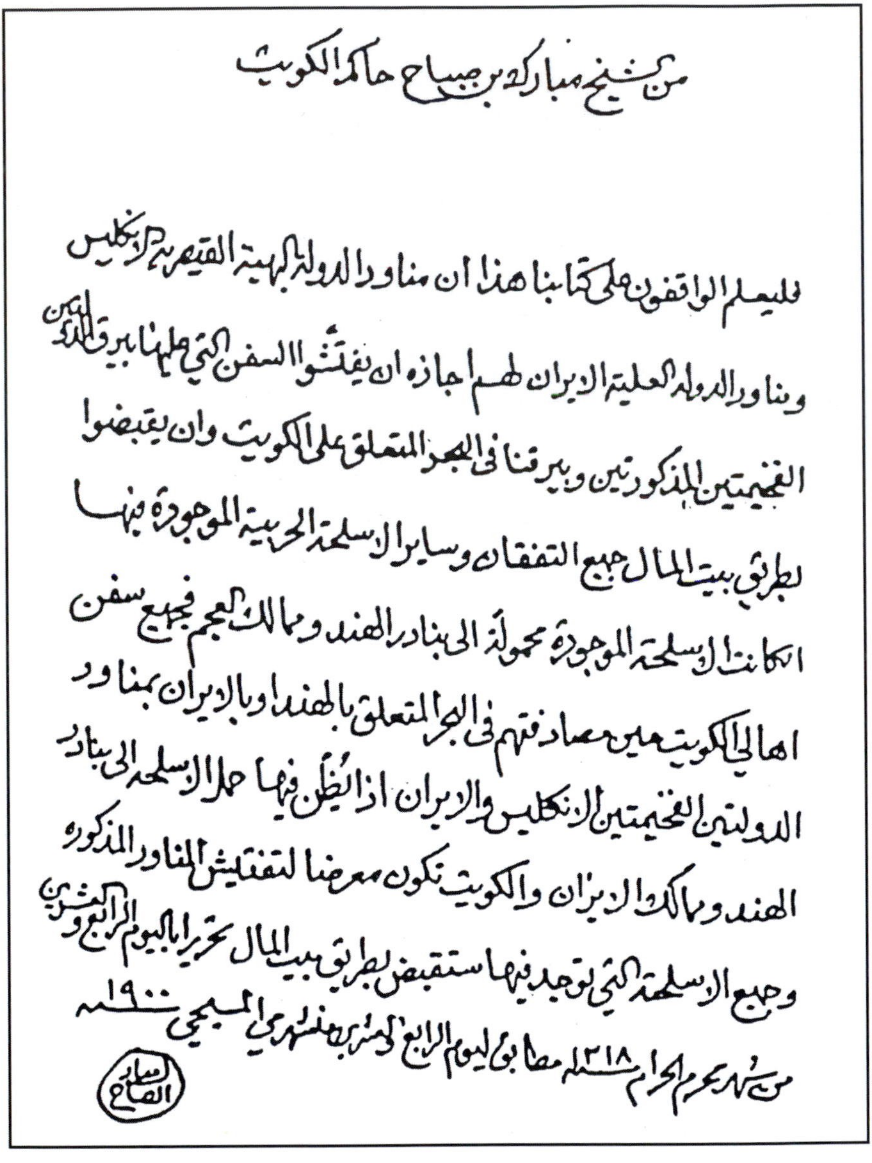

من شيخ مبارك بن صباح حاكم الكويت

ليعلم الواقفون على كتابنا هذا أن مناور الدولة البهية القيصرية الإنكليس
ومناور الدولة العلية الإيران لهم إجازه أن يفتشوا السفن التي عليها بيرق الدول
المذكورتين في بحرنا وبرنا في البحر المتعلق على الكويت وأن يقبضوا
بطريق بيت المال جميع التفقات وسائر الأسلحة الحربية الموجودة بها
إن كانت الأسلحة الموجودة محمولة إلى بنادر الهند وما لك العجم في جميع سفن
أهالي الكويت ومن مصادفتهم في البحر المتعلق بالهند وبالإيران بمناور
الدولتين التفتيشيتين الإنكليس والإيران إذا أيقن فيها حمل الأسلحة إلى بنادر
الهند وما لك والإيران والكويت نكون مع رضانا لتفتيش المناور المذكور
وجميع الأسلحة التي توجد فيها استقبض بطريق بيت المال تحرير باليوم الرابع والعشرين
من محرم الحرام سنة ١٣١٨ مطابق لليوم الرابع لشهر يناير من شهور السنة المسيحي سنة ١٩٠٠

Plate 15. A document showing the Sheikh's approval for British and Iranian ships to be inspected and searched for smuggled weapons, 1900.

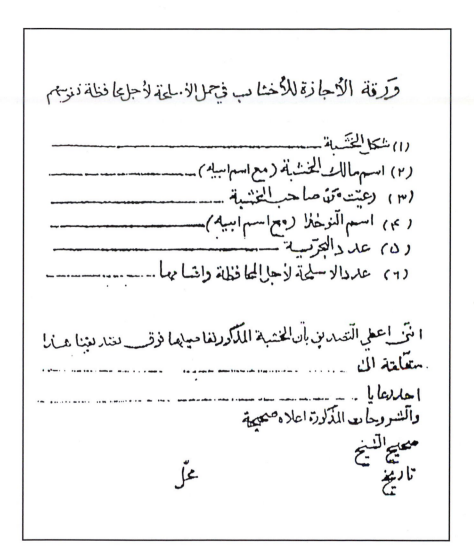

وَرَقَةُ الأَجازَة للأخشاب في حمل الأسلحة لأجل حِفظة سفينة ذنويهم

(١) شكل الخشتبة _____

(٢) اسم مالك الخشتبة (مع اسم ابيه) _____

(٣) رعيت ومَن صاحب الخشتبة _____

(٤) اسم النوخذا (مع اسم ابيه) _____

(٥) عدد البحرية _____

(٦) عدد الاسلحة لأجل المحافظة وانشا بها .... _____

انّنا اعطي التصديق بأن الخشتبة المذكور وقائد حميلها ذرق _____ لتدابينا هذا

ستعلقة الى _____

احداما يا . _____ ....

والشروحات المذكورة اعلاه صحيحة

ختيم الشيخ

تاريخ   على

Plate 16. A certificate issued by Sheikh Mubarak authorizing weapons for self-defence onboard ships.

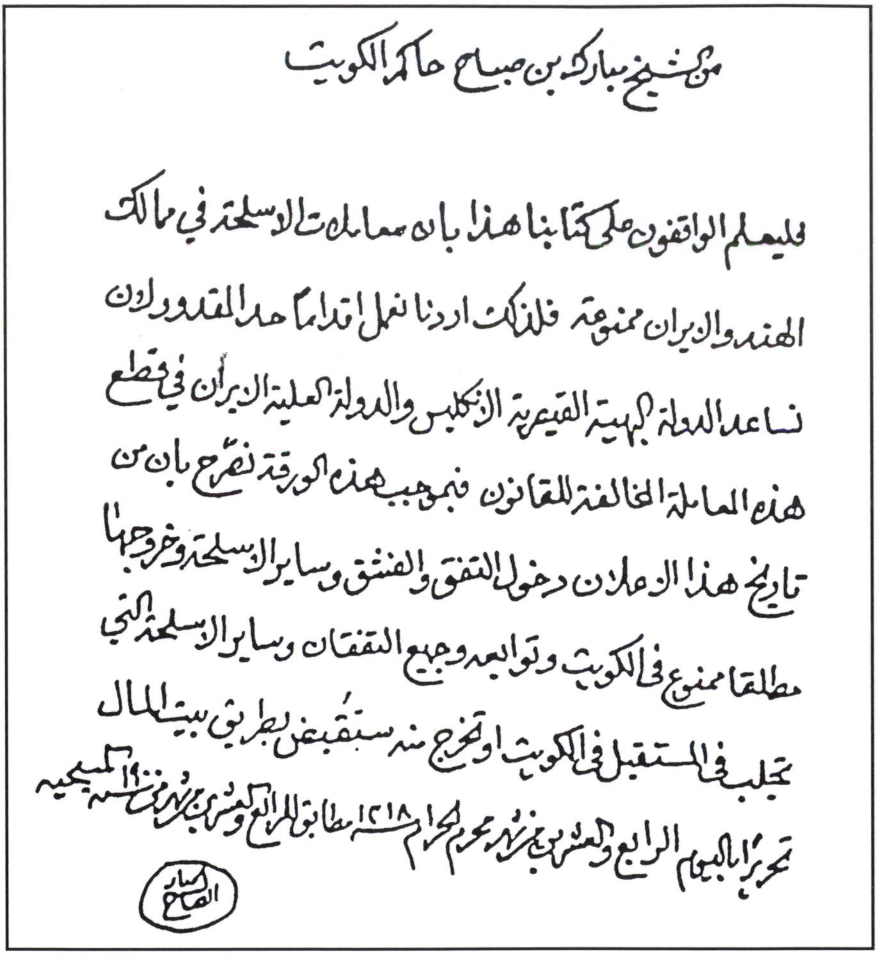

من الشيخ مبارك بن صباح حاكم الكويت

ليعلم الواقفون على كتابنا هذا بان معاملة الاسلحة في ممالك الهند وايران ممنوعة فلذلك اردنا نفعل اقداما هذا المقدم ولكن نساعد الدولة البهية القيصرية الانكليس والدولة العلية ايران في قطع هذه المعاملة المخالفة للقانون فنموجب هذه الورقة نصرح بان من تاريخ هذا الاعلان دخول التفق والفشق وسايرالاسلحة وخروجها مطلقا ممنوع في الكويت وتوابعه وجميع الثقفان وسايرالاسلحة التي تجلب في المستقبل في الكويت او تخرج منه سيقبض عليها بيت المال تحريرا باليوم الرابع والعشرين من شهر محرم الحرام سنة ١٢١٨ ...

Plate 17. The Sheikh pledges to oppose the arms trade, 1900.